D1250809

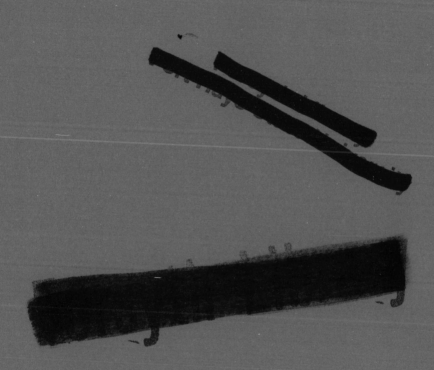

WITHDRAWN

R.B.Kitaj

R.B.Kitaj

EDITED BY RICHARD MORPHET

RIZZOLI
NEW YORK

To my Family and my Cities

R.B. Kitaj

Exhibition schedule:

Tate Gallery, London
16 June – 4 September 1994

Los Angeles County Museum of Art
23 October 1994 – 8 January 1995

The Metropolitan Museum of Art, New York
15 February – 14 May 1995

Cover: Detail from *Cecil Court, London WC2 (The Refugees)*,
1983–1984 (plate no. 65)

Frontispiece: David Hockney, *Kitaj in His Studio*, 1974
(whereabouts unknown)

First published in the United States of America in 1994 by
Rizzoli International Publications, Inc.
300 Park Avenue South
New York, New York 10010

Originally published in Great Britain in 1994 by
Tate Gallery Publications
Millbank, London SW1P 4RG

Library of Congress Cataloging-in-Publication Data

Kitaj, R.B.
 R.B. Kitaj : a retrospective / edited by Richard Morphet : essay by Richard Wollheim.
 p. cm.
 Catalog of a traveling exhibition held at the Tate Gallery in London,
the Los Angeles County Museum, and the Metropolitan Museum of Art.
 Includes bibliographical references.
 ISBN 0-8478-1846-2
 1. Kitaj, R.B.—Exhibitions. I. Morphet, Richard.
II. Wollheim, Richard, 1923–   . III. Tate Gallery. IV. Los Angeles County Museum.
V. Metropolitan Museum of Art (New York, N.Y.) VI. Title.
N6537.K53A4   1995
759.13—dc20   94-5321
                                                 CIP

Designed by Caroline Johnston
Printed in Great Britain

Contents

Foreword

We are delighted to be able to present this major retrospective of the work of R.B. Kitaj which will be shown first at the Tate Gallery and subsequently at Los Angeles County Museum of Art and The Metropolitan Museum of Art, New York.

Born in Cleveland, Ohio, Kitaj first came to England in 1956 and then settled here. The exhibition covers his work over thirty-five years, dating from 1958 until the present day. It demonstrates the originality, from an early date, of Kitaj's approach to sources of iconography and to the means of realising these in paintings. It also shows the very personal vitality of his handling of paint, of his language of colour and of the graphic strength that underpins his acts of depiction. A notable feature of the exhibition is the charcoals and pastels which occupy such an important a place in the revival of figure drawing in Britain in recent years. Kitaj's paintings of the 1990s continue to concentrate on human relations, on the art of the past, on the life of ideas and on the revelation of self, now combined with a new freedom of touch employing a colouristic range that extends from the near monochrome to the sumptuous.

The selection has been made by Richard Morphet, Keeper of the Modern Collection at the Tate Gallery, in close collaboration with the artist. He is also the editor of the catalogue, for which he has written an introductory essay.

We owe an immense gratitude to Kitaj for the very considerable time he has dedicated to the whole project, and this includes his considerable input into the catalogue. He has written a number of texts, and has also designed the overall layout of the plates section. Where he has decided to write texts on individual works he has chosen a variety of approaches, some texts being historically factual, some wholly fictitious, some appearing opposite the colour plates, some in the catalogue list. Not every work has a text but again this is a deliberate choice of the artist and is not an indication of the relative importance of the work. In his writing, no less than in his art, Kitaj is a remarkable creator of characters and of situations. Our gratitude for the texts he has provided on individual works is extended by our pleasure at his willingness to give the extensive new interview published here, which ranges widely across his feelings and beliefs and which illuminates the motivations underlying his art.

Richard Wollheim has followed the development of Kitaj's art for over thirty years. We are delighted to be able to publish his essay on Kitaj's art, which benefits alike from his insight as a philosopher of art and from his close friendship with the artist. Our thanks also go to Joanne Northey, who has compiled the chronology.

We are very grateful to all the lenders who responded so willingly to our requests for loans to the exhibition and to its tour. It means a long separation for them from their works, and without such generosity we would not have been able to mount this exhibition.

We should finally like to thank Marlborough Fine Art (London) Ltd, and in particular Geoffrey Parton, who have been unfailingly supportive at all stages with information, advice and help.

It has been a privilege and pleasure to work so closely with the artist. His enthusiasm for every aspect of the exhibition has remained undiminished throughout. We are indeed deeply grateful.

Nicholas Serota
Director

The Art of R.B. Kitaj: 'To thine own self be true'[1]

RICHARD MORPHET

Introduction

This exhibition surveys thirty-five years' work by an American painter who for almost the whole of this period has lived in England and who is Jewish. Though simple to state, these facts of Kitaj's origins and habitat denote a complex interaction of identities, the dynamic of which has formed his art.[2]

Despite the length of his life in England, which is his home, Kitaj remains strikingly American in important ways. From Ralph Waldo Emerson to baseball and from Hollywood to Morton Feldman, his work repeatedly highlights the indigenous American culture in which he was formed and remains steeped. The bracing directness and pragmatism which he applies to any subject must also be transatlantic in origin. Nevertheless Kitaj's art has, for over thirty years, come to constitute one of the most distinctive bodies of work within the English scene, where it has been correspondingly influential. Furthermore, in the period's debate about the needs of art and the possibilities it offers, his opinion has been exceptional in its clarity, vividness and challenge. Either of these achievements – in image and in word – would be remarkable by itself, but the two together (and they cannot sensibly be separated) have had a decisive impact both on English art and on a wider culture.

In combining the roles of artist and of catalyst Kitaj extends a distinguished tradition established by Americans who have chosen to live in England, including James McNeill Whistler, Henry James, John Singer Sargent, Jacob Epstein, Ezra Pound and T.S. Eliot. Like all of these, Kitaj has not only affected the art of this country but also accentuated English self-awareness. Moreover, in respect of London he has reinforced a quality long held to be a special feature of English art, the sense of place.

Though himself a conspicuous representative of both American and English culture, Kitaj sees each with a clarity enhanced by what he feels is the perspective of an outsider. The sense in which he is an exile from America is obvious, but despite the fact that the course of English art since 1960 cannot be understood without reference to his contribution – and to his integration here – he feels essentially rootless. Central to this self-perception is Kitaj's preoccupation with his Jewish identity. This preoccupation developed in the 1970s and has since dominated his work. Even when not overtly stated, this theme permeates his art; with hindsight, it can even be seen to have done so for many years before Kitaj himself was conscious of it.

Kitaj's concern with the Jewish theme is powerfully coloured, and in many ways driven, by his horror at the Holocaust; in its originality and its insistence, his is one of the most powerful bodies of work on this topic.[3] But for all the exceptional reinforcement given to it by the Holocaust, the notion of not belonging to any settled society is, for Kitaj, inherent in the very nature of existence as a Jew. He quotes Abraham's words, 'I am a stranger and a so-journer', and those of Gershom Scholem (on Jews and Germans), who writes of 'This "being elsewhere" combined with the desperate wish to "be at home" in a manner at once intense, fruitful and destructive'.[4] On p.132 of this cata-logue Kitaj further quotes with approval Schönberg's observation that 'I have long since resolved to be a Jew ... I regard that as more important than my art'.

Thus a central motivation of Kitaj's art is the compulsion to declare, and therefore to characterise, an identity. On the one hand, this identity is the in-heritor of many traditions and it is further defined by the concentration and the passion with which it engages with any given subject. On the other hand, it is innately restless; as it is continuously 'displaced', its frame of reference is not constrained by the assumptions deriving from a settled origin. Thus it is able to draw with unusual freedom on markedly disparate sources, and to bring these together in new and unexpected combinations which, for the viewer, reveal a world of the imagination that is strange, distinct and com-pelling. For all its idiosyncrasy, this world, even when seen through a single painting, has a quality of completeness and conviction. Its source is a highly individual vision, but one through which we are able also to recognise significant aspects of the condition of our age.

The consistent theme of Kitaj's paintings is human experience, but while he draws repeatedly on documentary sources his paintings are not themselves documentary. So it is not surprising that his endeavour is fed not only by great artists but also by the great novelists and film makers. There is, indeed, much of the novelist and of the director in Kitaj's concern with conceiving charac-ters and situations. His methods of doing this include the creation of new con-texts for motifs originally of specific origin, the adaptation of pre-existing images by often disturbing distortion and the straight invention of faces and figures. His brushmark is often of considerable freedom, and Kitaj uses its combination of boldness and ambiguity to represent both physiognomy and feeling in unexpected ways. A striking aspect of the figures in Kitaj's paintings is his ability to project them as authentic presences, a projection that is at once physical and psychological. The admiration with which he speaks of Dickens and Tolstoy is a pointer to the wholeheartedness of the characterisa-tions he seeks to realise and to the breadth of the view of life that he seeks to encompass. Not only the figures but also the atmospheres that Kitaj creates in paintings have an immediacy and a plausibility that persuade us of their actu-ality. At times we feel almost that we have experienced them personally – per-haps, in view of their heightened intensity, in dream, that parallel location of the fusion of images drawn directly from life with the play of inner fears and emotions.

The richness of subject in Kitaj's art is complemented by marked visual abundance. Even in its most cool and immaculate phase, Kitaj's painting em-phasised its manual origin. It has long been the arena for the exercise of a touch that is lyrical and, through all its varied modes, intensely individual. Ki-taj's mark-making is alive with a nervous energy that is, in itself, one of his means of conveying the emotion of any subject he depicts. His paint surfaces are animated from edge to edge, packed with abstract incident within the de-picted forms, and satisfying both as complete compositions and to explore in detail. It may be, in part, their basis in drawing that over the years has increasingly given them an almost bodily sweep, with directional thrusts akin to currents, and a kind of organic internal momentum. Paint can rest like soft powder or be built forward in abruptly tactile deposits. It is dragged, scumbled and layered. Within an armature of cursive line, patches of colour are rubbed in, often filling it incompletely and thus setting up a lively visual counterpoint. Kitaj's colour, though often subtle and sometimes exploring the beauty of near monochrome, is more frequently conspicuous for its fullness and brilliance, even its luxuriance. These qualities are the vehicle for his art's distinctly declaratory quality in which, without loss of intimacy, the private can become almost heraldic and the bizarre believable.

The delight that Kitaj's paintings afford to the senses cannot be separated from their central aim – to address human experience in terms of thought and feeling as well as of visual fact. Energy, inventiveness, conviction, unpredictability, focus and range, all these are features of a sometimes difficult, always vigorous art of unusual fullness. The intensity of Kitaj's own engagement with a subject underlies the capacity of his works to engage, in turn, the attention and the imagination of the viewer. In the art of its period this combination of qualities has often been surprising and always impossible to ignore.

Early Work: 1958 to mid-1970s

Since the 1970s, Kitaj's art has been widely associated with that of other London painters, including Bacon, Freud, Auerbach, Kossoff and Andrews, with whom he shares a preoccupation with representing the human subject. At the outset of Kitaj's career, however, the originality of form and subject in his work made it difficult for commentators to know quite where to place it within contemporary art. Its look was highly unfamiliar, combining fractured surfaces with a variety of allusions. No less puzzling was the evident cohabitation in a single work of what looked like obsessive calculation with the free play of instinct. For superficial, if understandable, reasons, Kitaj's art was for a time mistakenly identified with Pop, but no less understandably one area with which commentators did *not* associate it was with the group of figure painters mentioned above, who concentrated on the direct act of forming the single image of a figure or scene out of paint, avoiding fragmentation of the motif and unaccompanied by added materials. (In the light both of these painters' already evident preoccupations and of the eventual modes of Kitaj's art it is interesting to read the first of Kitaj's published writings that has been traced, a glowing review in 1958 of a major retrospective of Kokoschka, held in Vienna, where both Kokoschka and Kitaj had worked early in their careers.[5])

The earliest works Kitaj made in England included incisive drawings from observation, but by the time he enrolled at the Royal College of Art in 1959, and still more prominently when he unveiled his first solo exhibition in 1963, he revealed a kind of painting that had no direct precedent. A single canvas would contain a multiplicity of discrete images, loosely disposed. These included individual abstract forms but above all a large number of figurative motifs which, while each carrying a strong sense of very particular origins and significance, interrelated in ways that were potent in suggestions to the imagination yet essentially unaccountable. Two further features enriched the effect: the painted images were in a variety of styles, and many of the images were taken physically from pre-existing sources and collaged to the canvas.

Kitaj acknowledged the influence of Surrealism, and its legacy is undeniable both in the form of these works and in their effects, which include the encouragement of free association and the disconcerting states of mind that illogical-seeming juxtapositions provoke. Furthermore, these enigmatic works had a number of points in common with advanced American art of the period. The scattering of configurations across the picture plane created an active 'field' obliquely related to that of Abstract Expressionism, while the introduction into a painterly surface of material not generally associated with the studio – thus insisting on specifics and 'confusing' aesthetics with the preoccupations of other worlds – paralleled the transition in the United States from gestural abstraction to Pop (as seen, for example, in the work of Rauschenberg).

The unusual openness of Kitaj's approach to source materials meant that the mass media were as acceptable to him as any other, where compelling imagery was concerned; magazine and newspaper photographs and images from film have continued to feed his art. But while the occasional appearance of such material in his early work and his willingness to quote directly from non-art sources suggested a method to younger painters whose taste was for Pop, his own trajectory lay in another direction. As an American, he did not see in transatlantic consumer culture an exotic appeal, and even his early work reveals that his gaze was principally towards the past.

Most importantly, the character of each of Kitaj's works demonstrated that for all its puzzling nature it had a purposeful programme, was not simply reflecting the look of a culture and was, of its essence, engaged with ideas. His paintings were noticeably preoccupied with past struggles against oppression. Kitaj dedicated his first exhibition 'To the Open Society / with reservations', and a writer looking back on the period has described some of his works as 'commemorative icons in the hagiography of martyred radicals', adding that 'Kitaj not only eulogises the individual dead but evokes the atmosphere of ideas in which they breathed'.[6] In particular, however, it was the provision by Kitaj of texts to support his paintings which confirmed that their function was intellectual as well as aesthetic. Kitaj's own catalogue entries gave bibliographies for particular works, as well as quoting at length from authors as diverse as Goethe, Fritz Saxl and Robert Creeley. But furthermore, a number of works contained, in collage, extensive texts handwritten by Kitaj himself, some of which were accounts of the iconography of the works of which they were themselves a part.

Perhaps the most striking proof of the distance between Kitaj's aims and those of Pop art in general was his passionate involvement, made evident alike in his early paintings and their accompanying texts, with the discipline of iconography (the study of the meaning of images). A pioneer in this field had been the German art historian Aby Warburg (1866–1929), to whose work and life Kitaj frequently alludes in the 1960s, in both art and text. It is significant in relation to Kitaj's emergent preoccupations that the move to London, in 1933, of the Institute which Warburg founded, and which bears his name, was owing to Nazi persecution and that its principal members, many of whose writings have been important to Kitaj, were thus Jewish

fig.1 Willem de Kooning **Woman and Bicycle** 1952–3 Oil on canvas *Whitney Museum of American Art, New York. Purchase*

refugees. It is also significant that one of Warburg's motivations in developing an iconographical approach in the late nineteenth century was to counter a simultaneously developing strand in art criticism, which stressed the importance of form at the expense of that of content. A main purpose of Kitaj's influential writings of the 1970s was to make the same point in his own day, but already in the early 1960s the startling new relationship his exhibitions proposed between idea and image can be seen as a statement in this cause.

Central to the work of the Warburg Institute is an awareness of the transmission of images over extended distances and times, and of the ways in which the transformation of a tradition can constitute a means of its continuation. In Kitaj's art, the conjunction of fractured forms with recontextualised images reads like a metaphor of the ability of ideas to survive, despite interruptions and threats of all kinds, and of their re-emergence in often surprising guises. The pen is mightier than the sword, and Kitaj's works of over thirty years make this point both through their repeated references to texts written by victims of persecution and through their use of images derived from books by or about them. Kitaj's obsession with the book as the vehicle by which both kinds of material is handed down permeates his work and at all periods is one of its key underlying themes. Indeed, frequently though Kitaj has used magazines as sources of imagery, a distinctive feature of his recycling of printed images during decades when this has been a common technique is the extent to which they are derived from books.

Though Kitaj's propensity to tell stories in art would later be more overt, already in his works of the early 1960s the sense of narrative interest was unmistakable. On his arrival in England in 1957, he had studied in Oxford under the art historian Edgar Wind, who had worked at the Warburg Institute both before and after its move to England. Kitaj's art is closely consistent with many of Wind's beliefs, for example, that 'it is precisely by means of fiction that the great artist becomes serious and imposes his seriousness on us in the form of feeling, of curiosity, awe and wonder'.[7]

Kitaj moved to England not only to study at the Ruskin School but also 'because James and Eliot and Pound had gone there 50 years before ... I wasn't going to go to paint in Paris or anywhere else; I was going to go to Oxford and become a kind of scholar-painter'.[8] Even more particularly, 'The intense passion for Pound and Joyce and Eliot, and the complexity of so much modern poetry, always led me to think you could do the same sort of thing in painting'.[9] Kitaj has stated that Pound and Eliot are among those modern writers whose compendious nature has interested him, 'those who try to get the whole world in'.[10] In Frederic Tuten's view, 'the paradigm of Kitaj's art is Eliot's *Wasteland*, with its structure of allusion, quotation, the mixture of lyric and colloquial voices, its quick cuts to scenes of urban love and terror. Eliot as the model of Kitaj's concern with the continuum of the past and present'.[11] Similar parallels exist between Kitaj's work and the poetry of Ezra Pound. The creative use of fragmentation by both writers is an obvious precedent for Kitaj. Already in the early 1960s Kitaj's paintings, for all their 'difficulty' – another quality shared with the poetry of Pound and Eliot – showed that capacity to draw the viewer into their particular world, and to do so by means at once of the intellect and of the emotions, that is one of the distinguishing features of his work, as of theirs. Timothy Hyman observed in 1979: 'I don't think anyone before Kitaj has made such convincing pictures of ideas ... Like the Cantos these pictures teeter on the borderline between ideas and mere play of ideas. Yet it was a new kind of picture, and one we could recognise, in its many-layered complexity, its interlocked rhythms of thought, as looking like the inside of our own minds'.[12]

Hyman pointed to a parallel with another aspect of Pound when he wrote that 'Kitaj's position as the Yankee outsider who has the energy to float a circus in London, and the courage to initiate its polemics, is uncannily close to that of Pound in the twenties'.[13] These words were written of the Kitaj of the mid-1970s, but they are illuminating, in retrospect, even about the Kitaj of fifteen years earlier, from his time at the Royal College of Art in London to the remarkable impact of his first exhibition.

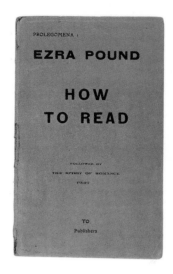

Arriving at the Royal College in 1959, Kitaj at twenty-seven was significantly older than his fellow students and had behind him not only art school experience in New York, Vienna and Oxford but also enormously wide reading and a broader experience of life. Marco Livingstone suggested something of the impact he must have had on his peers when he wrote that at the College: 'Kitaj's work revealed ways in which picture-making could, and should, be a vehicle for intellectual as well as sensual communication. The making of images was viewed [by him] as the construction of a language of signs which could be "read" in the way that words can be read. Kitaj was interested, furthermore, in the Surrealist notion of automatism and in the Abstract Expressionist corollary, the concept of gesture, both of which seized on image-making as a kind of writing expressive of the functioning of thought or of the assertion of personality'.[14] These words occur in a monograph on David Hockney and their relevance to the development of his work in the early 1960s is clear. As Hockney himself recorded: 'The one student I kept talking to a lot was Ron Kitaj. Ron was slowly doing these strange pictures, and I talked to him about them and about my work ... I'd talk to him about my interests; I was a keen vegetarian then, and interested in politics a bit, and he'd say to me, why don't you paint those subjects? And I thought, it's quite right; that's what I'm complaining about, I'm not doing anything that's from me. So that was the way I broke it. I began to paint those subjects ... And I thought, well, it's better; I feel better; you feel as if something's coming out. And then Ron said Yes, that's much more interesting.'[15]

fig.3 David Hockney **We Two Boys Together Clinging** 1961 Oil on board *Arts Council Collection, The South Bank Centre, London*

At a period when there was great concern with issues of form, Kitaj's challenging emphasis on the importance in art of ideas and of content was at least as influential outside the Royal College as in. Even the *Times* recognised this, observing in 1963: 'Mr R.B. Kitaj's first exhibition, now that it has at last taken place, puts the whole "new wave" of figurative painting in this country during the last two or three years into perspective. It supplies the purpose and authority that were rather lacking from its public image before ... Kitaj's work stands for a firm reaction against any appraisal of a picture by its formal qualities alone ... he demands the longer, more complicated experience which engages the whole intelligence.'[16] For Peter Greenaway, then an art student, the exhibition was a revelation: 'I was repeatedly told my paintings were too literary ... Art schools are so successful at breaking your confidence. And I suddenly saw this body of work that legitimised all I had hopes of one day doing. Kitaj legitimised text; he legitimised arcane and elitist information; he drew and painted in as many as ten different ways on the same canvas; he threw ideas around, like confetti ... There was unashamed political passion and extravagantly bold sexual imagery. His ideas were international, far from English timidity and English jokiness, and that timid and jokey English pop-art.'[17] For Clive Phillpot, 'one witnessed [in Kitaj's work of the early sixties] a certain kind of content, which had seemed to be out of reach of painting, suddenly streaming in as to a newly punctured vacuum.'[18]

This is not to suggest that equal emphasis on the importance of ideas in art could be found nowhere else in English art of the period. Such a concern had, for example, been central for some years to the work of Richard Hamilton, who was also conspicuously alert to the resonances between an image gleaned from the contemporary mass media and its manifestations or parallels in earlier centuries. Hamilton, too, created on a flat surface spatially convincing scenes composed of images developed from disparate sources and likewise integrated paint and collage. However, the two artists' interest in American ad-mass culture was markedly different in degree and, curiously, Kitaj, though ten years younger, was better known to a wide audience, at an earlier date, as a painter who gathered images of diverse origin into a single work (his first one-man exhibition took place almost two years before Hamilton's first as a Pop artist).[19] Another London artist preoccupied with the romance of imagery from the past and with the reinforcement and transformation of its meaning in newly created contexts was Eduardo Paolozzi, with whom in 1960–2 Kitaj collaborated on two works incorporating collage, one of them the painting 'Warburg's Visit to New Mexico' (private collection).[20]

Kitaj's art is distinguished from that made by both these artists in the early 1960s by the degree of psychological urgency with which it is charged. Even in the decade when he made those of his works that are the most difficult to 'read', his work communicated, as it has continued to do, a sense of raw psychic self-exposure. For many viewers who found the meaning of a work elusive, this heightened condition was compelling when combined not only with the beauty and variety of Kitaj's ways of handling paint but also with the extremes of pictorial mode that he was prepared to adopt.

In 'Specimen Musings of a Democrat' 1962 (no.7), for example, the greater part of the surface of the work is subdivided by a rectilinear grid, modules of which are occupied sometimes by rectangles of single painted colours, sometimes by painted imagery and sometimes by collage. The collaged sheets are variously printed, hand-drawn or handwritten. Their paper is sometimes white, sometimes coloured and sometimes printed with ruled lines; when cut into small rectangles the latter type, in particular, somewhat resembles index cards. Some of the imagery repeats from one rectangle to another, with changes in the medium employed. As in several of Kitaj's early paintings, the handwriting is insistently orderly. While extremely personal in character it is also suggestive of the standardisations and disciplines of whole cultures and systems of education, notably the American educational system within which Kitaj was formed and the more sophisticated trans-national world of scholarly investigation and exchange into which he was drawn in early adulthood.[21]

The very look of Kitaj's handwriting was expressive. Even before its collaged texts were read, the evident care and concern for clarity with which they had been inscribed communicated a sense of obsessive particularity about the content of a given work. That a painting should need so closely to be read (in both the senses of this word) and that it should operate simultaneously in the worlds of plastic and of intellectual exploration were ideas both expressive in themselves and rich in suggestions for subsequent art. In larger paintings, Kitaj disposed discrete abstract forms across the canvas either in lines, which he intended to 'look' like a poem (as in 'Cracks and Reforms and Bursts in the Violet Air' 1962, private collection), or in irregular networks (as in 'Halcyon Days (Med)' 1964, fig.4) and inserted, here and there, among these structures a variety of collaged images. For some years from the mid-1960s he made a number of very small paintings in each of which a single portrait head was very directly drawn in monochrome paint on a white ground. At another extreme, in 'Casting' 1967–9 (Museum Ludwig, Cologne) images of the heads of eight prostitutes were ranked one above another in a vertical column. The effect was akin to the printed broadsheets of early American brothels, for beside each head the prostitute's professional name was handwritten in paint. As always with Kitaj, however, the interest of the work's form is inseparable from that of its remarkable expressive effect. At the end of the decade, Kitaj made a small number of sculptures in connection with the Art and Technology project of the Los Angeles County Museum of Art. Like some of his prints, which similarly fall outside the scope of the present exhibition, these are notable for the directness with which they re-present, in another medium, single images drawn from the culture of an earlier period.

fig.4 Kitaj **Halcyon Days (Med)** 1964
Oil and collage on canvas *Museum Boymans-van Beuningen, Rotterdam*

So many were the vistas hinted at in the form and content of Kitaj's work of the early 1960s that it is not surprising that in a major survey of British art of the time John Russell could write: 'If I had to choose the artist who pre-eminently represents the open situation, I should probably single out R.B. Kitaj... I know of no painter now living from whom we can expect more.'[22] By the time these words were written, Kitaj had begun noticeably to move away from the literal fragmentation of image characteristic of his works of the early decade. Instead, his heterogeneously derived images were now fused into scenes combining apparent spatial integration with a flagrant 'illogicality' that was both enigmatic, unnerving and potent. This was to be Kitaj's principal painting mode until the late 1970s. Paint tended to be applied more thinly and forms to be organised in grander, more carefully delineated planes, using richer and more sonorous colour. Distinctive in their often threatening atmospheres and prompting conjecture as to the stories and meaning of their arresting scenes, these paintings appeared in the very years when some of the most discussed new art was adopting increasingly austere or cerebral modes and was emphasising an outward detachment. They seemed, by contrast, to be reviving the tradition of the large-scale allegorical or history painting. In the boldness with which they orchestrated character, narrative and setting they also disclosed a close affinity with film, and with what Kitaj has called its 'plural energies'.

fig.5 Kitaj **Maria Prophetissa** 1964
Oil on canvas *Whereabouts unknown*

A Watershed at Mid-Decade

Despite its dissimilarity to such tendencies as abstraction, Pop and Conceptual art, Kitaj's painting in the 1960s and 1970s was both conceived and perceived in the context of modernist art and literature; in method and assumption it drew liberally on the modernist heritage. Beginning, however, in the early 1970s Kitaj embarked on a fundamental reappraisal of the nature of his art. Of necessity, this process was inseparable from a reconsideration of his relationship to modernism, even though he continued to feel a profound debt to its major achievements.

What disturbed him was the enclosed character, as he saw it, of the modernist enterprise. He wrote in 1980 that 'something odd has happened in our own time. The power of the historical argument, of the necessity for art to be "modern", is awash in its own ideological juices ... It seems interesting to me that the period that separates us from 1900, surely one of the most terrible histories of bad faith ever, should somehow conceive and nourish a life of forms increasingly divorced from the illustration of human life which had been art's main province before'. From its central concerns in earlier centuries he felt that twentieth-century art had 'turned away ... to a great introspective romance'.[23]

How this problem bore on Kitaj's own art was well summarised in 1979 by Timothy Hyman: 'In the 1960s Kitaj had created a new kind of picture ... What then were the reasons for his repudiating the work that had made him famous? He has called himself "a grandchild of Surrealism and many other aspects of modernism which have ruined me". What seems to be in question is the whole direction of modernism – its diffuse "spatial" concern, its perception of the world as collage, as opposed to classical art's depth and focused intensity of meaning. For Kitaj, the scope had been bought at too dear a price.'[24]

Kitaj himself had observed: 'In a way I regret that Pound and Eliot often had more of an influence on my pictures than previous painting did. Sometimes I think I would be further on in my maturity as a painter if I had been as moved by Rembrandt when I was eighteen as I was by Pound.'[25] Other aspects of modernism which Kitaj sought to expunge from his art were its partiality to irony and its inaccessibility. As he had stated in 1982: 'My disjunctive compositions have no doubt been true to some of the aspects of my life – to the life of a displaced, recalcitrant cosmopolite – but I've felt my pictures have been far too difficult. So I mean to "straighten myself out" as Martin Buber would say ... As I grow older I yearn for a deflation, not of mystery or complexity, but of opacity.'[26] He reacted, also, against the obsession that had developed in English art from the late 1950s with avoiding the alleged danger of allowing a work to be 'literary' or to constitute 'illustration'. And more clearly than ever he saw that the reason why he had rejected the reductivism characteristic of so much contemporary art was his wish for a fuller engagement with modern life, more directly conveyed by the resulting art.

An important means to such engagement was the act of drawing, which in the early 1970s assumed great prominence in Kitaj's work. 'After half a digressive lifetime', he wrote, 'I have had to dismantle my own unhappy resources and begin to draw all over again; a drawing redemption in adversity'.[27] Reacting against his own large and influential output as a printmaker, with its bases in collage and in technology, he felt that instead 'I should have been drawing ..., trying to develop a talent I might actually have. I think I wasted ten years, until with Sandra's encouragement and example I went back to drawing from life, using the classic disciplines ... without worrying about whether I was being "modern" or not'.[28] 'For me', he had earlier declared, 'forward (not back!) to drawing the human form every day; that *natural* passage (so it seems to me) toward the other shore – the delineation of the face and fortunes and torments of us all.'[29]

fig.6 Sandra Fisher **Maggi Hambling** 1980
Charcoal on paper *R.B. Kitaj*

The outcome, as Frederic Tuten observed in 1982, was that Kitaj 'reinvigorated the tradition of drawing and of drawing from the figure ... These drawings are among the most beautiful we have seen in decades and their existence at this time raises substantial questions about where we have been in the past 30 years and where, if anywhere, our art is going'.[30] For Robert Hughes, Kitaj 'has emerged (along with such Englishmen as Lucian Freud and Frank Auerbach) as one of the few real masters of the art of depictive figure drawing now alive ... *Solid, chunky, driven, greedy*: these adjectives apply to Kitaj's appropriation of the world.' [present author's italics][31]

The first three words of the title of Kitaj's first exhibition, in 1963, were 'Pictures with Commentary'. The commentary was edited and in large part written by himself. Ever since, Kitaj's work as an artist had been interwoven with published essays and written interviews, offering a parallel critique that was compelling on account both of the force of its ideas and of their expression. In the mid-1970s the Arts Council of Great Britain invited Kitaj to select and to buy for their collection a group of British works which would then form the core of an exhibition articulating the works' common theme. Consistent with the direction his thinking about his own art was taking, Kitaj chose to focus on drawings made according to 'what I believe to be the most basic art-idea, from which so much great art has come. I was looking mostly for pictures of the single human form', which would 'glow like beacons of where art has been and like agents of a newer art life to come.'[32]

The title of the exhibition was the last three words of a line in W.H. Auden's poem 'Letter to Lord Byron': 'To me Art's subject is the human clay'. In the catalogue, Kitaj articulated this thesis with clarity and passion. His essay immediately became, and has remained, one of the key texts in the history of the period's vigorous debate about the purposes of art. Published in the same year as the national controversy aroused by the Tate Gallery's purchase, four years earlier, of Carl Andre's 'Equivalent VIII' 1966 ('The Bricks'), it marked a turning point in the British art community's recognition of the need for a more pluralistic concept of the nature of the significant art of any modern period. It was also one of a number of distinctively personal texts by Kitaj, published over the years, which established his as one of the most exceptional voices within serious discourse on several interlinked topics – the relationship between art and wider human experience, the relationship between present and past art, the conditions and consequences of persecution and of exile, and the recognition of the self.

Although Kitaj's writing is unimaginable divorced from his practice as an artist, in its own right it would make him a substantial figure in the cultural dialogue of our time. His writing combines inner necessity, urgency of feeling, breadth of reference and vividness of focus with a relevance to human affairs that operates independently of his art, yet at the same time is sharply illuminated by it. His highly individual expression shows qualities that are unexpected in combination. It is rough-hewn yet sophisticated, communiqué-like yet with a dynamic impetus that keeps the reader continuously engaged, and it employs a tone that is at once public in its weight and conversational in its intimacy. The writer comes across as having insatiable curiosity and as being fervent in his convictions yet at the same time agonised and dissatisfied – at once prophet and seeker. The opposite of withdrawn or esoteric, Kitaj's texts reflect the complexity of lived experience. They are unusual among serious

fig.7 Henry Moore **The Artist's Mother** 1927
Pencil, pen and ink with finger rub and scraping
on paper *The Henry Moore Foundation*
Photo: Michel Muller

fig.8 Leonard McComb **Egyptian Sculpture
Drawing** 1975 Pencil and watercolour on
prepared paper *R.B. Kitaj*

art-related writing in the degree to which they are pervaded by the idioms of
the speech of street, bar, workshop and sports stadium, as well as by those of
mid-century film.

The exhibition *The Human Clay* brought together the work of artists as
prominent as Freud and Hockney with that of others, of several generations,
who were much less well known. Although it constituted a plea for recognition of the importance of images of the human figure, Kitaj emphasised the
need for diversity in art, writing: 'Do not take this exhibition as a tightass pre-
sumption for one kind of holy art ... Some argument may be suggested here
but argument within the art, within a popular front ... There will always be
various lots of truths according to the odd lives we lead ... Artistic, like political argument will only be suppressed at our peril.'[33]

Despite these assurances, controversy surrounded, for some years, a concept which Kitaj introduced in the exhibition's catalogue, that of a 'School of
London'. Kitaj's main purpose in articulating this idea was to draw attention
to what seemed to him the insufficiently recognised richness of achievement of
the art being made in the city where he lived. However close the links between
artists, this richness was grounded, he felt, in a bracing diversity. He wrote:
'There are artistic personalities in this small island more unique and strong
and I think more numerous than anywhere in the world outside America's
jolting artistic vigour. There are ten or more people in this town, or not far
away, of world class, including my friends of the abstract persuasion. In fact, I
think there is a substantial School of London ... If some of the strange and fascinating personalities you may encounter here were given a fraction of the in-
ternationalist attention and encouragement reserved in this barren time for
provincial and orthodox vanguardism, a School of London might become even
more real than the one I have construed in my head.'[34]

Though Kitaj's meaning in proposing the idea of a School of London has
been misunderstood, it is not entirely surprising that many came to associate
the phrase with a smaller group of painters, including – though not restricted
to – Bacon, Freud, Auerbach, Kossoff, Andrews and Kitaj himself. All six of
these made art overtly concerned with the human figure and marked by intense engagement with the subject, and four of them also attached great importance to drawing. All six also combined the communication through their
own art of a strong sense of the life of their own day with a powerful response
to great art of the past. For them, as for others in *The Human Clay* (such as
Moore, Hamilton, Caro, Hodgkin, Blake and Hockney), this had always been
the case, but for much of the art community, including many artists, a curious
dislocation had developed, over the decades, between the making of art in the
present and awareness of the heritage of past art as a living thing. Kitaj's activity made a key contribution to the process of reconnecting contemporary
with past art which began to gather pace in the mid-1970s. The effect of the
arguments he advanced in print was sharpened by the telling implications of
the change in his own art practice.

The past two decades have witnessed a steady increase in the number of exhibitions of the art of earlier centuries and of associated publications. Over the
same period, the renewal of appreciation of the work of artists such as Menzel,
Corinth, Vuillard, (late) Sickert, Beckmann, Spencer, Dix, Hopper, Matisse of
the earlier Nice period, (late) Picasso, Hélion, (late) Guston and Balthus has
similarly demonstrated the hunger that existed for strongly wrought art that

openly addressed subjects rich in human interest, yet which had suffered periods of unjustified relative neglect. Though presented by some as reactionary in nature, Kitaj's related engagement with earlier art was in the cause of opening up an important way forward for art in the present and future, in which human feelings and circumstances would be no less memorably represented.

Of all past periods and places, it was with late nineteenth- and early twentieth-century France that Kitaj came, at this time, to feel most closely engaged. Above all, this was in respect of the work of two artists who, he stressed, had made some of their most extraordinary work in our own century, Cézanne and Degas. Kitaj's Cézanne was not the master of formal relations admired by Roger Fry, but rather a genius who broke new ground with a type of figural invention owing its very form to the deeply personal psychological intensity with which it was imbued. This could be seen particularly clearly in the late pictures of bathers. Ungainly but powerful, the figures in these paintings had both physical and emotional immediacy; their images gave a strong sense of transmission from great art of earlier periods; and, vitally, they spoke of Cézanne's inner life, yet did so in ways which left intact an essential mystery. Kitaj asked: 'How about late, late Cézanne? *What* was going on in that man's wondrous mind? Those clumped, hurt, awkward, stilted bathers with webbed feet, no ankles, moronic heads, slipping features, came from God knows which frame of mind.'[35]

Kitaj also stated that 'The drawings of Degas are one of those artistic achievements by which I measure all art'.[36] In particular, he was moved by the late pastels of nudes, 'these crazy-exquisite summations of a lifetime, these heavily contoured, highly emphatic, utterly invented visions of women. Like late Cézanne bathers, their facial features are incredible, like no women ever seen because, I suspect, the drawing hand was obeying a higher order, both in Degas and in Cézanne, born of reclusion and mastery and sensation. For me, these two misanthropes, in a sort of holy anguish, were gouging out the best works in my own now almost finished century.'[37]

It was when viewing drawings by Degas in Paris in 1975 that Kitaj experienced as a revelation the possibilities of the medium of pastel. Till then he had resisted using it, despite urgings from Sandra Fisher, but now for some years pastel took on a role in Kitaj's work as important as oil paint, and often as weighty. In their thoroughly wrought substance, their crumbled textures and their brilliance of colour, his pastels frequently attained the presence of canvases. An insistent materiality was enhanced by Kitaj's use of heavy papers. Their pronounced grain was accentuated by the pastel rubbed into them, while the body of many works was emphasised by Kitaj's tendency, in building a composition, to combine several separate sheets of paper. The edges of these sheets had been torn irregularly, with the result that the outer contours of discrete surfaces formed ridges that operated within a work both as pictorial information, like ambiguous drawn lines, and as a kind of shallow relief.

In renewing the tradition of the genre of pastel, Kitaj added a late modern emphasis in the frankness of his exposure of the relation between medium and ground and of the physical means employed in making marks. He used pastel to convey a wide range of effects, from enhanced plasticity to refinement and tender softness. Both the tactile freedom of pastel and its capacity for luxury would feed into Kitaj's paintings. As many remarkable drawings from observation show, pastel could also be made to yield a greater sense of closeness with

fig.9 Edgar Degas **Nude Woman Drying Her Foot** *c.*1885–6 Pastel on buff wove paper affixed to original pulpboard mount *The Metropolitan Museum of Art, New York. The H.O. Havemeyer Collection. Bequest of Mrs H.O. Havemeyer, 1929*

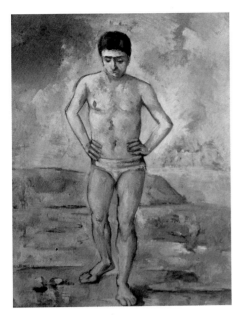

fig.10 Paul Cézanne **The Bather** *c.*1885
Oil on canvas *The Museum of Modern Art,
New York. Lillie P. Bliss Collection*

the human subject. A parallel, if unnerving, intimacy is achieved in the often large drawings derived substantially from the imagination. These show how well pastel was adapted to disclosing the sometimes disturbing reality of the artist's inner world. Some of Kitaj's pastels leave the viewer uncertain whether their images of fear and horror are released by the malleability of the medium or are dictated from within, as if by hallucination. This ambiguity is nowhere seen so powerfully as in the series of single bathers, in which a human activity familiar in the work of Renoir, Gauguin, Matisse and, of course, Degas and Cézanne, is re-examined in the light of mid and late twentieth-century experience. Timothy Hyman has aptly described Kitaj's single bathers as embodying an 'existential conception of the "estranged" figure, set in, or against, the void'[38] and has drawn attention to their debt both to Cézanne's painting 'The Bather' *c.*1885 (fig.10) and to its interpretation by Diane Lesko, which 'confirmed the strangeness, bordering on madness, of Cézanne's art'.[39]

A Jewish Identity

In 1980, Kitaj declared: 'I, for one, *feel* like a Post-Impressionist.'[40] However, in the same years as he felt this impulse towards a crucial reconnection with art of the period from van Gogh to Matisse, Kitaj had a parallel instinct, of growing intensity, namely that he must reconnect with his own identity as a Jew. The ability of the great Post-Impressionists simultaneously to convey the vividness of human experience and to project their own self-identity offered a powerful example to Kitaj as he sought to realise in his own art the nature of the experience of a people and, in particular, that of the one person among them whose life he knew from the inside.

Kitaj has observed: 'I take it that one's condition is the truest subject of one's art.'[41] He has drawn attention to Emerson's view that 'That is always best which gives me to myself. The sublime is excited in me by the great stoical doctrine, *obey thyself.*'[42] Brought up in an agnostic milieu, Kitaj did not reflect intensively on his Jewish heritage till he had reached middle age. He associated Jewishness with religious belief (which he did not have, and is now 'trying to figure out'), but his self-awareness and the direction of his art seem to have reached a turning point at the moment when his study of the history of the Jewish people led to a closer examination of the nature of the Holocaust and of the roots of this Nazi perpetration of mass murder in the decades that preceded it.

As expressed in another context by Amos Elon, the key realisation was that 'Jews had been singled out to die not because of their religion, or their politics, or because of what they did, but simply because they were there, they existed.'[43] Elon goes on to describe how this understanding led to 'a bleak, hard, pessimistic view of life', described by Jacob Talman 'as a "divine and creative madness which not only stills all fear and hesitation but also makes for clarity of vision in a landscape bathed in a lurid, distorting light"'.[44]

Although these observations were made in reference to specifically Israeli experience, they illuminate the changes that came about in Kitaj's art from the mid-1970s. Looking back in 1984, he recalled: 'I had always thought someone born Jewish was a Jew only if he wanted to be one. [This] classic as-similationist pose had been destroyed by the Holocaust ... The famous phrase ringing in my mind – "The Englishness of English Art" became for me the "Jewishness of Jewish Art".'[45]

In the light of this insight, Kitaj saw that the nature of Jewish experience had for many years been a central subject of his art without his realising it. Remarkably many of the radical activists and truth-telling commentators on whose images his works had centred, such as Rosa Luxemburg, Aby Warburg, Isaac Babel and Walter Lippmann, were Jewish and had reflected in their lives and writings what Kitaj calls the strange predicament of their people. In the words of Avram Kampf, writing about Kitaj, 'Like himself they seemed to be assimilated Jews not fully at home among the people among whom they were active. They seemed to be outsiders of a profoundly idealistic cast of mind, pos-sessed of a certain style of feeling, bound by a strong loyalty to their utopian dreams and a mysterious commitment to the absolute'.[46]

Kitaj's determination now to make the Jewish theme explicit in his art was strengthened by the realisation that: 'the decline of a Jewish collective memory was itself consumed in the Holocaust, which in turn becomes our most press-ing memory, our Crucifixion. The innermost meaning of that event, according to Buber, was a message from God for *teshuva*, a turning and renewal. Like Kafka, I've never made a "frank deposit into the bank of belief"; not yet, but somehow ... I've stumbled into an understanding that my own art has turned in the shadow of our infernal history. That history is still being written and I believe it may also be painted.'[47] Kitaj summed up this clarification of the focus of his art when he said: 'I'd like to try, not only to do Cézanne and Degas over again after Surrealism, but after Auschwitz, after [the] Gulag.'[48]

Historians of the aftermath of the Holocaust, in which millions of Jews were murdered by the Nazis during the Second World War, have observed how after its enormity had been reflected in memorials and in a wide range of immedi-ately post-war art a lengthy period elapsed in which artists addressed this theme much less often than the extremity of its nature might have led one to expect. The remarkable works which Kitaj would now produce, permeated by its implications, form an important and distinctive part of a delayed response in art and literature which began to surface some quarter of a century after the event.

Paradoxically, Kitaj's need to concentrate his focus onto Jewish experience had the result of widening the accessibility of his subject matter and of univer-salising its message. His art dealt with events that stood out within recent memory and was clearly powered by the present pain of an individual. These factors enhanced its impact; but above all, Kitaj's insistent theme was man's inhumanity to man. As he put it: 'the threatened condition of the Jews wit-nesses the condition of our wider world.'[49]

Kitaj's development of the theme of Jewish identity had the effect of pulling together all the strands of his work up to that time, and not of his art alone. For his passion for the printed word, too, could now be seen as characteristi-cally Jewish: 'Even a false scholar ... like myself seems to arrive, by some nat-ural (inherited – Jewish?) order of things, at painting by way of the word, which may come on some days before art ... as it was said to in the begin-ning.'[50] He added that: 'Harold Bloom has written, in a fearful essay about the survival of the Jews (as a Jewry), of their "text-centredness", their "text-obses-

fig.11 Kitaj **I and Thou** 1990 Oil on canvas
The artist

fig.12 Franz Kafka **A Man Seated at a Table with his Head on his Hands** Drawing J.P. Stern, *The World of Franz Kafka, courtesy Weidenfeld and Nicholson Limited*

siveness". I believe that one of the most touching gifts this refractory people of mine has left to our painting art, to its cosmopolitan modernism, is justly described by Bloom's terms.'[51]

All these themes come together in a painting such as 'If Not, Not' 1975–6 (no.29), in which a landscape strewn and embedded with motifs attesting desperation and destruction, and dominated by the image of the gatehouse at Auschwitz, discloses a debt to Eliot's *The Waste Land*. But the urgency of Kitaj's sense of his identity as a Jew led naturally to his increasing absorption in the lives and work of Jewish writers. Two of these in particular, Kafka and Benjamin, came to have a significance for him as great as that of Degas and Cézanne and to exceed in importance that of Eliot and Pound.

In his novels, Franz Kafka (1883–1924) conveyed the feelings of disorientation, fear and guilt of the individual who, in the modern world, finds himself an outsider to the prevailing system, by which he is oppressed. Kafka's writings make clear how his sense of alienation and of uncertainty about his own abilities reflects his perception of the position of Jews in the Central Europe of his day. Kitaj has written of Kafka: 'I feel closer to him than to any other. The artists I dwell on every day of my life, such as Giotto, Rembrandt, Degas, Cézanne, Matisse and Picasso fail me in this one ... respect – their condition was not the condition of the Jew ... Above all, Kafka encourages me to know myself and to puzzle out my own Jewishnesss and to try and make that over into an art of picture-making ... Kafka is the magical element in my equation. He did what no painter has been able to do really clearly ... the Jewish condition becomes the subject of Kafka's art, it informs its form ... Kafka was the only artist I've ever heard of, the only artist I know, who assumes the condition of Jewishness in forms which speak to [the painter in] me.'[52]

Kitaj discovered the German writer Walter Benjamin (1892–1940) in 1965. Benjamin's suicide as a victim of the Holocaust was the final tragic and telling action of a mind which would in any case have fascinated Kitaj through his wide-ranging texts. Benjamin was a non-religious Jewish bibliomane, influenced by Surrealism and immersed in the past and present of Paris, where he lived in exile from 1933. 'In the life and work and death of Benjamin', Kitaj wrote, 'I found a parable and a real analogue to the very methods and ideas I had pursued in my own painting: a shifting urban complex of film-like fragmentation, an additive, free-verse of an art, collected in the political and cultural urgencies of the diaspora Jew ... Benjamin spoke to my sense of exile of mind and heart, an un-at-homeness in great sensual cities which might lead to an art and *maybe* even a Jewishness of Jewish art.'[53] And elsewhere: 'Benjamin the oddball Marxist never interested me but ... his peculiar Jewish life spoke to me ... The tormented conjurer Benjamin was crucial in my turn towards a Jewish aspect in art ... He sent me back to read the wondrous Kafka I had not read since Vienna and forward to Scholem and the endless questions of assimilation, Diaspora, Homeland and Apocalypse which would disturb my painting.'[54]

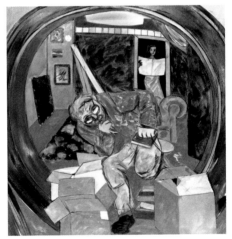

fig.13 Kitaj **Unpacking my Library** 1990–1 Oil on canvas *Joe Kitaj, Los Angeles*

In 1989, Kitaj published the longest and the most trenchant and impassioned of his many distinctive texts, the *First Diasporist Manifesto*. This 128 page publication, strikingly illustrated by photographs and by numerous reproductions (mostly cropped details) of his works in all media on Jewish themes, is not only the fullest statement of the Jewish dimension in Kitaj's art and thought but also in many ways a summation of his aims, overall, as an artist. For since the central subject of Kitaj's art is his own experience and understanding, to realise his Jewish identity was also to make possible a clearer understanding of the nature of his art as he had pursued it since long before he became conscious of its Jewish essence.

Some advised Kitaj against publishing a book on this theme and he himself came to regret its publication, because he feels it is 'like an unfinished painting'.[55] But the form, the expression, the originality and above all the richness of idea in this text guarantee lasting appreciation of its significance. Like Kitaj's art, it integrates intensely personal history and feeling with consideration of issues of importance for the community at large.

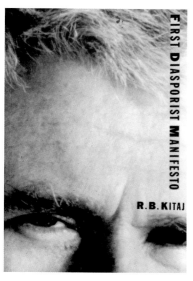

fig.14 R.B. Kitaj, *First Diasporist Manifesto* (front cover) *Courtesy Thames and Hudson Ltd*

In the twentieth century, art had come increasingly to be discussed and even judged in terms of its relation to style. Kitaj's *Manifesto* was the climax, to date, of the expression of his conviction that, on the contrary, the determining factor may be content and its imaginative communication. Thus, in proposing the existence of a hitherto unidentified 'ism', he was seeking to identify approaches to art which, though united by predisposing circumstances that could not help but affect an artist's work, had no common look.

'Rootedness', he wrote, 'has played its intrinsic and subtle part in the national art modes of Egypt, Japan, England, Holland and the high Mediterranean cultures and city-states. I want to suggest and manifest a commonality (for painting) in dispersion ... If a people is dispersed, hurt, hounded, uneasy, their pariah condition confounds expectation in profound and complex ways. So it must be in aesthetic matters. Even if a Diasporist seems to assimilate easily to prevailing aesthetics, as he does in most currents of life, the confounding, uneasy side of his nature may also be addressed, that deeper heart, as magical as anything the Surrealist or Mystical-Abstractionist ever sought within himself.'[56]

He personally wished to be 'a tribal remembrancer, wrestling with my Diasporic angel'.[57] He also suspected the existence in Diasporism of 'a *depressive* connection which formulates its own aesthetic',[58] and in identifying among its Jewish exemplars Primo Levi, Soutine, Kafka, Celan, Bomberg, Benjamin and Rothko he could logically also have included himself.

But although it was his own Jewish identity that had led Kitaj to its insights, a central conclusion of the *Manifesto* was that Diasporism is a condition not dependent on racial, national or religious affiliation *per se*. 'Jews do not own Diaspora', he wrote, 'they are not the only Diasporists by a long shot. They are merely mine.'[59] Indeed, 'I consider "Guernica" to be a Diasporist painting, at least as much as it is Cubist, Surrealist, Socialist/Antifascist, Picassoist',[60] and 'Beckmann was not a Jew but he foretold, within free modernism, that a Diasporist art of painting would synthesize the perils, freedoms and all but inexplicable paradox of identity some of us would cleave to in art of our own. Diasporism may be more appropriate to paradox than even Surrealism was, because its life is lived while it is painted.'[61] As Marco Livingstone has stated: 'The application of Kitaj's thesis not just to Jews but to all people classed as outside the mainstream of power in their society, including women, foreigners, homosexuals and those of non-Caucasian racial origin, creates a potent image to anyone who feels both a part of that society and somehow also alienated from it.'[62]

fig.15 Pablo Picasso **Guernica** 1937
Museo Nacional Centro de Arte Reina Sofía, Madrid

In the 1970s, as we have seen, Kitaj responded to the powerful sense of concentration achieved by the great artists of the late nineteenth and early twentieth centuries in the human images they created, and he reacted against the fragmented forms of his own early work. Among the consequences of these developments was a new interest in representing the single figure. Stirred by his sense of the strangeness of the situation of anyone who, through circumstance or specialisation, becomes 'located' in a culture not their own, he embarked on a series of imaginary portraits in a uniform slender, upright format. As he wrote in the *Manifesto*: 'Diasporism has inspired those representations or fictions of types of people to whose pictures I have given titles ending in *ist* – Orientalist, Neocubist, Arabist, ... Cézannist, Sensualist, Communist and Socialist, Kabbalist, Caféist, Hispanist, and so on. I believe in a type-coining power for art. Some have been friends; all have been Diasporists (mostly not Jewish), folk who complicate one's world in strange and wonderful ways. These people have not taken Pascal's advice, which is something like: all the trouble in the world is caused by people who do not know how to stay in their own room. I'm glad they didn't because their dispersed lives have broken ... patterns and searched out cosmopolitan treasure.'[63] This series of works relates to Kitaj's fascination with 'secret lives', and also to his need, when engaged with a Degas or a Kafka, to know in detail not only how they went about making their work but also about the patterns, habits and obsessions of their personal existence. It epitomises the conviction, which underlies all aspects of his work, that whatever a creative person makes is one with his or her life as a whole.

Since 1980

From the early 1980s, the urgency of Kitaj's engagement with the complexity of human experience and often with intense psychological states seemed to find additional expression, in his painting, in the forthrightness with which the drawing of the image was exposed in the finished work, in the freedom with which paint was applied and in the richness, sometimes even the jolt, of his colour. For more than a decade now, his work has been dominated by crowded yet boldly articulated multi-figure compositions. He foreshadowed these when he wrote in *The Human Clay*: 'There will always be pictures whose complexity, difficulty, mystery will be ambitious enough to resemble patterns of human existence ... When I said ... that I was looking for examples of the basic art-idea, single figure invention, I did not mean to presume that a higher order is embraced there alone. In fact, the opposite may be the case for me. Ultimate skill and imagination would seem to assume a plenitude in painting when the "earthed" human image is compounded in the great compositions, enigmas, confessions, prophecies, sacraments, fragments, questions which have been and will be peculiar to the art of painting.'

By contrast with Kitaj's typical paintings of the 1960s and early 1970s, those since 1980 have tended to conjure broadly credible scenes of figures in spatially unified settings. It would, however, be a mistake to conclude that Kitaj has lost that inclination towards drawing on a multiplicity of sources for the imagery of a particular painting, which in earlier periods was manifested so openly by the 'illogical' nature of a picture's internal relationships. On entering Kitaj's studio, the persistence of this urge is immediately evident. Pinned to the walls are reproductions of details of the art of the last many centuries, while around each painting in progress the floor is covered with books open at particular pages, bearing images from Cézanne or Degas, but also from Giotto, from Ingres, from Hopper, from Brueghel, from Michelangelo, and with Matisse 'as a sacred presence'. In his paintings these motifs, recast, fuse with stories half of the imagination and half of the acute realities of our own era, as well as with re-enactments of the disturbances and occasions of Kitaj's own life. The result is an art abundant in suggestion, in which images combine a pronounced immediate reality with a mysterious, insistent half-familiarity.

In combining previously unrelated images on a single canvas so as to make there a new reality, Kitaj's painting, particularly of the 1960s and 1970s, anticipated, at a superficial level, the approach of some new art that achieved great prominence in the 1980s. In using disparate sources, however, Kitaj's aim has never been to mirror the confusing bombardment of image and message that we all experience in the modern world, or, through his juxtapositions, to convey a sense of irony. The distinction was well made by Stephen Spender when he wrote: 'The post-modernism against which [Kitaj] has reacted has its own kind of seriousness; but the tragic is precisely what it avoids or evades. The tragic implies both looking at the life of experience inside oneself and at the outer world of the disasters of war and violence – and constructing a vision which will meet and include both. It deals in wholeness.'[64]

fig.16 Kitaj **Certain Forms of Association Neglected Before** 1961 Oil on canvas *Whereabouts unknown*

Kitaj's painting of the 1980s, with its fractured painterly surfaces and urgent graphic currents, was dominated by large allegories of the suffering inflicted in our century by anti-Semitism. After broad but disturbing treatments of the theme in works such as 'The Jewish School (Drawing a Golem)' (no.57) and 'Rock Garden (The Nation)' (no.59) Kitaj increasingly introduced imagery from his personal life, such as portraits of himself (e.g. in 'Cecil Court, London WC2 (The Refugees)' (no.65) and of his friends (e.g. 'The Jewish Rider', no.71). The latter painting is one of many in which, in this decade, Kitaj employed the motif of the chimney. Sometimes it was shown smoking, as in Nazi extermination camps. At other times, vulnerable figures were pictured as trapped inside it. Kitaj's aim was to find a symbol of Passion as powerful for the Jewish people as that of the Cross for Christians; indeed, in some works, the two motifs are tellingly juxtaposed.

Intermittently from the mid-1980s, Kitaj painted a number of pictures with titles beginning with the word 'Germania'. These explore aspects of the history, in the modern era, of the persecution of the Jews in the country where the motor of this tragedy was located (nos.73, 75). Also in the 1980s, in Germany itself, Anselm Kiefer was addressing the same theme. Though very different from Kitaj's, Kiefer's art likewise aimed to confront the perturbing actualities of the recent past and to this end similarly employed directness of image and vigour of touch as the means of powerful allegory.

fig.17 Kitaj **Passion (1940–45) Writing** 1985 Oil on canvas *The artist*

Following his recovery from a heart attack, Kitaj embarked in 1990 on what can be seen as an identifiably new phase in his painting. His range of subjects became more panoramic and the flow of ideas more of a torrent, as the number of works in progress at any time markedly increased. At the same time, the autobiographical element grew more pronounced. This can be seen in the number of paintings on family themes, in the explorations of Kitaj's im-

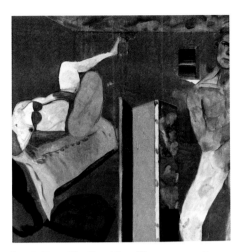

fig.18 Kitaj **The First Time (Havana, 1949)** 1990 Oil on canvas *Private collection, courtesy Marlborough Fine Art (London) Ltd*

mediate London locale, in the sequence of small and inventive canvases on aspects of his own health (described by Kitaj as 'little hypochonds', nos.94–101), and in many paintings of recollection. The latter extend from confessional 'snapshots' of his earliest sexual encounters to the retrospective overviews given in works such as 'My Cities (An Experimental Drama)' (no.104) and 'Greenwich Village' (no.105). 'The Wedding' (no.102) commemorates Kitaj's marriage to Sandra fisher in 1983. Set in an ancient synagogue, it is an affirmation of hope for the future, yet its relation to such earlier works as 'Cecil Court, London WC2 (The Refugees)' cannot fail to remind us of the theme of displacement which unites the family histories of the majority of those shown participating in the ceremony.

In the 1990s, Kitaj applies paint more thinly but with much greater freedom of gesture, sometimes with cascades of discrete marks. Conspicuously exposed within the painting, drawing is bolder and more inventive. Unlike with the impasted faces and figures of the early 1980s, drawing is the principal vehicle in these paintings of distortions of customary physiognomy, in which the human image is twisted, dislocated and sometimes virtually remade. Strangely, this substantial invention of images is a means of endowing the resulting human presences with distinct credibility, as well as of heightening psychological expression. As his statement on p.56 shows, the nature of the development of Kitaj's art into the future is reassuringly unclear.

Heresy and Example

Kitaj's entire career can be viewed in terms of a continuous interplay between the mainstream and unorthodoxy. Nonconformity and resistance have the upper hand, but their relation to the broad currents of the day is dynamic, sometimes even formative, and for all Kitaj's reclusion, he is far from isolationist.

Kitaj's work as an artist began at the same time and place as Abstract Expressionism reached its high point, but there, in the New York of 1950, 'my provincial heart was set on learning to paint like Hans Memlinc ... Those faces still set me dreaming, still stand for the adventure I was looking for when I began.'[65] Like the Abstract Expressionists, however, Kitaj would place urgency of subject and of its articulation at the centre of his art, would draw richly on imagery from the past, and would respond to the crisis of our century by means of works combining a sense of the tragic with unusual exposure of the self.

In the early 1960s, when Kitaj exhibited works steeped in the perceptions of Warburg and his circle about the layered meanings of images drawn from a wide range of sources, he was not only flying in the face of a hostility among artists to the 'literary' which was then approaching its apogee but also causing bewilderment to the Warburg Institute. Yet Kitaj's art was both foreshadowing the massive revival of source-accentuating art that was to follow and making what is now recognised as a valuable addition to that very chain of image-meaning that is the concern of iconologists.

The relationship of Kitaj's work to Pop, Conceptual and what has been

fig.19 Kitaj **A History of Polish Literature** 1962 Collage and lace on board *The artist*

called 'Post-Modern' art has been touched on above. In each case, the approaches he took to making art showed others that certain things were possible. Thus, though the resulting works and art forms had no substantial connection with his vision, it is undeniable that his work acted as a force for change. There is similarly a link between the exceptional openness of Kitaj's examination of his personal and inner life, in his art and writing, and the foregrounding of such concerns by many younger artists who have attained prominence in recent years.

As we have seen, Kitaj has been, at least as strongly, a force for change in the direction of a return to traditional approaches to pictorial art. But while he is a major contributor to the 'school' of figure painting and drawing that lies at the heart of the network of London artists he helped identify, the restlessness of his exploration of a wide territory and the forms of its expression in his work make him perhaps its least orthodox still-resident constituent. Similarly, while his articulacy has long enhanced outsiders' awareness of the special richness of American, British and Jewish cultures, Kitaj is a highly unorthodox representative of each. Nevertheless, his position in each culture is both integral and in many ways exemplary.

Kitaj could have restricted his attention to only one of these areas, just as he could have been 'only' an artist or 'only' a writer. But part and parcel of what is bound to be seen as his significant contribution to the reclamation of a central place in art for urgent representational content is his determination that that content should be able to encompass any aspect of life experience. John Ashbery reflected this purpose when he wrote: 'How wonderful it would be if a painter could unite the inexhaustibility of poetry with the concreteness of painting. Kitaj, I think, comes closer than any other contemporary, and he does so not because he is painting ideas, but because he is constantly scrutinising all the chief indicators – poetry, pictures, politics, sex, the attitudes of people he sees, and the auras of situations they bring with them – in an effort to decode the cryptogram of the world.'[66]

This instinct to be all-inclusive means that Kitaj's work overflows many of the bounds customary for particular disciplines in the arts. It is significant that he paints in a library and that he writes in a café, and also that he uses his bibliomania to look outwards, as much as to look in. Kitaj's work is at the opposite extreme from that of many twentieth-century artists who sought purity of form. 'Mondrian', he has written, 'has been a great source for one of the pervasive ideas in much of our art – the idea of detachment – an art which has been urged towards autonomy ... [but] it has always seemed to me that maybe an even larger spiritual purity than an art of detachment may lie in the very direction of sweating people in their unbalance rather than away from that life.'[67]

Much modern art aspires to the condition of the object. Of its nature, an object has a quality of enclosure. Kitaj has minimal interest in this aspect of art; his concern, rather, is with the art of *picturing*. A pointer to his affiliation to one end of the object/picturing spectrum is his instinct towards reproducing paintings in the form of selected details only. Such a mode emphasises the immediacy of a scene and a preference for the unknownness of a picture, its potential as opposed to its status as a thing.

Kitaj is therefore conspicuously anti-classical. He has said: 'I don't believe in a return to order ... Disorder maybe. Serious painters surprise themselves, upset themselves and others.'[68] His criterion for judging success in a work of art is not how 'final' its form is: open, loose, impassioned work often achieves greater distinctiveness and bears more of the stamp of life. The key consideration is whether an image is memorable – and *how* memorable it can be made.

Such a work need not be compendious. 'For two years now', he recorded in 1980, 'I've only been drawing ... most often the single human face or body on single sheets of paper. When you get it right, as a handful of men have, you get the whole world in ... Then you can do *anything*. When you get the whole world into a representation of the human form ... you also *let* the whole world in and the art becomes more *social*.'[69]

Essential in this endeavour is that the artist engage fully not only with the motif, but with himself. An observation of Kitaj's, already quoted, merits repetition: 'One's condition is the truest subject of one's art.'[70] The artist should avoid being dictated to by outside imperatives of style. Equally, it makes no sense to aim to make a work a universal statement.[71] 'I have ... come to believe that the universal is very often a result of particularist criteria – cultural traditions and destinies, personal experience, historical drama and milieux. In other words, it's defined by who made the thing, the particularist himself. Art seems [dull to me] when it gets that equation backward: International Style strives, cart before horse, for the universal, and the life-force is left behind.'[72] Or again: 'For me, what is good in art is expressed by a cast of mind, an imaginative personality which has seized the terms of a picture in ways that can surprise and engage my own nervous system. It is the persistence and independence of personality which will always confound history ... This cast of mind or manifest personality in a picture subsumes form and content for me. *It collapses time.*'[73]

This is the reason why the abundance in Kitaj's art of images drawn from pre-existing sources is the means to so much more than a succession of striking juxtapositions; in the pressure of Kitaj's personal concerns, the images become, in more than one sense, remade. Equally, his many images of sexual acts and exchanges derive their effectiveness as art from the fullness of his projection into the sensations of these encounters, as well as from that of his curiosity about their circumstances. Part of the strength and the originality of these works is in their directness. In an interview of 1982, Kitaj agreed that: 'some of the most "searing", most poignant images are ... those where the border between the erotic and the pornographic is indistinct',[74] 'where the distinction need not exist in my understanding of sexuality in art. My erotic life and my life in art have always seemed to ignite each other and as I grow old I can see in my own sexual decline a quickening of the art impulse, a transfiguration of mind over sexual matter. I hope the marriage between sex and art can be better than ever.'[75]

fig.20 Kitaj **Communist and Socialist** 1975
Pastel on paper *The artist*

Rootlessness and Transmission

The erotic pictures are only the most pronounced examples of a general truth about Kitaj's art, that in order to become engaged in the inner world of a work by him one does not need to have mastered a range of specialist knowledge, whether in literature, politics or art itself. Even in those multi-referential pictures where one cannot know exactly what is going on without being told, one is immersed very directly in the atmosphere peculiar to the work from one's first sight of it.

These atmospheres are not only the creation of a gifted storyteller; they are expressions of one or more of the various cultures of which, whether by birth or through identification, Kitaj is an inheritor. His receptiveness to climate, in this sense, permeates both his art and his writing. It enhances the ability of his work as a whole to transmit passions and ideas from the past (both distant and recent). Passion has precedence, for in evoking an atmosphere Kitaj so charges the work with the emotions it has for him that these command immediate recognition. Once engaged, however, and shown how much these issues *matter*, the viewer is led to consider the beliefs and particular preoccupations of circles and individuals both dead and alive. Kitaj's work not only testifies to the survival of their thought but becomes itself a means of securing attention to it in the future.

Kitaj has described himself as a 'false scholar'.[76] Yet the urgency with which he opens perspectives on areas of past thought and feeling combines with the vividness of the vistas he thus presents to give his work a role complementary to that of scholarship in provoking the viewer to think and to learn. In art and literature alike, Kitaj both animates the tradition and enriches it.

Paradoxically, for an artist who thus asserts continuities through time, Kitaj's work draws equal attention to disjunctions and to discontinuity. To set up the new and illuminating relationships that his paintings propose, he wrests motifs from their original contexts. It is as though a central motive of his art is to examine what happens when unrelated things interact. That they do so interact in his imagination, as in his life, is a result of the rootlessness Kitaj feels in his very being.

Rootlessness is closely connected to the experience of constantly moving on or, if not actually doing so, of living under the felt threat that moving might become unavoidable. This sense in Kitaj is linked to what Timothy Hyman has described as 'the consciousness, through all his work, of an undefined, but incurable, malaise'.[77] Kitaj himself has been quoted as saying 'I do like to watch people who are un-at home'.[78] On some levels one might say that Kitaj, though he pours his being into his art, is himself un-at home in his own work. In recent reflections on boxing, he wrote: 'I became an artist for chrisakes, which I'll regret to my dying day because my art feels more dislocated than my jaw did that fateful day in the late Forties.'[79]

Kitaj's work is permeated by the senses, in various combinations, of instability, danger, disjunction and sexual tension; these are registered with a kind of excitement, even an exhilaration. One reason for his interest in the brothel, locus of many of his images, may be the fact that pleasure is combined there with unease, in a setting where many contrasting personal histories touch fleetingly, within an essentially rootless situation. Kitaj's art demonstrates, however, that rootlessness has its positive aspects. Ideas are themselves a kind of home that can nurture those who dwell in it. This helps account for the significance to Kitaj of places where ideas (and the lives attached to them) intersect – the great cities, and the libraries, museums, rare-book sellers' and cafés which, along with brothels, recur in his art.

The fusions and disconnections, the flux and surprising possibilities that are intrinsic to these temporary meeting places link the rootlessness which Kitaj feels to the fertility of cosmopolitanism. This was one of the qualities in modernism that attracted Kitaj to it and, no less significantly, that made the Nazis and Stalinists hostile both to it and to Jews. If rootlessness is at the centre of Kitaj's art, so is a cosmopolitanism in him that has enriched the British art scene, in which, for all his protestations, he has thoroughly taken root.

Failure and Success

In the text he has written about his painting 'The Jew, Etc.' 1976–unfinished (no.31), Kitaj states: 'In this picture, I intend Joe, my emblematic Jew, to be the unfinished subject of an aesthetic of entrapment and escape, an endless, tainted Galut-Passage, wherein he acts out his own unfinish ... One of Joe Singer's jobs relates to a tradition of our exile, which influences this picture, whereby living messengers are trained up, who take the place of books, in order to preserve a freshness of teaching, not endangered by date or dogma.'[80] This text emphasises the transitional and fragmentary character of the forms of expression that may result from a situation so high in risk. But it also demonstrates that these are not necessarily weaknesses. One of the distinctive features of Kitaj's vision is his view that in art uncompletion, even failure, can be positive attributes; as he observed in the catalogue of *The Human Clay*, 'I grow to love the way we fail'. Moreover, 'even if we do seem to fail ourselves and others, life is short and art is long and one's miserable failures may look like trumps some day'.[81]

The subject of Kitaj's art is his own condition, itself a manifestation of the human condition. The latter is noted for its imperfection. It follows that any expression which reflects this state has value if, for all its faults – perhaps, indeed, on account of them – it succeeds in being true to life. Kitaj is willing to be exposed, even embarrassing, in favour of vividness of feeling. With that important purpose in mind, he sees being flawed as a strength in art. Consistently with this view, he has reversed the negative meanings conventionally applied to many words. Those to which he has given a positive connotation include 'disturbed', 'upset', 'difficult', 'tormented', 'tragic', 'vulnerable' and 'damned'. In a single short text, his introduction to the catalogue of *The Artist's Eye*, the exhibition he selected for the National Gallery, London, 'stunted', 'awkward', 'crazed', 'stilted', 'desperate', 'unhappy' and 'anguished' were all words that he used in a positive sense.

A further quality often disapproved of in art, but to which Kitaj accords a central and enriching role, is inconsistency. He wrote in 1968: 'I would like to develop into a switch-hitter and divide my time among the very complex, the very fresh and simple, the clearer meaning, the very difficult ... and more.'[82] Marco Livingstone has referred to 'the marriage of clarity and mystery which has become Kitaj's most prized goal'.[83] Kitaj must be counted among the principal advocates both of the provision of explicit accounts of the content and meaning of works of art and of the contradiction of such an approach through its replacement by fiction, or by silence. Each of these approaches is creative, but so is his wish to employ the three in combination, a choice which says much about the protean nature of his art.

A key factor in the attraction, for Kitaj, of the two great proteans of modernism, Matisse and Picasso, is their freedom from the constraints of consistency. 'When I worry at my waywardness, my false steps, my lack of consistent method, I find solace in those two geniuses of my century who seemed to be able to do anything they liked, however various, who were never satisfied with signature tunes. I always tell students that it's no coincidence that the two greatest, most inventive modernists happened also to be the two greatest draughtsmen of the human figure in our time, as well – and you can add to that, greatest sculptors, collagists, protegés of Cézanne, and much else.'[84]

Individual paintings by Kitaj can be the result of a direct statement of motif or idea identified from the outset, or they can proceed by intuition. Livingstone[85] quotes Kitaj's approval, writing of William Empson, that: 'One of his types allows for the poet (artist) to *find* his intentions in the course of writing (read – painting), to *discover* his idea after he has begun. This is *very* important for my own work. Why should I not discover intentions, ideas, meanings long after[?]'.

This partiality of Kitaj's to unpredictability is part of his wish as an artist to be able to escape restrictions and to take on anything at will. That wish, in turn, is inseparable from his need to be several people simultaneously – American and European, traditionalist and modernist, painter, sensualist and writer, celebrant and melancholic, settled and rootless. The strengths of his art are, in a sense, powered by the very unresolvability of such oppositions. As Kitaj wrote in his *Manifesto*, 'Diasporist art is contradictory at its heart'.[86]

Such openness to the virtues of opposites makes it unsurprising that for all the insistence of his polemics Kitaj is the reverse of a dogmatist. As he told Frederic Tuten: 'I always mean to speak for myself alone'.[87] His initiative in *The Human Clay* was a powerful call for recognition in practical terms of the importance of traditional approaches, yet those who saw this as an attempt to overturn all that modernism had stood for were mistaken. As he explained in 1980: 'Modernism is very dear to me. Fascism and Modernism are enemies. Fascism is *my* enemy. The enemies of my enemies are my friends.'[88] Kitaj's whole enterprise opposes the notion that art is a contest the purpose of which is to identify the one right way to make art in our time; in his view, any way is right which results in memorable work that is true to the nature of the artist who made it.

Kitaj's art is, indeed, done 'after Auschwitz', as he proposed. Man's inhumanity to man is far from always the specific subject of a work, but the implications of what has happened still penetrate his vision, even when his subject is explicitly lyrical. This was already the case long before the period when the Holocaust and its implications moved to the centre of his thoughts. His art therefore always has a darker undertone. It is not, however, true to say that its message is bleak. For not only does it celebrate the survival of ideas through many vicissitudes, it insists on the inexhaustible interest of human behaviour, motivation and experience, and does so in ways which celebrate humanity it-self. Kitaj writes in 1993: 'Jews will always be in trouble, but so will Blacks, for instance; I don't expect to put Tragedy behind me but I'm more and more interested in the Human Comedy and hope to devote some of my old age to that. I've got a young family and they keep me almost cheerful.'[89]

The central subject of Kitaj's art is states of mind, imagination and feeling. His works are affirmations of existence; that they go far beyond being mere markers is owing to Kitaj's ability to fuse striking pictorial invention, vitality of line and richness and beauty of colour and paint with an urgency of feeling that drives and determines all the elements in a picture. In so doing, Kitaj reveals himself with an openness that is unusual in degree. He exposes not only his beliefs but also his vulnerabilities. Uninterested in the constraints of the classical and aiming neither for an orderly development nor for a consistent 'look', he has produced an oeuvre notable for its generosity. It is an ardent, overflowing art, yet one in which awkwardness is a means of expressive energy and in which what is at times an almost wild extravagance does not overwhelm – indeed, reinforces – a work's purpose or sense.

Life is both exhilarating and grim. This century and this decade have confirmed how appalling it can be. Kitaj's is not an escapist art, but it is made in the belief that art, as much when it bears witness as when it evokes well-being, can be a source of strength. As Kitaj wrote in the *Manifesto*: 'We learn about life and its events by uncovering ourselves. Beyond that, or during that discovery, lies art in all its dramatic, controversial and depressing ambiguity ... The timeless Beckett may be paraphrased: (Art), that double-headed monster of damnation and salvation ... I even suspect art can mend the world a little.'[90] Interviewed in 1986, Kitaj concurred in the view that we cannot know the world. He voiced exceptional admiration for the work of Francis Bacon which, he agreed, was predicated on that assumption. For himself, however, he expressed the hope that the same assumption 'will carry me through less nihilist waters ..., towards an (ungraspable?) redemptive art'.[91] It will be surprising if many who see this exhibition do not feel that Kitaj has already grasped such an art, that he first did so more than three decades ago, and that the development here surveyed offers the exciting prospect of work no less memorable in the years ahead.

Notes

All books published in London unless otherwise stated.

1. William Shakespeare, *Hamlet*, Act 1, scene iii.
2. Kitaj arrived in England in 1957. Details of the times and places at which he has subsequently lived elsewhere, notably in the United States and France, are set out in the Chronology on pp.57–64.
3. cf. in particular Vivianne Barsky, '"Home Is where the Heart Is": Jewish Themes in the Art of R.B. Kitaj', in Ezra Mendelson (ed.), *Art and its Uses: The Visual Image and Modern Jewish Society (Studies in Contemporary Jewry: An Annual, VI)*, New York and Oxford 1990, pp.149–85 and Ziva Amishai-Maisels, *Depiction and Interpretation: The Influence of the Holocaust on the Visual Arts*, Oxford 1993.
4. In R.B. Kitaj, *First Diasporist Manifesto*, London and New York 1989, pp.121, 117.
5. 'Kokoschka', *Art News and Review*, vol.10, no.5, 16 Aug. 1958, p.5. Singling out for special admiration Kokoschka's work of 1917–24, Kitaj observed that whenever Kokoschka chose a new idiom, 'one of the most enlightening quests is posed. Namely: where does Kokoschka stand in relation to problems with which his younger contemporaries have been grappling? The Elbe landscapes with their sister canvases attempt to invest simple gestures of paint with a coloristic intensity inclined to plumb the depths of subject thirty years before de Stael. As I found myself staring into face after face, at a flicker of teeth, at a rapt refusal on the part of two eyes to seem alike, I was reminded of what de Kooning has called "the intimate proportions of anatomy".'
6. Frederic Tuten, 'Neither Fool, nor Naive, nor Poseur-Saint: Fragments on R.B. Kitaj', *Artforum*, vol.20, no.5, Jan. 1982, pp.61–9.
7. John Bayley, 'Introduction', in Edgar Wind, *Art and Anarchy*, 3rd ed. 1985, pp.xi–xx.
8. Kitaj quoted in Jerome Tarshis, 'The "fugitive passions" of R.B. Kitaj', *Art News*, vol.75, no.8, Oct. 1976, pp.40–3.
9. Ibid.
10. In a letter to Marco Livingstone, quoted in his *R.B. Kitaj*, Oxford and New York 1985, p.21.
11. Frederic Tuten, 'On R.B. Kitaj: Mainly Personal, Heuristic and Polemical', in *R.B. Kitaj: Pictures*, exh. cat., Marlborough Gallery, New York 1974, pp.5–7.
12. Timothy Hyman, Introduction, in *Narrative Paintings: figurative Art of Two Generations*, exh. cat., Arnolfini, Bristol 1979.
13. Timothy Hyman, 'R.B. Kitaj: Avatar of Ezra', *London Magazine*, vol.17, no.3, Aug.–Sept. 1977, pp.53–61.
14. Marco Livingstone, *David Hockney*, 1981, p.18.
15. Nikos Stangos (ed.), *David Hockney by David Hockney*, 1976, p.41.
16. 'An Eagerly Awaited First Exhibition', *Times*, 7 Feb. 1963, p.16.
17. Peter Greenaway, 'My Great Advantage over Veronese Is that I Can Make the People Move', *Art Newspaper*, vol.2, no.9, June 1991, pp.10–12.
18. Clive Phillpot, 'Kitaj Retrospective', *Art Journal*, vol.42, no.1, Spring 1982, pp.55–7.
19. Significant of this difference is the fact that in the major international survey exhibition *54/64: Painting and Sculpture of a Decade*, held at the Tate Gallery in 1964, Kitaj was represented by four works and Hamilton not at all.
20. Both works are reproduced in the catalogue of Kitaj's solo exhibition at Marlborough Fine Art in 1963.
21. Concern with meticulous procedure underlies 'Specimen Musings of a Democrat' in an unusual degree, in that it was inspired by the systematic visualisations of the medieval Catalan, Ramon Lull.
22. In Robertson, Russell, Snowdon, *Private View*, 1965, pp.193–4.
23. Introduction to *The Artist's Eye: An Exhibition Selected by R.B. Kitaj at the National Gallery*, London, exh. cat., National Gallery 1980, pp.[3–6].
24. Timothy Hyman, 'R.B. Kitaj: Decadence and Renewal' in *R.B. Kitaj*, exh. cat., Marlborough Gallery, New York 1979.
25. 'R.B. Kitaj and David Hockney Discuss the Case for a Return to Figuration', *New Review*, vol.3, nos.34/5, Jan.–Feb.1977, pp.75–7.
26. Tuten 1982.
27. Introduction to *The Artist's Eye* 1980.
28. Interviewed by John Russell Taylor in 'Profile: R.B. Kitaj. The State of the Artist', *Times*, 23 May 1983, p.13.
29. R.B. Kitaj, 'A Return to London' (interview with Timothy Hyman), *London Magazine*, vol.19, vol.11, Feb. 1980, pp.15–27.
30. Tuten 1982.
31. Robert Hughes, 'Edgy Footnotes to an Era', *Time*, vol.118, no.17, 26 Oct. 1981, pp.76–7, repr. as 'R.B. Kitaj' in Hughes, *Nothing if not Critical*, 1990, pp.269–72.
32. Kitaj in *The Human Clay*, exh. cat., Arts Council of Great Britain 1976, pp.[5–8].
33. Ibid.; 'popular' appeared as 'Popular' in that publication.
34. Ibid.
35. Tuten 1982.
36. Introduction to *The Artist's Eye* 1980.
37. R.B. Kitaj, 'Degas and the Nude', *Modern Painters*, vol.1, no.2, Summer 1988, p.93.
38. Timothy Hyman, in *R.B. Kitaj: 'The Sensualist' 1973–84*. Oslo 1991, p.8.
39. Ibid., p.13.
40. Introduction to *The Artist's Eye* 1980.
41. Tuten 1982.
42. Ralph Waldo Emerson, Divinity School Address, quoted in 'Prefaces by R.B. Kitaj' in Marco Livingstone, *Kitaj*, 2nd ed. 1992, pp.161–2.
43. Amos Elon, 'The Politics of Memory', *New York Review of Books*, 7 Oct. 1993, pp.3–5.
44. Ibid.
45. R.B. Kitaj, 'Jewish Art – Indictment and Defence: A Personal Testimony', *Jewish Chronicle Colour Magazine*, 30 Nov. 1984, pp.42–6.
46. *Chagall to Kitaj: Jewish Experience in 20th Century Art*, exh. cat., Barbican Art Gallery 1990, p.106.
47. See n.45 above.
48. See n.29 above.
49. *First Diasporist Manifesto* 1989, p21
50. 'Prefaces by R.B. Kitaj' in Livingstone 1992, p.161. Kitaj has also observed that: 'My Prefaces also have a source in the Jewish tradition called Midrash – commentaries, exegesis, emendation on sacred texts, sometimes highly contradictory and open to diffuse forms of imaginative genre.' (In Krzysztof Z. Cieskowski, 'Problems in Kitaj, Mostly Iconographic', *Art Libraries Journal*, vol.14, no.2, 1989, pp.37–9).
51. Livingstone 1992, p.161.
52. Tuten 1982. Words in square brackets added by Kitaj for the present catalogue.
53. See n.45 above.
54. In interview with David Cohen, 'The Viennese Inspiration: In Search of Self', *R.A.: Royal Academy Magazine*, no.29, Winter 1990, pp.34–6.
55. Kitaj to the author, 1993.
56. *First Diasporist Manifesto* 1989, pp.25–7.
57. Ibid., p.39.
58. Ibid., p.73.
59. Ibid., p.21.
60. Ibid., p.87.
61. Ibid., p.91.
62. Livingstone 1992, p.41.
63. Ibid., p.75.
64. Stephen Spender, 'R.B. Kitaj', in *R.B. Kitaj: Pastels and Drawings*, exh. cat., Marlborough fine Art 1980.
65. Introduction to *The Artist's Eye* 1980.
66. John Ashbery, 'Hunger and Love in their Variations', in *R.B. Kitaj*, exh. cat., Hirshhorn Museum, Washington 1981, repr. in John Ashbery, Joe Shannon, Jane Livingston, Timothy Hyman, *R.B. Kitaj: Paintings, Drawings, Pastels*, 1983.
67. *The Human Clay* 1976.
68. Cohen 1990.
69. See n.29 above.
70. Tuten 1982.
71. 'Only dilettantes try to be universal' – Isaac Bashevis Singer, quoted by Kitaj in his introduction to 'Prefaces by R.B. Kitaj', in Livingstone 1992, pp.161–2.
72. In interview with Andrew Brighton, 'Conversations with R.B. Kitaj', *Art in America*, vol.74, no.6, June 1986, pp.98–105. Words in brackets substituted by Kitaj, 1993.
73. Introduction to *The Artist's Eye* 1980.
74. Tuten 1982.
75. Kitaj to the author, 1993.
76. *First Diasporist Manifesto* 1989, p.39.
77. Timothy Hyman, 'R.B. Kitaj: Decadence and Renewal', in *R.B. Kitaj*, exh. cat., Marlborough Gallery, New York 1979.
78. Quoted by Dan Hofstader in 'Annals of Art: Dungeon Masters', *New Yorker*, 12 Nov. 1990, pp.53–92.
79. R.B. Kitaj, 'Art in Sport: Boxing', *Art Review*, vol.45, Sept. 1993, p.17.
80. For the full text, see p.132.
81. Kitaj to the author, 1993.
82. In Ethel Moore (ed.), *Letters from 31 Artists to the Albright-Knox Art Gallery*, [Buffalo NY] 1970, p.18.
83. Marco Livingstone, 'R.B. Kitaj', in *The Proper Study: Contemporary figurative Art from Britain*, 1984, p.89.
84. Kitaj to the author, 1993.
85. Livingstone 1992, p.18.
86. *First Diasporist Manifesto* 1989, p.35.
87. Tuten 1982.
88. See n.29 above.
89. Kitaj to the author, 1993.
90. *First Diasporist Manifesto* 1989, p.15.
91. Brighton 1986.

Kitaj: Recollections and Reflections

RICHARD WOLLHEIM

If I decipher correctly some words scribbled in an old engagement book for 11 January 1963, that was the day on which an old friend of mine, John Richardson, arranged that the two of us should go down to Dulwich to see a new painter, who, in the course of a brief meeting, had impressed him deeply.

The new painter, it was predicted, would soon cause a stir. From all accounts he seemed totally unlike the normal run of London art students of that period, at any rate as I knew them. Elbowing each other out of the way as they tumbled out of art school, they prided themselves on being tough and grumpy, they were suspicious of the past, and they had their gaze set firmly on Manhattan. By contrast, he had scholarly leanings, and was something of a bibliophile. He frequented the musty second-hand bookshops with which London was still full, where he could regularly be found with his nose up against the shelves of old art books or works of curious appeal. He was deep into the ideas of Aby Warburg, fragments of whose writings and journals he meticulously transcribed, in a simple, sloping handwriting, onto the clear or unmarked areas of his canvases. Before coming to England, he had stud-

fig.21 Kitaj **Wollheim and Angela** 1980 (detail) Charcoal on paper
The artist

ied art, first at Cooper Union, and then, after military service, in Vienna, where he had been, at one remove, the student of Schiele. He had gone to the Ruskin School in Oxford, and, while there, he had followed the lectures of Edgar Wind. He had been a postgraduate student at the Royal College, which he had just left. He was not tough or grumpy. He was not suspicious of the past. Nor was he at all glamourised by America: he was American.

Some of this I must have learnt, along with Kitaj's name, sitting in one of the pools of light into which Richardson's dark green sitting-room in the Albany was divided, and some I learnt only as we were making our way through wintry south London. We drove in a mini-van, which I had bought a few months before, expressly to get to my analysis, and which at this time I used a lot. It was a restless period for me, and I had got into the habit of driving, with friends or alone, to what then seemed outlying parts of London: to Dulwich, during the short hours of daylight, to see the Poussins; to Greenwich, and its magnificent, sprawling palace; to the East End to stand at night in the shadows of the great Hawksmoor towers; or, in the early hours of the morning, to go to seedy clubs in Notting Hill or in the decaying seventeenth-century squares of Wapping, now cleaned up forever. Sometimes these expeditions were a success, sometimes they completely failed, leaving me disappointed, or exhausted, or frightened. Now we were driving along to see a character out of Borges or Canetti, and this was a trip that I was sure to enjoy.

Kitaj opened the door to us.

I have preserved no initial impression.

I cannot, for instance, remember how he addressed us, or whether he had a beard, or wore spectacles. But soon I was intrigued by a gesture, which, affectingly, he has preserved into middle age. Recurrently he wiped the palm of his hand, sometimes the back of his hand, across his mouth and chin, and, when he did it, it was as though he was trying to rub deep into himself some physical memory, some distillation of the moment, which was lying on the surface of the skin. It was the gesture of someone who felt that he could not afford to miss a moment's worth of experience, but who, rather than squander it in the moment, would rather save it up and then relive it in his own time. It was the gesture of an artist.

It was a small house, and we, two city-slickers as we must have seemed in our dark suits and satin ties, followed Kitaj down a short linoleumed passage. At the end of the passage we were led into a room, where a young boy wearing a cowboy hat was looking with great intensity at a film on television. It was Lem, the future screen-writer, who has been one of the great joys of Kitaj's life. The boy was holding a black plastic gun, trained on the screen, and he had one of the central characters in his sights. Kitaj was ahead of us, and, as he walked between the boy and the screen, with a little flick of the wrist he turned off the set. The screen shrunk to a pinpoint of light, it blacked out, the gun drooped in the boy's hands, and, with total good humour, as though he had learnt from his father the art of preserving the moment, he got up and left the room.

The three of us who were left sat down. We talked for a few minutes. About what I do not remember, but it could not have been idle talk. Kitaj spoke emphatically, and with great seriousness. When he disagreed, he said nothing, but his silence was so intense that it changed the subject. Then, without a word, he got up and left the room. After a while he returned with a big tray he had prepared for us, which was weighed down with a giant teapot and mugs and plates and knives and something very simple to eat. It was like a Tolstoyan celebration.

For what happened next I have to rely on an immediate and quite uncorroborated experience, which nevertheless I feel impelled to trust. It opened on to something deep and involuntary in Kitaj's character.

For a few minutes Kitaj was standing there in front of us, holding the tray, and the china began to rattle, and briefly it might have been thought that he had not the slightest idea what to do next. Then abruptly the young painter bent forward, and, with something like the gauche determination of an old English drawing master, someone he might have known from the Ruskin or from some illustrated book of memoirs, he hooked his foot around a chair, he pulled it towards him, and, seemingly regardless of the fact that it was piled high with books, he set the tray down on its uneven surface. Then he straightened himself up, and he stared at us.

I do not intend the comparison to the old teacher to be taken as an invention of mine. I am sure that it is not, and that it is how Kitaj, on some level of consciousness, envisaged himself. You had only to look at him, and you could see that he was in the midst of a sudden inward impersonation. His briskness and his candour had deserted him, and I would have sworn that briefly, in those few minutes, his face aged thirty, forty years.

We stayed in all about an hour or so, and, by the time we left, I did indeed have impressions of the man. Two impressions, and both overwhelming: that of an iron will, and that of a deep, yearning romanticism.

In talking of romanticism, which I take to be essential to the genesis, and so to the understanding, of Kitaj's art, I could be readily misunderstood. Some might think of it as an attachment, indeed an excessive attachment, to appearances. But misguidedly: for that is at best half the story, and it is the less interesting half. What it leaves out is the inwardness of the attachment, or the alchemy that transpires on the inside. For when this youngish student from Ohio assumed, not casually but not after deliberation, the stiff, homespun look of someone who had drawn with Tonks or the elder Nicholson or had known Sickert, or when, over the years, he would go on assuming the manners, the daily habits, the prejudices, the little short-cuts of existence, by which, or so books informed him, or so he divined, the life of the serious artist had always been sustained, he did so in the spirit of an initiation, an immersion, an internalisation. There is, when we reflect upon it, nothing so odd in the fact that a painter should feel that the mastery of appearances would give him a kind of inner understanding not to be found elsewhere.

Not to be found elsewhere: and – it must be added – of which he felt himself to stand in particular need. To this very day, Kitaj will talk of his two great friends, Freud and Auerbach, as born within the charmed world of European art, and, by implication, of himself as brought up outside it. While he, a provincial boy, as he sees himself, was wasting his time with New York Surrealism and de Kooning, they were 'devouring' – a word he loves, for the fierce image it conveys of knowledge – the Old Masters. So to the conclusion: time had been lost, there was ground to be made up, and, to make it up, he has, at different stages of his life, resorted to different devices, different practices, different little bits of magic. For it is as the paraphernalia of magic that we should think of those pages, clipped from *Life* magazine, which are still pinned to the door frame of the studio, or of the Skira books and the monographs, pulled down from the bookshelves and laid out open on the floor while he paints: small rituals ministering to that quiet process of introjection which forms the inner lining of what those indifferent to the ways of art will continue to think of as mere ventriloquism.

Years after I had got to know him, when the Godwin house in which he still lives was being rebuilt around him, Kitaj said to me, 'I want a house that has the look of somewhere where Goethe, or Hölderlin, or one of those great Romantics, might have lived, with old oak floorboards, a kind of grey, that thick' – and he held up in front of my eyes his thumb and forefinger a good four inches apart, as though planks that thick had all the virtue of the older art engrained in them. And he continued to hold his fingers open like a clamp, until Weimar or Göttingen might have floated before his eyes, and then, without warning, he laughed at the idea. Kitaj's belief in tradition, in the handing down of art from one artist to another, is as deep, as profound, as unwavering, as that of Ingres or Picasso, and with them too it had magical associations. But it has never quelled his sense of irony.

A few years earlier, and he had believed that the virtue lay in travel. He explained to me his method. On a Friday or Saturday he would go out to Heathrow airport, and he would look up at the departure screens and see when the next flights were leaving for Barcelona, or Frankfurt, or Amsterdam, or Copenhagen, his own great imaginary cities, and he would buy a ticket, and get on a plane. The weekend would pass in pilgrimage as he roamed around the city, haunting the cafés and the squares and the museums and the red-light districts, inhaling the smells of the foreign food, which he never ate, and the foreign tobacco, which he never smoked, and, in the brothels, noting the endless positions, and the variations upon the positions, that sex and greed and fantasy and the threat of disappointment can impose upon the human frame: the human frame naked, half-naked, fully clothed.

And all the while he sketched. He sketched in the mind and out of it, and, as he did so, the fragments, the details, the very things out of which, as he sees it, art is constructed, accumulated.

When, from our present vantage point, we survey the art of the twentieth century, we can make out, falteringly, two different traditions or tendencies, each of which issues, in its own way, in an art of the fragmentary.

One tradition consists in the artist's taking an aspect of art, an aspect that has always been one aspect amongst others, and then making – or sometimes discovering – objects, or series of objects, that have this one aspect to the exclusion of all others. Or, if that is said to be an impossibility, for strictly speaking nothing can have just one aspect, then a more accurate way of describing these objects would be to say that they claim our attention solely in virtue of this one aspect: the remaining aspects, which they certainly have, they renounce, and we likewise are invited to disregard them.

The aspect that the artist isolates in this way is invariably something basic. Over the years, over the centuries, it has not been ignored. It has received attention. But what it has never received, and indeed never asked for, is undivided attention, so that, when the claim is made, we have a form of art that is not only new, but distinctively modern. Looking back over this first tendency and its art, we can recognise a miscellany of aspects that have, at different times, or by different artists, been picked out and given this kind of treatment. For instance: that it is the decision of the artist whether he has finished the work; that the spectator of the work has a contribution to make to its appearance; that the work derives from an idea, or a conception, in the head of the artist; that works of art belong to a tradition, or that artists borrow images from earlier artists; that there is something arbitrary about what the work is made of, or the materials that supply its medium.

Effectively the founder of this first tradition is Marcel Duchamp – or, rather, the simulacrum that the art world has created for itself of this uncommitted, dandified figure, who deserved better than to have followers. And, as to who the followers are, we are likely, depending on our taste and judgment, to pick on any of a number of bewilderingly different-looking artists. However, what gives them unity – or what gives the list we draw up its authority – is that, in each case, the art is fragmentary in that it is the concept of art under which it has been made that has been fragmented. For what we are invited to accept as art, or to regard as art, is something that satisfies just one of the fragments into which the

concept has been discomposed. The residue of the concept, and everything that has traditionally gone with this residue in the way of reference, or association, or aspiration, is now declared superfluous. And, if we are now inclined to ask whether this was perennially so, and whether it is simply the clear-sightedness of twentieth-century man that has allowed us to discard something in the traditional concept that was always expendable, or whether this amounts to a real conceptual change, these are questions that we are discouraged from asking. Asking them is said to show an essentialist attitude, which is said to be bad. This first tendency is hotly historicist.

The second tradition or tendency understands the fragmentary very differently. The fragments that this art has at its disposal or for its raw materials result from subdivision, as fragments must, but from subdivision not of a concept, but of a material thing. And here a distinction can be made within this tendency. However, the distinction does not seem fundamental, though, at certain moments in this century, it has been taken very seriously, both by artists and by critics. The distinction hinges on whether the thing, the material thing, that is fragmented is a work of art or perhaps something that might, in other circumstances, have been a work of art, or whether it is a mere article of everyday life. For example, contrast Rodin, who brought to his sculpture fragments of cinquecento art, and collage as practised by the Cubists, where it is the bric-a-brac of studio life that is transformed into art. But this distinction does not go very deep, for even with these two cases where the contrast is visually stark, there is a convergence. There is a convergence as far as the motivation of the artist is concerned. In each case, behind the fragment, there is the same desire to emphasise the physicality of the work, and the same desire to provide the work with a richness of significance or context.

Physicality, enrichment: these are the central values of this second tradition, and it is they that ensure that it and the first tradition are ultimately irreconcilable. Many recent artists have been unable to accept this as a fact, and they have struggled, this way and that, to bring the two traditions together. They have tried to fuse them, to conjoin them, to juxtapose them, but, to my eye, no serious painter – and I deliberately exclude painters of lesser intent, who have been able to concoct a variety of superficial compromises – has been able to secure more than a momentary, unstable truce.

Very few works in either tradition have dedicated themselves solely to the delectation of the senses. Most have had a didactic side. They have taken the viewer by the elbow, and extolled their own merits. Over the centuries, the work of art has always been something of a teacher, but not always a teacher about itself.

But the truth is that the first, or conceptual, tradition has very little to propose to its adherents except didacticism: didacticism, tempered by play. Most movements in art have offered their practitioners some distinctive subject matter. This is true of movements so randomly different as Impressionism, International Gothic, Cubism, the Nazarenes, Abstract Expressionism, the Euston Road – no matter how we jumble the categories, there has been something assigned to the painter to paint. But the conceptual tradition has so purified the subject matter of art that ultimately the artist is called upon to repeat, over and over again, the basic art lesson. The tradition has, of course, drawn into its ranks many artists of temperament and of high visionary intent, and they, being who they are, have produced works of subversive richness. But, in so far as the tradition is strictly observed, the subject matter of every work that the artist sends into the world, is, no matter how wittily it is embellished, or how provocatively executed, reducible, with little discernible remainder, to some favoured answer to the question, What is Art?

It is this self-denying aspect of the conceptual tradition that has led Kitaj to distance himself from it. A few earlyish prints, themselves the product of a period of uncertainty, and now disowned, manifest a sort of Duchampian defiance: but defiance without the accompanying Duchampian abstinence. Abstemious as a person, which, if not on the most conventional understanding, he certainly is, Kitaj has looked in art for something more satisfying than austerity. For him the desire to make works that are about art has always been a distant second to the desire to make works that are art, and he finds it hard to see how a work could be art without its having a subject matter other than itself. From the beginning, the choice, and the elaboration, and the realisation, of subject matter, have been at the centre of Kitaj's art. This is no more than we should expect from the artist who is known to have put Hockney, then a young art student, on the track that he has made his own, when, asked to advise him what he should paint, he told him to paint whatever interested him in life.

All this is mostly to do with preference or taste, and has very little bearing upon art. Kitaj's alienation from the conceptual tradition is rooted more in the kind of person he is than in the kind of artist he is interested in being. My own wager would be that, if he had been a banker, or a baseball player, or an actor, or a mathematician, if he had never put brush to canvas or dreamt of doing so, he would not have spent many Saturday mornings looking at the work of Donald Judd or Sherrie Levine.

But, when we turn to Kitaj's relations with the second tradition, or with the art of the material fragment, more comes into play. For now we have to understand something that not only holds a positive appeal for him but has an appeal that goes beyond taste or even temperament and reaches into the deepest recesses of his art.

When Kitaj, now a man in his mid-thirties, first emerged as a distinctive presence upon the London scene – a role which he was soon to abandon unreluctantly – and he appeared at dinner parties with his neat, stubbly beard, and his salty humour, and his highly distinctive turn of phrase, which his

written prose catches so well, as well as with his own special sack of learning, it became something of a platitude to say that he was the Ezra Pound of contemporary painting. He did little, as far as I can recall, to discourage it. Nor did he have any real reason to do so. For an idea that has always come to him naturally, so much so that he still asks, incredulously, What is so wrong with it?, is that painting that was truly modernist would want to fashion itself upon the undisputed achievements of modernist literature, and, in particular, of modernist poetry. Eliot, Joyce, Yeats, Kafka, Wallace Stevens, Lowell, would not, he feels, be half-bad models for a young painter.

And in thinking this, Kitaj, who is a lover of books, no less so because he buys more than he will ever finish, and loves to have them standing around him, like the marbles that an eighteenth-century traveller might have brought back from the Grand Tour, has always had, and always drawn upon, his own conception of what is distinctive, what is perhaps superior, about the Moderns. For him the central achievement of modernist literature is that it has relaxed the ways of organising the material it confronts. Instead of the traditional modes of combination, it has cultivated juxtaposition, and the contrast of images, and the pursuit of incongruity. It has been an art of fragments.

If the modern poet and the modern novelist work with bits, with shards, with slivers, the question is, why, or in what way, do they set the modern painter an example to follow? And Kitaj has made it amply clear, from his own practice and from things he has said, what his answer would be. The fragment serves three purposes. It attaches the work of art to its past by embedding some of the past in the present: it reproduces the condition of modern life, and, in particular, of modern urban life, to which modernist art is wedded: and it allows the artist to capture intimations of the uncanny, and the daemonic, and the dreamlike, which are integral to any art of a confessional kind, which modern art is committed to being.

Let us then look at how Kitaj, in his own work, uses the fragment to tap these three wellsprings of modern art.

In the first place, in borrowing from earlier art in order to establish a solidarity between his own work and the past, Kitaj does this to no fixed amount and in no fixed proportion. There is no telling how much of the earlier art he will appropriate, or how large a part of the new work this will occupy.

Sometimes a whole figure will work its way into the picture. In a painting dating from student days called 'The Perils of Revisionism' (private collection), Michelangelo's Sinner (fig.22) wanders down from the wall of the Sistine Chapel and dominates the composition. At other times, an older work will, without making its intervention apparent at any particular point, structure a whole painting, as when the great left side of Uccello's 'flood', representing the Ark (fig.23), provides the armature for 'Greenwich Village' (no.105). Or, yet again, there will be the casual introduction of figures that have been loitering in the artist's mind too long: as with the falling figures along the left edge of 'Erie Shore' (no.16), which derive from Gustave Doré. These figures are spies from the past, policing the present.

Sometimes the borrowed element will be something less specific, or less articulated, than what would be reproduced in an art book as a detail. It will be, for instance, an area of free brushwork, or a particular contour, or a rhyming of forms: or it will be something that is not to be identified with anything locatable on the surface of an older picture. Kitaj has described to me his attachment to certain pigments that were once, but are no longer, in common use amongst artists. One day, as we were talking in his studio, Kitaj brought out of a wooden box, which had seen some service, two twisted tubes of Marie-Collart green, virtually dried out, and he turned them towards me so that I could see the labels with the makers' names barely legible. For a moment more, he fondled the tubes as though they might intervene, in a way that, say, Henry James would have understood, between himself and the practitioners of an older art. Then he threw the tubes back into the reliquary from which he had taken them. He gave it as his view that I might understand something so crazy as a romance, an extra-pictorial romance, with a colour.

Secondly, there is, I have suggested, the use of the fragment for what we might think of as the better portrayal of modern life. But this needs to be qualified. For if we compare, in this respect, Kitaj with his friend from student days, Hockney, we may note that, at that period of his career when Hockney set himself most strenuously to chronicle modern life, what he went after was contemporaneity. Poised (in the great phrase that Hazlitt records Northcote as using to describe the portrait painter's art) like a 'mouser', he pounced upon what was most distinctive of the passing moment: it was the transient feel of what it was like to be alive at that time at that place, which no other kind of historian had any means of recording, that he aimed to get his claws into.

Not so Kitaj. For him, modern life is the life of that legendary metropolis, of that mechanised Babylon, where all the great writers and painters, and all the great idlers and noctambulists, and all the great madams and their clients, real and fictional, of the last hundred years and more, would have been equally at home: where Baudelaire might have strolled with Svevo, and Walter Benjamin had a drink with Polly Adler, and John Ashbery written poetry at a café table, and where Cavafy and Proust and Pavese could have negotiated with Jupien for the sexual favours they craved. In Kitaj's world-picture, the term 'modernity' has a denotation that has been distended over time: it is used to refer to everything that it has ever been used to refer to since it first gained circulation as a tool of criticism, now more than a hundred years ago.

Finally, as to the use of the fragment to convey the darkness of the mind, the way it is haunted by incomprehensible passions or relentless obsessions, this is for Kitaj a continuation of his interest in a form of art which he brooded over be-

fig.22 Michelangelo 'Fall of the Damned' (detail) from **The Last Judgement** 1536–41 Fresco *Sistine Chapel, Rome* Photo: from L. Goldscheider, *The Paintings of Michelangelo*, Phaidon Press Ltd

fig.23 Paolo Uccello **The Deluge** *c.*1445–7 (detail) Fresco *Chiostro Verde, Santa Maria Novella, Florence* Photo: Scala, Florence

fore he knew about the Italian Renaissance or about Cubism: Surrealism. When something has meant a great deal to Kitaj, he often, in talking about it, uses phrases that we know are destined to be repeated. 'Surrealism' I have heard him say, 'is a stream in which I chose to swim for many years.' But it has been Surrealism according to his gospel. For the 'classical' Surrealists, for Breton, for Ernst (except for the *Semaine de bonté*), for Magritte, Kitaj has little time. The Surrealism that is his kind of surrealism is that of what he calls the 'Symbolist-Surrealists': van Gogh, Picasso, Giacometti, Miró, Balthus, de Kooning, artists who apprenticed themselves, not through abandon or delirium, but through fierce self-scrutiny, to what Kitaj, in a letter, once referred to as 'the primacy of artistic craziness'.

Everything said so far touches upon the role of the fragment as a way of enriching, or enlarging the subject matter of painting. But in Kitaj's art, the fragment reaches out beyond subject matter, and it is that in terms of which both technique and organisation have been conceived: conceived, questioned, reconceived. Any adequate account of Kitaj's art would have to show how, for each identifiable stage, subject matter, technique, and organisation, find a new form of co-existence, which, in turn, is the result of a new rethinking of the fragment. I shall make a few observations towards such a project.

fig.24 Kitaj **The Bells of Hell** 1960 (detail) Oil on canvas *Whereabouts unknown*

In 1990, I mentioned to Kitaj that I had recently become friendly with the Californian painter Wayne Thiebaud, the Chardin of contemporary painting, and I said something about his views on painting. 'Don't tell me,' Kitaj said, 'he thinks of himself as a formalist. All American painters think of themselves as formalists: they all do it, whether they're Brice Marden, or whether they're Edward Hopper, or whether they're... Chuck Close'. And he might have added, 'Or whether they're R.B. Kitaj'.

I take it that the essence of formalism lies in thinking that the structure, or arrangement, or lay-out, of a painting can be perfectly adequately talked about independently of any reference to what is represented or expressed in the painting: independently, in other words, of its subject matter. A formalist doesn't have to, though many formalists do, think that structure is the most important thing about a painting, or that the merit of a painting depends on arrangement. It wasn't formalism that led Roger Fry to say that Breughel's 'Christ Carrying the Cross to Calvary' was marred by a small dark circle, some way up the right-hand side of the picture, inscribed on a yellowish ground, which threw the composition off balance. But what made him a formalist was thinking that this description provided a completely unexceptionable way of talking about the representation of the small knot of spectators who, even as Christ stumbled under the weight of the cross, were gathering on the stony hillside round Golgotha so as not to miss what would be, when the sun was high, the great event of the day. If this is the right way of conceiving of formalism, then without a doubt, for two decades or so, Kitaj

tended to think about his work in formalist terms. He 'composed' his paintings, and the mode of composition changed over the years.

In the late 1950s and the early 1960s, Kitaj relied heavily upon the smudgy, hand-drawn compartment, broadly reminiscent of American Surrealism, and derived specifically from a number of historical sources, all very much in a Warburgian taste: some doodles that Erasmus drew in the margins of one of his manuscripts, Native American pictographs (fig.24), and the mnemonic tables of the Catalan magus, Ramon Lull. Paintings such as 'Tarot Variations' 1958 (no.2), 'Specimen Musings of a Democrat' 1961 (no.7), 'Reflections on Violence' 1962 (no.10), and the upper half of 'Kennst du das Land', of the same year (no.9) all illustrate this procedure.

However, in the mid-1960s the procedure is abandoned, and instead the picture is divided into a number of hard-edge cubicles. This method of composition, which is fully evolved in paintings like 'The Ohio Gang' 1964 (no.12), and 'Walter Lippmann' 1966 (no.15), remains in favour for almost two decades, and it is responsible for such lucid, spectacular works as 'The Autumn of Central Paris (after Walter Benjamin)' 1972–3 (no.19), and 'To Live in Peace (The Singers)' 1973–4 (no.23). It expires in one of Kitaj's eeriest and most moving works, 'Sighs from Hell', an elaborate pastel of 1979 (no.47).

But by the late 1970s, Kitaj had come to be irritated by the carpentry, by the continuous 'trueing', that this method imposed upon him, and he gave it up, in large part as the result of a simultaneous upheaval in his technique. If this was a blow for freedom, it also involved real sacrifice, and it was a turning-point within Kitaj's development comparable to that within Hockney's when, a few years earlier, he had tired of the sort of work involved in the construction of the large double portraits. But, even when the hard-edged method was most in the ascendancy as a way of organising the picture, Kitaj never used it in an exclusively formalist fashion. If the organisational role of the cubicles into which the surface was divided was to be accurately experienced, they had to be thought of, not just configurationally, but also as representing windows, or screens, or table-tops, or the panelled awning of a café. At least from a painting like 'Kenneth Anger and Michael Powell' 1973 (no.21), the manner in which the painting was fragmented was pictorial in the full sense of the term, it was no longer simply geometrical.

Technique, and changes in technique, tell a very similar story. There is the same slow, unwitting departure from formalism, driven by the same desire to integrate the matter and the manner of the painting, the what and the how.

As a young man, Kitaj was a thick painter, largely in homage, he tells me, to de Kooning's 'Women'. Then, during the time he was at the Royal College, he changed. From now onwards the paint is thin and often dry, and it serves the cause of formalism admirably. It gives the cubicles into which the painting is divided an impersonal surface, and it accentuates the linearity of the picture, which is sometimes taken to Florentine lengths. Animation of the surface is confined to the highly decorative alternation of smooth and stippled paintwork. In paintings like 'The Arabist' 1975–6 (no.30) and 'The Orientalist' 1976–7 (no.33), there is a very elegant, somewhat Art Deco, use of black, reminiscent of the earliest Nice paintings of Matisse.

Then, between about 1977 and 1988, there were two convulsions in technique, both of which gave birth to some deeply arresting work, but which ultimately are most interesting for what may be thought of as the synthesis in which they resulted.

The first of these revolutions, the seeds of which were sown in the mid-1970s, took the form of working, at first intermittently, then for a period continuously, in pastel. At this stage, various influences converged upon Kitaj's work. One was the revival of drawing from the model, which now displaced the Old Master reproductions and the aestheticised photographs of brothels as the major source of imagery. Another was the work of various figurative painters living in London, with whom, at this period, he continuously compared notes on their respective progress towards a new figuration. A third, and perhaps the most important, influence was the constant example of Sandra, later his wife, who all this while dedicated her days to the cultivation of drawing. What this technical innovation produced was a highly ambitious series of images of the female body, which swelled up to command the entire sheet. Superficially it looked as though the art of the fragment had been left behind.

These large-scale drawings raise an interesting question about the precise content of Kitaj's intentions. He sees himself, rightly, as part of the long European tradition of the human figure, which he believes to have been reinvigorated at the turn of the century by, above all, Cézanne. ('My Cézanne', he said once, 'is not Rubin's Cézanne'.) However, sometimes in enumerating this tradition, Kitaj allows the names of Giotto and Masaccio to slip in, thereby suggesting a more specific tradition: one concerned, not just with the human body, but with its majesty, its monumentality.

The question whether Kitaj's work actually belongs to, and is not merely influenced by, this tradition within the tradition is difficult to answer. It is as difficult to answer as the very same question raised about the work of Matisse after his Italian trip. I suspect that, in the case of both artists, the answer is complicated by a distinctive form of fetishism, whereby skin is experienced as a kind of clothing, nakedness as a manner of dressing-up. And, in Kitaj's case, a further complication is his amazing gift for physiognomy, or for the depiction of emotion or character, so that the face – now leering, now placatory, now malignant, now idiotic – becomes like a mask, forever clamped over the natural features. In this way the head acquires an informational priority over the body. Nothing could be further from Giotto or Masaccio.

But certainly the last word in deciding precisely how Kitaj stands to the monumental tradition lies somewhere in the recesses of these giant pastels.

I do not know what Kitaj now feels about these works, his 'Degas's'. What is clear is that, though the draughtmanship evident in these works was never to vanish, for a while it was eclipsed. This was when, some time in 1980, a second revolution overtook the first. Paintings appeared that were as unexpected as the eruption of a dormant volcano. Consider 'The Jewish School (Drawing a Golem)' (no.57), 'Cecil Court, London WC2' (The Refugees) (no.65), and 'John Ford on his Deathbed' (no.66), all worked on between 1980 and 1984. The paint thickened, the underpainting was exposed, linearity was dissolved, and scale was distorted or even reversed: there was a certain studied raucousness of colour. But the most remarkable change in pictorial conception was that the picture was now thought out, or was allowed to think itself out, in a way that dispensed with composition in any schematic sense. There was organisation without composition.

Kitaj has denied that this phase was expressionistic. He was aiming, he says, at a 'casual', by which he means a less controlled, facture. But he certainly allowed himself a more dissonant subject matter. The strangeness of the external world, upon which the earlier paintings had depended, is displaced by the teeming uncertainties of the inner world. Ambivalence of the passions had never been very far from his work, so that it would be possible to characterise its overall subject matter equally well as the human tragedy and as the human comedy. But from now onwards Kitaj welcomed the inconsistencies in his own temperament, which his increasingly reclusive life fostered, and, over this decade, and spilling into the next, he encouraged one piece of cultivated exaggeration to stand in for many other, perhaps profounder, themes, which still lay half-submerged. Kitaj astounded the critics when he, the eternal wanderer, the self-styled diasporist, started to search for an identity, of which he had never seemed to sense the lack, through the reconstruction of a Jewish culture, which he had never known.

One of the currents that certainly underlay this new identification was something that had always been a strong element in Kitaj's make-up, sometimes overwhelming even his dedication to work: a powerful empathy for the suffering of the world. And it is, I believe, this emotional generosity, stronger than any partial or ethnic affiliation, that underlies the latest works in the present exhibition. For the most part studies in anxiety and turbulence, in the contemplation of illness and death, and in the deep recompenses of family love, these paintings set personal concerns within an undefined, an unconstricting, an unidealised, sense of common, earthy humanity.

In the summer of 1992, Kitaj asked me, 'Are you familiar with that phrase "old-age style"?' I said I was. He said that that was what he was now interested in. I said that he was rather young for that. 'I'm working on it' was his reply.

It is an open question in the psychology of art whether there really is such a thing, such a single thing, as old-age style: and, if there is, why should a man in his late fifties or early sixties fall victim to it? But, whatever the explanation, there is to be observed in many of the works that Kitaj has painted under the shadow of the present retrospective something that looks 'late': that is, a fusion of pictorial concerns, purchased at the price – a price that a number of very old and very good painters seemed prepared to pay – of inelegance, of moodiness, even of a certain peremptoriness. This

effect is one to which, once again, technique made its contribution. A major innovation, dating from the late 1980s, brought it about that from then onwards every painting should visibly preserve its own history. No longer would there be a final state of the picture, a face set upon it, to which the canons of formalism could then be applied.

The innovation was the use of very soft pit charcoal, or the 4B Conté stick. Applied directly to the canvas, and then fixed, the stick left behind a line of such saturation and sonority that it served as a lure for the artist. Kitaj has talked of the way the very intensity of the line inspired him to preserve it, and, when necessary, to refreshen it. This in turn led him back from the rough scumbling of the previous years, and the paint is now applied in a succession of thinned, translucent layers, through which the line could, in his phrase, 'breathe'. An alliance of underdrawing – line preserved – and overdrawing – line refreshed – induced a new kind of looseness.

This is not the moment to discuss these last paintings in any detail. Some of them have not been publicly seen before, and they need first to face a broader tribunal.

But I should like, in conclusion, to connect these paintings with the only *specific* complaint that I have known Kitaj to make about his own work. More than once he has said to me how he regrets his inability to imbue his painting with a sense of place. In saying this, he was, I know, thinking wistfully of Hopper and his violet-shadowed evocations of Main Street as evening draws in. For a man so haunted by geography, here was a bitter admission. However, in certain recent paintings the *genius loci* casts its spell. The unity of mood that this implies – no small emotional achievement – I trace to the new unity of pictorial surface, to the dawning of what I see as a precarious all-overness, which the very tenacity of mood itself confirms.

Kitaj Interviewed by Richard Morphet

R.M. If the Kitaj who settled in London in the late 1950s could have seen laid out the works that he actually painted in the decades leading up to 1994, what aspects of them would he have found the most surprising?

R.B.K. Someone once said that all American expatriates end up on a farm in Connecticut. Still, in spite of great London exceptions to that, I might have been amazed that most of these works of mine laid out into our very own *fin de siècle* would be painted abroad. Many years ago in London, Clement Greenberg told me that my pictures could only have been painted by an American. Well, we all know that Clem had the greatest eye since Cyclops and such an eye might even detect in the pictures themselves an American Diasporist. I think I would also have been surprised by the growing influence of precursors I hadn't taken on board when young – late Cézanne above all. It would be a long haul into middle age when my ideated sensations (Berenson's fancy term I've always rather liked) would coalesce around those few painters who renewed the depiction of the human form, from the last two years of van Gogh to the pictures Matisse painted up to about 1920. In that not so distant period ending around twelve years before I was born, I would find my radical coefficients (you should forgive the expression). These were precursors I would create for my own result who seem to me far more unusual and still more crucial than any art made in my lifetime so far. They would help drive me out of what bores me in this here modern world and into my own modern art which would even entertain a Jewish period, God help me, which might have surprised me most of all, because in 1959 I couldn't recognise the symptoms of such a thing without fear and trembling.

R.M. To me, you seem intensely American (in your frank directness, in your concern with specifics, in your concern with universals, in your idealism...) and at the same time intensely European, even English. Where do you think the balance of emphasis lies, or is this a non-question, either because you feel these different aspects are so fused or because you feel they are transcended by some identity that is more fundamental?

R.B.K. Well, first of all I feel *un*balanced most of the time. I guess my art, for what it's worth, may be largely about this lack of balance, in the disorders and refusals which dislocate it or animate it. Dislocation seems to be an aesthetic mood in my pictures. There is no unmediated culture now anyway – one is hybrid, impure. I have also convinced myself that there is nothing more fundamental in art than the examined life

and that were it not for the prevalence of (yet) unexamined life, that is, we never seem to know ourselves well enough, more of us would quit art because we would not be able to rise to the vocation, like failed priests. Before he began on his great work, Proust asked himself in a notebook: 'Should it be made into a novel, a philosophical study, am I a novelist?' So, the fundamental identity you ask about turns out to be my own predicament, which I try to address by painting, not things, but *about* things which interest me, often fantasies I chase after. Yes, my American–European–English predicament interests me so much that I pray all its unhinged inflections will cough up specific universal pictures from time to time.

R.M. To me, as to others, you seem a key part of what London is (and has been for over three decades), and you are obviously exceptionally sensitive to the past and present of any place where you are, as well as being keenly responsive to much that is happening here. How is it, therefore, that you feel in any way not at home here?

R.B.K. Home is one of those concepts like love, and God... which inspire both yearning and mistrust. Let me tell you a little story: I tried to convince my old friend Howard Hodgkin to accept election to the Royal Academy and Howard said: 'Oh, it's OK for you. You're American and you think it's romantic'. He really hit home. I love romance and fantasy. This whole goddamn retrospective is about romance, which is my truest home, and my art lives there with me. Sometimes I feel at home in London and sometimes not when I get homesick for various fantasies. The Manhattan of my youth is gone and Paris was and still is a grand illusion of mine, but all things are possible in romantic art where one traps 'involuntary memory' and ideas and regrets and desires. Absurdly, I'm trying to do some portraits of characters in the Bible. I'm not a Bible scholar or thumper, but there were a lot of homeless people in that book, starting with the banished Adam and Eve and their son Cain, who was a ceaseless wanderer, as Abraham and Moses would be. I don't want to lose myself in that mythic tribe, but those founding narratives of exile seem unfinished to me, prophetic of my own unfinish and also, I'm not averse to what Aby Warburg called the Social Memory. Home is an affair of the imagination for me, of which my pictures are both poor reflections and my most hopeful shots. But you have detected something: a sense of loss? Making odd or even wrong choices in life, as in art, becomes an aesthetic.

R.M. Before you first came to Europe, did you feel a sense of Europeanness in you in any way that would have been unusual for an American-born person of your generation (or even for such an American born of parents from non-American backgrounds)?

R.B.K. Yes. I brought myself up on the Lost Generation, especially Hemingway and Fitzgerald, and in high school I was damn well going to Europe to do what they had done, only this time in painting. I had discovered Joyce, Pound, Eliot and Surrealism as a teenager, just before I came to Europe, and movies like *The Red Shoes* gave me exactly the unreal melodrama of the artistic life in Europe I wanted it to be (and still do). Michael Powell, who made it, was to become a dear friend and I told him he was the pusher who addicted me when I was about fifteen in a movie theater just off Times Square. When I arrived in Paris at eighteen, on my way to Vienna to study art, I didn't spend much time at the Louvre. I just got on the Orient Express with 'The Third Man' twanging in my mind. Maybe I would meet a Valli or a Moira Shearer. Art and adventure are always confused in my life and I can't get them sorted out, thank God. I've always been a Magazinist (as Poe called himself) and post-war Europe seduced me also in the journals of the period like *Art News*, the Surrealist *View* and *Partisan Review*. I've still got them all in my London attic.

R.M. When you were a student at the Royal College of Art, how different did you feel from your fellow painting students, in terms of the extent of your knowledge of past art and of your sense of the importance of the relationship between art and literature?

R.B.K. There were at least two students at the College who were great readers and they damn well knew that books and art are inseparable companions in many art lives. Those who think otherwise don't know their stuff. The two colleagues were Adrian Berg and David Hockney. I believe it's common knowledge that I encouraged more than a few young painters to introduce dramas and ideas that interested them into their pictures (as I was doing myself). One wished to subvert the dead hand academic notion, widely prevalent then and less now, that the world is flat beyond the picture-plane. All the bright young painters at the College were doing abstraction at first – even Hockney. I bought an abstraction from his two-week abstract period from him which is still on my wall now. But abstraction, I pointed out, was also profoundly based in books. Years before, in New York, I'd read the classic texts, written by Mondrian and Kandinsky in those wonderful Wittenborn publications edited by Motherwell (another bookman) and I knew that the founding masters of abstraction, including Malevich, were inspired by the most arcane books of mysticism.

R.M. You must have been extremely influential on a number of them. How influential were *they* (i.e. their distinct attitudes and interests) on *you*?

R.B.K. I think I was the only one who had a little family, so I left College early every day and went home to Dulwich Village and I only got to know very few of those gifted students in any deep way... I used to imagine they were such lucky bastards screwing around swinging London bedsitterland. Their optimism and tearaway ambition engaged me, and perhaps an unexpected British sensuality even. Americanism was in the air then, as you know, but there was no one in London who could add to what I already knew more or less profoundly, like Hollywood Kulchur, American politics, Action Painting and the various Manhattan reactions to it picking up steam around 1960 and, well, American life, art and literature in general. Popular music never interested me and the slick American razzle I grew up with, which was Popping art didn't dazzle me. I fled from it, into my own neuroses, and my art would mostly respond, as Flaubert said it would, to deep and always hidden wounds. Adrian Berg and I shared a little workspace at the Royal College and he introduced me to some poetry I hadn't tried before, like Auden, G.M. Hopkins and especially Yeats. Adrian would serenade me with the Yeats he knew by heart and I became fascinated by the Irishness. Above all, there was the Blond Bradford Bombshell and I believe we've always worked upon each other over these thirty-four years in quite complex ways. But that's another story, at least a slim vol. A third student I was very close to was a South African named Raymond Woodhead. We shared many attitudes and passions, including girls. He quit art, went to study philosophy and romance at Oxford and became an adventurer.

R.M. In the 1960s, what degree of engagement did you feel with the work of Bacon, Freud, Auerbach, Kossoff and Andrews (by comparison with the degree of engagement you felt in later decades)? Insofar as such engagement was less at that time, what factors do you think underlay this?

R.B.K. Bacon is special in my life and I believe the others you mention would say the same, although I was never as close to the wicked witch as they were and he badmouthed us all. He got under my skin long before I came to England. In NY in the early fifties I'd already decided that Bacon and Balthus were my favourite post-war painters and still feel that today. Harry Fischer introduced Bacon to me over lunch at the Reform Club around 1962. We lived in the same district for his last twenty-five years and gossiped in the supermarket and streets. I think he was born for his era, post-horror, post-war London and Europe. He may have been the greatest Surrealist, its unorthodox apotheosis anyway, and like Surrealism, I believe he sought to stun his audience. He was a stunning creature, a kind of mutant, not a human type I'd ever encountered – Gide's Immoralist arisen in painting. Like 'The Immoralist', his mode was the gratuitous act, only this time on those relentless canvases, strong stuff for friend and foe. As to the others, my engagement was more gradual. I think I know why... because I'm a late developer. In Dulwich, in the early sixties, my neighbour, the poet Christopher Middleton, had Hugh Kenner to supper one night. Kenner had just visited Ezra Pound and he told us a great line Pound drawled about Eliot: 'Tawm was a crocodile... If he'd a been born a gazelle it woulda kilt 'im'. Well, I'm a crocodile like Tom Eliot... Berenson's books and Edgar Wind and Karl Parker (at the Ashmolean) had taught me something about the Italians, especially their drawing, but I began quite late to digest Rembrandt, Goya, Manet, van Gogh, Cézanne, etc., (the painterly painters). I was well into my thirties. These London guys had been studying the masters as a religious devotion since teenage and they'd entered into the very lives and paint of the great painters, you can take it from me. That's one of the main things that make London painting so powerful good now, it ignores trends, which is a good trend here and unusual elsewhere. This London predilection confirmed my own slow resolution. So, when I first encountered Auerbach, Freud and the others in the early sixties, I was growing up too. By the early seventies I was buying examples of their work.

R.M. In what lines of descent do you see yourself as a painter/writer?

R.B.K. Oh, I see myself in most exalted lines of descent of course, among those mad scribblers Delacroix, van Gogh, Gauguin, Whistler, Sickert, to name just five. The collected writings of Matisse and Klee are also favourites on my shelves, and I've already mentioned the crucial books written by Mondrian and Kandinsky in another context. Painters who write are also enacting a kind of play within a play... the larger drama is the work of the great confessional writers for me... Rousseau (a discovery of my old age), Proust, Montaigne, Kafka, Gide, the Russians, Canetti and the like. I came upon the confessional mode quite young. In the army, I read Gide's superb Journals on guard duty in the Fontainebleau forest. Kafka's Diaries changed my life later on, and Robert Lowell's poetry also helped lead me to think an autobiographical art of painting was not only possible but deep in my bones. But painters have always written, Picasso wrote a lot of Surrealist stuff. At the top of the heap was Michelangelo. Aside from two volumes of letters and some lost theoretical writing, he wrote about four hundred poems, many of which seem very bold to me in English translation from what is said to be idiosyncratic and dense in the original, full of paradox and often about his art in surprising ways. He has inspired me to try to write poems about my own pictures, to somehow extend the life of a painting while I'm still alive, maybe because I don't want to die yet and poetry is a special life-force after the painting has been taken out of my hands. I've failed so far because my poems seem poor, but I'll keep trying. Meanwhile, I've written some short stories or prose-poems for some of my pictures, as you know. I like the idea that they have no life apart from the picture. They illustrate the picture the way pictures have always illustrated books in our lives.

R.M. In what lines of descent do you see yourself as a painter/bibliophile/collector?

R.B.K. As everyone knows, pictures and books can change the inside of one's head, so I collect them around me in expectation. They excite me like one's other vices do. I come alive among my vices in heightened anticipation of pleasure which always seeps into the habit of painting. Every good painter I know is a talented reader. Some of them keep libraries and collect pictures. It has always been so. Velásquez, Rubens, Rembrandt and others were obsessive collectors. Rubens kept buying rare books all his life (duplicates of Ovid for instance) and for Rembrandt, collecting pictures and books and things was an 'ungovernable compulsion'. The supreme collector of pictures must be Degas. One of my happiest possessions is the set of original vente catalogues from 1918 which J.M. Keynes signed to his lover Duncan Grant (Keynes bought for the National Gallery at the Degas sale). Degas collected hundreds of pictures, mainly by his contemporaries, from Ingres, Delacroix and Manet to Cézanne, Gauguin and van Gogh, but also three by El Greco. When the light failed at dusk, he put on his top hat and made the rounds of the art dealers. Picasso was a great collector of everything. Dealers would carry Courbet and Degas to Mougins in suitcases for him. Is there not ambiguous cross-purpose in many of our moods?... acquisition/austerity, deviance/domesticity, moralist/immoralist, sad/high, and so on. Each mood is a touchstone for the making of art, I can tell you. The collecting mood has been one of them. Sometimes my pictures shine from its radiant touch, I pretend; sometimes my pictures, feeding on art and books, seem to choke from overeating, over-reacting to better painters and writers crowding my walls, piled up on my floors.

R.M. In what lines of descent do you see yourself as an artist who, coming from another country, establishes himself in a country which he then gives insight into through his art and uses as the base for reflections, through his art and writings, on universal themes?

R.B.K. History is full of artists who lived out their lives in places far from their origins. But there is a more unusual pattern in the outstanding modernist schools. At the risk of being a real bore, I would submit that entire milieux in New York, Paris, London, etc. have been profoundly affected by the Alien in their midst and drew infinite aesthetic, even tragic power therefrom. Consider key pictures like Picasso's 'Gertrude Stein' and Matisse's grand experimental portraits of outsider women (G. Prozor, Y. Landsberg, E. Mudocci, S. Stein, the Cones, etc.). There's a pattern, as I said, a social history of art as a function of cosmopolitan refuge. These great cities are wondrous safe havens for a transient, alien, vulnerable modern aesthetic.

R.M. Great art is scattered across the world and vital human issues are the subject of debate in stirring forums. Yet the more widely your themes range to embrace such subjects, the greater seems to be the intensity of your withdrawal into the private world of your studio/library. Is there any contradiction here?

R.B.K. My working method is really a palliative. It's a kind of diminution of despair and boredom in a muddled but very charmed life. Part of me still believes that no man is an island but more and more, I cultivate this working method, this diminution, by staying in my room because I have so few social graces and I get into trouble when I go out into the world. That the terrible beauty of solitude has brought forth art is well known. Less known may be an asocial imperative within which imagination may thrive, but I'm just guessing. Rembrandt advised his pupils never to travel... 'not even to Italy'. An unfinished painting can be quite a florid adventure anyway, but with these memories of past art and past life and of rumours of true things (Kafka), I pretend to make it new. Someone in baseball said, what was was *was*, and what is is *is*, so you just paint it if you can seize the day.

R.M. There is to some extent an interesting parallel here with the methods of Freud, Auerbach, Kossoff and Andrews, in the sense that while all (like you) are deeply concerned with human themes and respond very sensitively to the individuality of other people, none of you are among those numerous artists who are seen everywhere at art gatherings. It is almost as though there is a direct relationship between a kind of withdrawal and an increased intensity in the ability to bring to life (paradoxically) specifically the human subject. How true do you think this is of you?

R.B.K. I used to enjoy a moderate social life (I think), but after the age of fifty, less and less. Now I really prefer not going out in society. I'm not good company anyway, with a wayward and melancholic temperament. My mother calls me Schopenhauer. When I discovered the Confessions of Rousseau in my fifties, I knew his feeling exactly when he confesses that he was out of his element among people of wit and fashion. When Rousseau's great heir, Proust, began his long years of withdrawal, he wrote: 'The artist who gives up an hour of work for an hour of chatter knows he is sacrificing a reality for something which does not exist'. Karl Kraus was funnier when he said the world contained two kinds of people, those who wanted to murder him and those who merely wanted to chat for a while. I don't know why one is so damn serious about painting, especially given the absurd vanity of showing pictures in public. I guess vanity is serious because I never met a painter who did not contrive to show his pictures. I believe that all things are relative and therein lies an impetus for the attractive solitude of painting: One withdraws into rooms lined with cork, visions, books, to paint pictures relative to paintings by masters who have altered the course of one's life. Of course failure is a constant, breakthroughs are rare and time is running out within the attrition of ageing, but the mirage of an old-age style beckons. Read Cézanne's last letters and you'll see what keeps a painter going it

alone: 'I glimpse the Promised Land. Will I be like the great leader of the Hebrews or will I be allowed to enter it?'

R.M. What is the source of your unusually strong impulse towards self-revelation?

R.B.K. This question raises another question which fascinates me: Why is every painter so keen to show his pictures? I would have thought (on the odds) that at least a small proportion (of us) would just be content to paint and not show, but I've never met or heard of such an odd creature. Does that not mean that *all* painters insist on some form of self-revelation? Or is being an artist really about money, fame, the love of women/men, etc. as Freud said? We are all like flashers imprecating 'Look at my pictures, Look at my pictures'. This is true of saints and sinners in my experience. I think it is a very funny situation, one of our unremarked human comedies, which leads me to remark upon another secret art happening which relates more to what I think you're getting at: the very widespread myth that one's personal life is irrelevant to the painting. To me, this is one of the least attractive (and most boring) ideas in the art discourse of my lifetime. I believe that a painting is an autonomous thing like everyone says and that it is at the same time an extension of oneself, a vital organ that got away. Fairfield Porter, a wonderful art critic (and painter) in my youth, said that painting is a way of making the connection between yourself and everything that includes yourself. In my case, painting can connect me with my own past, as in Tolstoy, Proust and Freud. Painting, like psychoanalysis, reflects the unconscious. It's about yourself and reveals something of yourself. The Surrealists were not the first to discover that. Cézanne's famous 'little sensations' are about his unconscious... and so for the Romantics before him. The source of the impulse you ask about is my unconscious I guess. Blame my ego... The romantic egotist in me (the Rousseau bloodline?) passes on little sensations/confessions which reveal more than other painters care to confess. I can't help myself. Well, maybe I can... 'The Couch', and 'The Confessional' and 'The Commandments' are designed to help you help yourself and I've invented what may be a special genre of confessional exegesis associated with my own painting which also excites my painting forward, I've found. Self-revelation confronts the art question. Self-revelation is one of my aesthetics. Van Gogh wrote: 'What lives in art and is eternally living is first of all the painter and then the painting'.

R.M. What do you feel about the extent of the absence of this impulse, in any overt form, in the work of the majority of artists?

R.B.K. They're smart and I'm dumb. Maybe the confessional passion is rare in painting because painters are brought up to believe that frankness must be wholly expended and exhausted in the *way* one daubs, leaving no energy for making a fool of yourself, as Tolstoy says artists should be prepared to do. My problem is that I already regret not having given in to still more foolish temptations and wayward adventures than I did in my life and art. And so I may be less stringent than my fellows about observing sacred dogmas like art for art's sake, painterly painting, truth to materials and especially the 1st Commandment: Show, don't tell! I find this special need for impersonality in art interesting and oppressive and against my nature. Many artists I adore, from Whistler to Eliot to Matisse have spelled out an impersonal imperative in their writing. My favourite painter in the clouded years after Matisse and Picasso died is Bacon. And even he, heavyweight champion of disreputable risk and the awful undertaste of absurd life, sounds oddly bland when he repeats over and over again (both in conversation and interviews) his injunctions against 'illustration', against interpretation, against saying anything about pictures that can't be pictured. He was a real bore about that stuff. This, what shall I call it... this quietude so popular among painters is like too much of a good thing and I guess I do dissent from it by exposing my private parts once in a while in reaction. But if a painting, reflecting off one's unconscious nervous-system, speaks for itself anyway, how can a little exegetical gossip about one's own nervous-system detract (if one is a natural-born gossip like van Gogh)? And another thing: Why should everyone (critics, historians, poets, biographers, curators, etc.) be allowed to talk about a painting revealingly except the guy who made it? C'mon fellas, give a sucker an even break... in spite of our orthodox codes of silence (omertà?), there's a compelling tension between what an artist paints and what he feels he ought to paint or what he thinks he has painted in the personal circumstances of his life... so, why not tell what happened if it excites you?

R.M. What do you think about the (to my mind absurd) view, held by many critics, that open self-revelation by an artist is in some way at odds with plastic imperatives in a work of art?

R.B.K. I only have two plastic imperatives: I don't like plastic and I don't like imperatives. I read Mondrian's *Plastic Art and Pure Plastic Art* when I was eighteen years old in NY. I've still got the same lovely copy designed by Paul Rand and it's still overflowing with plastic imperatives after all these years, dumping on the evocation of 'subjective states of feeling', 'particularities of form', 'fantastic feelings' and 'imagination based on appearances, events, or traditions'. All this stuff which I cleave to for dear life in art veils 'true reality' for Mondrian. And then he says: 'Art should not follow the intuitions relating to our life in time'. It may sound quaint and old hat now when anything goes, even coming from a heroic figure like Mondrian (and I think he *was* a heroic poet).

Not to be open about my reality, my obsession, would be to settle for a risk-free lesser art. I know the kind of criticism you're talking about. It wants Clint Eastwood or Alan Ladd to ride into town. No one knows who he is or where he comes from. He just does his art real good, says nothing and ex-

plains less. Then he rides away towards nowhere. Look, *Shane* is one of my favourite macho things too but my life in art is more like a Michael Curtiz movie starring W.C. Fields as Franz Kafka and scripted by Errol Flynn who wrote *My Wicked, Wicked Ways.*

R.M. What are the sources and the characteristics of your unusually intense interest in acts or moments of initiation as subjects for art?

R.B.K. 'In my beginning is my end' is a famous phrase repeated in Eliot's 'Quartets'... There are sexual initiations which obsess me as they obsessed many of the artists closest to my heart from Tolstoy to Picasso. Against all common sense, against all but a drop in the bucket of the art wisdom of my lifetime, I've sought to indulge this obsession for painting because I think the sexual self belongs to painting as much as the tragic self or the absurd self or the yearning self or the regretful self does... and one's many selves begin at the beginning and may not even end at the end if you leave a few interesting pictures behind in your wake.

R.M. When one looks at a large number of reproductions of your works, the view of life that many of them give is quite alarming, because of its recurrent emphasis on violence, cruelty, etc., as well as on raw exposure (both of yourself and of others). This is far from unacceptable – the vision is convincing, powerful and thought-provoking – but what comment do you have on the fact that your vision seems weighted towards the disturbing side of things?

In your art, the most conspicuously joyful manifestations seem, very tellingly, to be images of your immediate family and personal circle. There is also the powerful implicit affirmation, running through all your work, of the rights and dignity of man, a perspective which is the reverse of disturbing. Nevertheless, taking your images as a whole I am left with the balance of emphasis I have described.

R.B.K. That's because I live in an exposed state (in spite of growing reclusion), alarmist by nature. Don't ask where it comes from, I'm just lucky I guess. If there's a sense of foreboding in many of my pictures, and some bright colour, it's because that's the story of my life, foreboding and bright colour. I'm not exactly a *révolté* personality but I do find myself tending to the opposite of Matisse's most famous ambition – you know, his line about an art of balance like a good armchair etc. I can't strive for balance with any conviction because I feel off-balance and out of tune most of the time so maybe that's why my pictures are prone to sink into neurotic unease and dissonance rather than serenity and harmony. Quite aside from what you rightly call the disturbing side of things, I feel like a figure of fun within myself, a comic figure. I wish it were otherwise. Please understand, I don't like to alarm the booboisie, as I think Mencken called them... I leave that to the perpetual revolutionaries in art, but some few of us are not born optimists. Have you ever seen a happy, joyful, optimistic Munch or Bacon painting? Bacon once told me that when he got up each morning, he knew he was going to be unhappy all day. Melancholy is the unfocused consciousness behind a lot of good art, says a very old tradition, and it swims in the same borscht with ecstatic mania and rapture. I envy the sublime artists but I'm not really sure who they are or what they are up to in their sublime art because appearances are deceptive. In any case, I am intrigued by Dr Freud's equation of art with what my friend Wollheim so rightly calls 'the phantasy of the unhappy or the unsatisfied'. And at the same time I should dearly like to deliver a little comedy and happiness into painting in some memorable way because life seems laughable it hurts so much.

R.M. Can you expand on your expressed aversion to technology?

R.B.K. Progress might have been all right once, said Ogden Nash, but it has gone on too long. My favourite modern technologies are medical anaesthesia and movies. The rest of it is way too fast for me to catch up with in the practice of art and anyway technology is too industrial for my taste and inadequate to my romantic project and pessimistic frame of mind. Hockney says I should get a fax machine and I tell him I would rather install gaslight. Montaigne teaches us *the right not to know what we do not know*. These technologies, which I have the right not to know, fail me also in my colloquy with past art, by which I mean easel painting and my version of Bohemia which has always been a haven for frail art in a heartless climate. Some of my best friends in art are supreme technologists whose adventures I watch in awe, but my own adventure has been to court disaster wrestling the demon progress. I want to be like Paul Klee's famous angel who backs into the future gazing at the past. What a way to die!

R.M. In the 1950s your education and inclinations steeped you in the work of the great masters of earlier centuries (as well as in much of our own), but would you say it is true that for you the 1960s were a period of relative reduction in that engagement?

R.B.K. No, there was no reduction in my discourse with either older or modern art during the sixties. If I had to choose one shining beacon I never lost sight of (even on Malibu Beach in the swinging sixties) it would be the late little crucifixion drawings of Michelangelo, not then, not ever. These drawings, like late Beethoven Quartets, underwrite whatever faith I have in art (which comes and goes). They also predicate the art I feel closest to like Cézanne Bathers and the drawings of Degas which would encourage me to find a home, a synthesis, for my cursed literary art, my lack of method, my wandering attentions. I'm still trying to cobble a home for these vagrant things.

R.M. Your development of the literary form of the 'preface' to individual works seems to me a distinctive contribution to our culture. You have referred to nineteenth-century practice which in some ways points in this direction, but what precedents do you see for the frank inclusion *in the work itself* of

(on one level) its own explanation, as in 'The Red Banquet' 1960 [Walker Art Gallery, Liverpool], where the sort of information the Tate might nowadays give beside a work, written by a curator, appears on the work's own surface, as part of the art?

R.B.K. Oh, it was Eliot without a doubt. When I was a kid I thought that if he could append notes to the greatest poem this century, I could append notes to my paintings and drive dogmatic formalists nuts into the bargain, because young artists are supposed to rebel. Thank God I only did it a few times, although the collaged notes were early harbingers of the prefaces twenty-five years later. My vagrant spirit or nervous attention span or something warned me that enough was enough already. Early on, I came under attack for being literary and obscure and I think the notation was also a primitive response to that by pretending to sort out some of my iconography (don't forget I was an amateur Warburger then) right in the public's eye. Those notes make me wince now, but I suppose they had a late Dadaist twist and in the best instances (like 'Reflections on Violence', no.10) I think the notation spices the visual discourse of the painting. Of course there is a mighty precedent in the distant past which I was only dimly aware of in 1960 and that is the rich tapestry of rabbinic exegesis called Midrash, which originally took the form of commentaries on the Bible, sometimes inscribed right on the scriptural page as notation alongside the verses themselves. I'd never heard of Midrash in 1960 but I had noticed some of the Christian forms of this ancient Jewish practice in the art-historical world of the Warburg milieu I'd discovered as a daily student at the Ashmolean Museum, say, in medieval illumination. My real-life romance with Catalonia inspired two or three paintings based on the visionary notations of Ramon Lull, or at least the crypto-surrealist *look* of them. Anyway, all this stuff landed unsafely in my first exhibition at Marlborough (London) in 1963, which I called *Pictures with Commentary, Pictures without Commentary* and the shit hit the fan because painters are meant to be 'Redskins' (I can't remember whether that term was first used by Philip Rahv or Harold Rosenberg), instinctual noble savages or something. Much later, when I fell upon the Midrashic world, I felt that some extra-sensory Jewish magic must have got to me way back then in my ultrasecularist youth. To make an overlong story short, Midrash itself developed into a fantastic literature of commentary, parable, 'alternative' interpretation, poetic digression, allegory and tall tales, their explicative energies thriving on ambiguity, irrelevance, contradiction and speculation. It was in this spirit and because my mind remains divided about my art that I began to write prefaces, or afterwords, to my paintings. Rothko was called Yahweh's stenographer, so maybe the impulse lies deep in the soul. At the end of the day, I go to the café or diner to relax with this writing hobby I have, examining a painting after it's born, as one does looking at one's picture in the studio. The writing becomes a less than finite illustration of the picture.

R.M. Marco Livingstone's book (*Kitaj*, p.21 in 1992 edition) quotes a passage from you saying how, among writers of the past, you are particularly interested in the compendious aspirations of 'those who try to get the whole world in'. Your work as a painter is somewhat unusual in the degree to which it often addresses simultaneously autobiography, the life of the imagination and the history of the times. So while you obviously have a special fellow-feeling for painters and your art draws deeply on the great heritage of Western art, is there any sense in which you feel that among the artists of the twentieth century your particular enterprise makes you closer, even as a painter, to writers than to painters? It would theoretically be possible for you to feel this regardless of the fact that, as art, your work makes such an exceptional contribution.

R.B.K. There are some things I would like to do in painting which writers and movies have always done. I don't see why painting can't aspire to more than a few conditions because it can remain painting no matter what it aspires to. From the very beginning of abstraction, painters have luxuriated in the awareness that they could now feel as free (or even as pro-grammatic) with their abstract gestures and forms as com-posers had always been with theirs (Pater's famous prophecy of art aspiring to the condition of music) – and perhaps it's no coincidence that jazz improvisation will share a café table with the high period of abstraction (and not only abstrac-tion!) in art history. The spectres in books and films have all my life caused me to feel free to pursue their most unusual, intimate, migrant, screwy and fearful ideas in my painting. One's temperament may seek arousal anywhere. But no, I still feel closer to Cézanne and Degas and Picasso and Matisse than to the writers I love... It's just that the subjects of writ-ers are often more interesting and exciting to me than the subjects of painters tend to be (except for the human form itself) and I'd like to find ways to paint subjects which interest me or represent actions which don't happen much in paint-ing – having to do, for instance, with baddies and goodies and all the grand in-between characters in life, or comedy as relevant to painting as, say, Chaplin or W.C. Fields is specific to film, or any of those extraordinary, layered freedoms which are thought to be the special province of writing and poetry and drama. The vagaries of love and its subtexts interest me greatly but relations between men and women are rarely tried out now in painting. Movies attempt that as a great (flat) visual art so why shouldn't our painting do it in the frozen silence of its own confines and traditions? One's major work is arguably oneself and embraces one's whole compen-dious, scary life in the world and all *its* subjects. I feel like one might break through some invisible aesthetic wall into a Narnia and the utter freedoms there practiced by Dostoevsky and Hitchcock but not much yet by painters, to allow the works of the tribe of painters some *other* options and fewer orthodoxies. You see, I've always been an heir to the Symbol-ist tradition which long ago proposed the confusion between

the perceptions of the different senses. The composer Messi-aen used to say he could see the 'colour' of a musical tone and Miró wrote that his painting should have a 'high poetic and musical spirit ... like the singing of a song'. But I may be too old now and too late. There is only one writer I feel as close to as I do to any painter and that's Kafka.

R.M. When used to describe a work in any of the arts, the word 'voyeuristic' often carries the implication of disap-proval, but do you share such a view? Is there any way in which an element of voyeurism is a positive creative element in your work?

R.B.K. We're all voyeurs at the movies, aren't we?... sitting in the dark watching other people saying and doing the most intimate things. It doesn't have to be a big step from Blanche Dubois and Stanley Kowalski to the stuff of painting. And you can take it or leave it; You can avert your gaze and walk out if you don't like Balthus Lolitas or Bacon buggery or Picasso rosettes. I think that constrained art is lesser art... Baude-laire's notion of 'artificial paradises' is one of my favourite ideas and I believe favourite things belong in painting and that great paintings in themselves are often about deviance from norms anyway, extreme experience, you might say. I believe with a certain very fashionable dead Frenchman that managing the uses of pleasure may be, in fact, more than a little of one's heretical work. In any case, since when is a painter not a freethinking spectator, like Eliot's cursed free-thinking Jew?

R.M. Would you agree that your work shows an unusually pronounced interest not only in what great artists of the past produced but also *in how they went about producing it* (includ-ing all the key circumstances of their working situation, their lives, etc.)? And related to this, would you agree that your work shows an unusually pronounced interest in how you yourself go about doing things? Could it be that the very unusual form of many of your works in the period 1960–2 stemmed in part from a determination to make the artist's own intellectual procedures themselves a visible part of the subject matter of a work?

R.B.K. Yes, I'm really curious about the lives of painters and writers and the inner workings of artists I admire (the quick and the dead) especially as I become more of a hermit. One creates one's precursors, as Borges said. And yes, one's own life of the mind deserves an outing in one's paintings – but then I think *every* one of the zillion paintings on earth ex-poses more or less clearly something of what's going on between the artist's ears, don't you agree? There is an order-ing consciousness in each painting, however great or not great at all. To paraphrase Nietzsche, each painting becomes what one is in the head and there is nothing whatever that is impersonal. In fact, the image, my images anyway, spin off the life of my confused and feeling mind... I mean I can feel that excitement the way Bacon felt his images working off his nervous system and dropping into his paintings as he put it. I don't pretend for a moment that an exciting intellectual burst or even the rare ideated revelation translates like magic into memorable painting but it feels orgasmic good sometimes. I guess those embarrassing early pictures with exposed notes, collage and stuff were primitive youthful follies, neurotic symptoms, as they say, in the endless pursuit of one's subjects. Edmund Wilson wrote a very influential book called *Axel's Castle* I've had all my life which traces the Romantic-Symbolist persona as it centres itself in great modern works, as distinguished from classicist and naturalist art where, he says, the artist tries to keep out of it – but I don't really believe the artist is ever absent from the thing he makes and thus I'm willing to address the life quite freely in the picture, as a late Romantic or someone like that, more than a lot of painters wish to do I guess.

R.M. Are you able to define the particular character of your work of the last three or four years, by contrast with your preceding periods (including your work of the 1980s)? To what extent would you say that your work of the 1990s shows a greater gestural freedom, a greater looseness/assurance of touch, a fuller-than-ever pouring in of multiple subjects, and a greater directness?

R.B.K. Jesus, I hope what you say about my 1990s is true but I'm too uncertain to agree with you. During the seventies and eighties, my art and I became crazed with two beautiful obsessions as you know – drawing, mostly from life, and the Jewish Question. There were whole patches, whole years even, when I just drew the human form, trying to recapture the drawing mania of my youth as a skill (for lack of a better word) so that I could fire up my faltering art engines again. In those same years I read everything I could get my hands on about the Jews – I suppose you could say I entered a Jewish period, but neither my drawing nor my new-found consciousness in art were to be endgames. To make a boring story shorter, I emerged around 1990, from an unseemly depressed passage, punctuated by a heart attack, facing death for the first time, scared as hell and newly interested in mortality and maybe even a second-squad immortality, or at least the ungainly prospect of doing some pictures a few people might remember from one's absurd life (absurd also in the hubris that one might leave idiosyncratic tracks). A rush of painting ideas and a new ego-driven freedom seems to have crept up on me by 1990, suggesting the onset of an old-age style of sorts... more free than ever to be myself I think, to be one's own fool – yes, more loose and assured in my neuroses and their sensation-induced touch. But of course one charges one's fee for the experience of a lifetime, as Whistler famously said at the Ruskin trial... one drags that dubious experience (into the nineties) like the man had to drag all that junk (grand pianos, donkey carcasses) across the floor in Buñuel's great *Chien Andalou*.

R.M. Is it the case that in the last three years or so you have tended to have more paintings on the go simultaneously than has been normal for you in the past? If so, in what ways do you think this has affected the ways in which individual pictures now emerge?

R.B.K. Yes, I wander around my house of life like Mario Praz or maybe James Ensor... and having all these unfinished pictures around reminds me of how like a painting can be to an unfinished friendship, an unfinished marriage, an unfinished life... In fact the aura of examined life in painting has never seemed more obvious to me than now, in the clutter of these recent years, and to be quite honest, I feel loathe to finish anything, for starters because I don't know how to properly – I mean, why *should* one finish a friendship or a marriage or a book or a painting until death stops it all in its tracks? And speaking of death, I get myself over to Amsterdam about twice a year now to check out what van Gogh did in those furious two years before he died. So much of it is piled up in his museum there, like the pictures were stacked up unsold in what was left of his life by 1890 when he killed himself. If he had died when he got off the train at Arles in 1888, he might have been remembered as a minor Impressionist in the circle of Pissarro. I've never tried out so many pictures before and they do seem to depend on each other in rushing ways I'm not used to and so I go to Holland to create this precursor. I can't create the Agony and the Ecstasy of those two years because my pictures are not God-struck like his were... but I run there to feel the heat (along with some Rembrandt) and then I come home to London to my house full of pictures and hope the heat's still on.

R.M. In what ways, if any, has your practice of drawing changed in the 1990s? Has your practice of drawing become to a greater extent subsumed into the act of making marks on canvas?

R.B.K. Well, I've always drawn on canvas and the drawing got covered up by paint, and, of course, one draws *with* paint. Then, about 1990, by accident I stumbled upon a way of drawing on canvas with compressed little sticks called pit charcoal which allowed me a degree of incisive freedom I'd never had before – the freedom to keep the drawing alive through the whole life of the painting, not unlike my experience in pastel. When I used to teach life drawing, I'd say to students that it was a kind of youthful arrogance, even a mug's game, to proudly accept the line one had drawn as the last word. If there is no fixed contour in 'nature' then what is there to register, to write down, I would propose to kids trying to draw like eighty year old Matisse. One could make a splendid defence of the unmediated spontaneous line of course but I meant that when you draw from the human form, you can't really be too sure what you're seeing well enough to commit final lines with impunity so you may as well keep the thing alive, and that the supreme late drawings of Michelangelo, Rembrandt, Cézanne and Degas enter some geriatric ether of misreading their subjects. A few lifelong tendencies of mine like that began, I think, to converge in my old age – misreading life into pictures and an almost futile urge to revise mistakes – one's awful (life and art) patterns.

Drawing is only a symbolism for one's own sensation-induced powers of thinking and feeling after all. Not letting go of the drawing, going back and back at the thinly painted surface with my charcoal and drawing brush seems to portend more exciting inventions with which I can forego the pleasure of painterly or gestural painting as the spirit moves. I'm addicted more to drawing and colour and their discontents than I am to the kingship of paint, and since there are so many truly fine painterly painters around, I feel that great tradition is in safe hands and so I can pursue my drawing hybrids without laying it on thick.

R.M. In your developing late (only relatively!) style, to what extent do you seek a quality of grandeur, a quality I associate with (among others) Beckmann, Pollock, Bacon, Auerbach and Kossoff, but *not* with all painters one admires?

R.B.K. I doubt if I'm capable of grandeur, of the sweep and scale and large gesture the term conjures up in the painters you cite. I'm much more attuned to stuff like frankness and memory and regret and the examined life than to what we call grandeur. Beckmann is a painter I like and admire very much, but I prefer his more intimate easel paintings to his triptychs. And as for Bacon, is he not in one sense a modern conjurer, *literally* through glass darkly, of the grandeur of his hero (and mine) – Michelangelo? I mean, there's no sleight of hand in Michelangelo's 'Last Judgment', or Giotto's, or in Cézanne's last three large, glunky 'Bathers' in my book of grandeur, but a lot of goodness and love and pity I think. We late, nervous moderns seem to me to crowd a Ship of Fools, a leaking, cosmopolitan St Louis, drifting toward putative freedom but mostly kidding ourselves like those Jews did – at least I feel that about myself. True grandeur may have leaked out of this Godforsaken century of human foulness, leaving a bereft, aberrant and sometimes fascinating modernity, maybe a few grand designs in Matisse and Picasso. But don't listen to me muttering. In fact, I do have some delusions of grandeur but when I retire from the professional stage (which I plan to do), I intend to commit them to small parlour compositions, imitations of life, in which I want to tell the truth about myself (more than hitherto) as best I can before I die. My delusions will consist in the hope that the more true to myself I can get in old age, the more chance I'll have to cheat death, which is what the fool's gold we call art does, no? In one of Cézanne's last letters he said that to sing small was all that was left for him to do, which was also a delusion because of the grandeur of the Bathers and the Mountain he was painting madly. I do believe with an uncertain passion that it's more important for the soul of art to be more true to oneself than to art.

R.M. To what aspects of your debt, as a painter, to Sandra would you draw attention, in addition to her having led the way for you in her use of pastel?

R.B.K. Richard, you know me well enough to guess that my debts, 'as a painter', are hopelessly lost in my debts as a man.

Sandra urged me to try pastel and Degas, on a crucial visit to the Petit Palais, blew my mind as we used to say in bygone days, and so I tried it out twenty years ago with mixed results so far. Sandra and I are very unlike and I think that Freud says somewhere that's good, but I forget why. Her love and her love of life and of art shame me into trusting art a little more than I might do to dispel demons... into trusting this life-in-art. In the last year or so I've begun to form a little theory, a kind of aesthetic hunch, which goes something like this: There is a very strong idea around (Bacon was its dark prince) that good art happens when a painter takes no prisoners, when a painter lives only for the painting he wills to do. Uncompromising is the word one hears. And God knows, painters, like so much of the common herd they spring from, can be ruthless as hell. Mind you, I'm not talking about art for art's sake, which is a gentler concept. But I have felt the pull of this 'idea' myself, a real attraction to what I will call a kind of *nihilism* for lack of a better word – Fuck you all, I'm beyond the pale; I'm going to get my kicks out of this absurd art game... I'm going to pleasure myself, and don't count on me to defend any higher morality in art than that because I'm the Immoralist and because I *am* the bloody culture itself. It's a complex thing, but I've begun to sense that, as wild a card as I've been and am, as scary as life can get, its art comes in surprising various ways and one of the most unusual ways some of us make art is in the divine bosom of 'love', in the milieu of one's children, one's mate if one's lucky, loyal friendship, and so on. One is gifted with these *other* creatures, Sandra and Max for instance, the ones I live with, against the storm, against one's own nihilism and its precarious modern diabolisms. She and I (and the boy) don't just cross like ships in the night sending cursory signals. I know it will sound sentimental, but there is, I believe, a 'we' in art as well as an 'I'. Buber's *I and Thou* may foretell a new/old aesthetic, unexplained in our narcissistic painting histories.

R.M. What effects would you say your post-1989 practice of taking long walks through London in the early morning has had on your work as an artist?

R.B.K. After my little heart attack, the doctor told me to walk fast some miles each day to help keep death at bay, so that's what I do after sixty years of hating exercise – a suspension of disbelief perhaps, but as someone said about mortality – the stakes are high. When you get older, you also start thinking about how you've lived your life anyway, and so I wrestle with that angel on my walks, all the regrets, all the countless mistakes in life and art, the lessons unlearned... But the damn walks in London early morning streets are so bracing that hope springs daily in my pessimistic heart and the Black Dog has a hard time keeping up with me for a change. May I take you on one of my walks at about four miles per hour? (William) De Morgan's white house at the head of my road is the first thing I see in all English weathers and all London lights and so the Lady Art presents herself to me right off because that house has become my economy-size Mont Ste-Victoire, a view I've begun to essay because I feel it's so there, or here, or something. London Without End is really what the walks do for my art. Auerbach always encourages me to paint London, but unlike Frank I'm afraid the subjects will outlive my resolve: Erich Mendelsohn's great modernist long-house, My Heart Hospital, The Church Where Dickens Was Married, Turner's House, and so on and on the prowl. The truth is I've always prowled big cities for subjects which may excite what we call art. Some of these paintings are begun, awful failures among them. Halfway through my walk I stop to visit with my friend Susan, a bag-lady who sleeps in a doorway across from the Brompton Oratory where she attends Mass. I think she's always been an SW7 person, with a posh accent. My whole experience of psychiatrists has been very brief – only about a dozen forty minute visits, and nothing to write home about. Susan is my best shrink by far – I tell her some of my troubles and it only costs me a quid. On my way again past many scenes in these districts of my wild lost youth, I'm thinking hard about the painting back on my easel and what I might do to it that will be remembered in art history (something for the museums said Cézanne). By the time I buy my Herald Tribune at Gloucester Road, Titian himself better watch out. This thought only lasts about five minutes. As I cross the Fulham Road, my nerve has failed and Guido Reni better watch out. There's a lot of other stuff on my walk and then I get back home for breakfast with Sandra and Max. I begin the working day by falling asleep sitting at my easel in front of my painting.

R.M. Why do you have to leave the house in order to be able to write? Since that is the case, how is it that you are able to paint without going elsewhere to do it?

R.B.K. I've been a Caféist all my life and now I can regain some of my youth spent in cafés in places like Vienna, Paris, Barcelona and New York. I leave the house to seek my fortune in adventure and I often find it in the café or hamburger joint, alone with a book and my journal and my sketchbook. I stay home to paint the adventures which pile up in my old head.

R.M. How close an affinity do you feel with Chagall, a painter who invented his own imaginative world with which he merged both the factual story of his own life and, in memorable works, the tragic history of his people in his own era; and who also responded to the Jewish theatre, producing, among other works, a series of tall upright paintings of individual 'types'?

R.B.K. It's a funny thing, I really never gave Chagall much thought until they called that big Jewish exhibition at the Barbican, From Chagall to Kitaj. When I saw the posters all over London, I thought: God, what have I done? The poster, with a rather nice early Chagall on it, is in my little boy's bedroom and it makes me think what I've always thought – that Chagall was a painter who never much interested me.

My reasons are hardnosed and wholly unoriginal – the usual suspects: Pont Neuf prettiness and the French cuisined shtetl schmaltz of those long years from some damn good early modernist Yiddishkeit to the Riviera showbiz of his later wholesale trade. Greenberg talks about lack of concentration and pressure in Chagall. But Greenberg and Schapiro both say that Chagall, in his biblical etchings, is a master for the ages and although I can't quite see it myself, I wouldn't wish to argue otherwise either. You want affinity? Well, Chagall is one of the very few gifted Jewish painters who painted pictures about Jews. Sometimes I think Matisse painted more Jews than Jews do. The other ten or twenty good painters from Pissarro to now who happen to be Jewish don't go out of their way to do that. And I don't blame them at all. Every painter wants to be a master of the universe. But I guess when I entered my Jewish period, I was, in a way picking up a dying torch, not exactly from Chagall himself but as a new species of Jewish painter for my own era – one who almost stumbled upon Jewishness and became excited and alarmed by it and unable to exclude it from the art equation. I wanted to invent my own new attitude in the wake of that generation whose world had perished. Chagall was the exact contemporary of my grandparents, who came from the same Russian-Jewish clay he did. It seems like a sad fairy-tale to me with a tragic ending, and I can't pretend that I haven't got that tale and its bright coloured dread somewhere in the back of my art, passed down from the grandfathers and grandmothers into my pictures. But I don't think I've got a Chagall book in the house, and there's a lot of books in my house. Maybe I should buy one.

R.M. The relative recentness of the great Sickert retrospective at the Royal Academy in 1992 is a good context in which to ask whether you feel, as I imagine you must, an unusually strong response to his work among British artists of the last hundred years, and if so why. I imagine reasons must include his continuous simultaneous interest in the stuff of paint and the human subject; his gift for making figures truly present in a painting; the intensity of his response to the great Venetians, to the continuity of tradition, and to Degas; his genius for bringing London to life; his interest in maintaining ambiguity as to the subject or meaning of a work, even using a certain deliberate contradictoriness; his determination continuously to reinvent his own personality; and the highly original and individual nature of his contribution as a writer.

R.B.K. I do love Sickert and I think I've been learning bittersweet little lessons from him since I came to England in the fifties. But maybe not big lessons. I went many times to the Sickert show, early in the morning when I could be alone with him but I never brought my sketchbook as I've done so often at our great Academy exhibitions – Cézanne, the Venetians and so on (my friend McComb is often the only other RA drawing there). In fact most of the qualities you attribute to Sickert (except the crucial London one), are present in other painters, for instance Cézanne, my most favourite, who clasps me to his living breast and won't let go, denying me the companionship of sweethearts like Sickert except for stolen moments, even as I stagger toward the end and ought to lighten up a little before I drop. I love Sickert's London. I could eat it up. I wish I were there (sometimes I am). I love the lunacy of his late style too, and yes, I love his writing; He may be the greatest painter-scribbler of all except for van Gogh. I've been telling publishers they're crazy not to reprint *A Free House*, almost fifty years out of print, and what a grand book, full of keen life and lost traditions of real fine art and full also of obstreperous bull: Ooh aye, there's the rub... I think Sickert retarded his genius, as I've retarded mine, and so have many good painters who don't or can't quite stay up in the air long enough as they said Nijinsky could do. Sickert accuses Cézanne of *unfinish*, would you believe, like Cézanne's critics did, only with great wit: 'The Frenchman is nothing if not *entier*'! But that was early on. Later, Sickert himself became a dab hand at unfinish in the long long shadow of his beloved Degas. Sometimes I think that if Sickert had been a rich man like Degas, Cézanne, Manet, etc., if he had not to sell, to teach, to write for his living (and he hinted this more than once), he might have concentrated his genius more often – it's just an idle thought.

R.M. It seems to me that the driving force underlying your treatment of the Jewish theme is the thoughts and feelings that have sprung from your realisation that persecution or exclusion of Jews was based not on their religious beliefs but on the fact of their simply being Jews. The result has been a body of work which, while it ponders the richness and complexity of Jewish history, focuses, above all, on the issue of inhumanity per se. Thus although you dwell understandably on the exceptional horror of the Holocaust, your key theme is not specifically Jewish but is universal, namely the question of human values. Do you agree?

R.B.K. I'd love my pictures to be universal but that will be decided when I'm dead. I have a hunch that pictures only achieve universal interest by way of the muddle of obsessed attentions (the stuff that excites one in life) to which a very skilled painter exposes his or her picture... That attention might be variously Christian, African, Neurotic, Alien, Decorative, deeply English or any complex sensibility – you name it, but I wouldn't trust an art too much if it was damn well determined to be universal, like Esperanto, which a lot of art now looks like... because you are what you are and what can be more human than that? When I was about sixteen I was touched by Joyce's great line – to forge in the smithy of my soul, the uncreated conscience of my race... I think that's how it goes. What slowly began to dawn on me in the sixties was a funny question – Why are the Jews always in trouble? After the worst thing that ever happened to them (or anyone) in four thousand years of awful things, they seemed to have acquired a billion new enemies they never had before. I didn't want to gloss over what was unpleasant anymore in some kind of sheer art; I couldn't respond to bland international

style and, anyway, I was vitally attracted and excited by this troubled people and their extraordinary history, of which I was an up-to-the-minute member in neurotic standing. Another funny thing was (and Jews can be pretty funny), that my obsession with the Jews revealed itself to me as an art-obsession, as an *aesthetic*, as a dynamo cranking up some of my pictures, some of my life in art – what Harold Bloom identified as an Unrest-Cure.

So the moment of art proceeds from whatever attracts and excites one... That's what you give your *attention* to and so you paint it. A painter may give a lot of attention to the naked human body, to the primacy of colour, to God, maybe to a mountain in one's own native district. This attention is more formidable than mere *subject* and can bear the weight (in my mind at least) of style in its pursuit of what we call forms. Attention and aesthetic become one. What you call the question of human values resides for each of us (*sui generis*), I like to think, in something like Kandinsky's wonderful formulation: Concerning the Spiritual in Art. Concerning my own spirituality in art, in some pictures the Jews have been my Tahiti.

R.M. It seems to me that you have nevertheless increasingly found that you are able to deal effectively with a universal issue of such weight only in terms of the felt experience that is particular to you as an individual. Is this why the issue of Jewish identity is such a persistent theme of your art?

R.B.K. Yes, that's true. And, along the yellow brick road to that peculiar Oz, inexactly called 'identity' which I never expect to reach, I encountered at least two forces of destiny. The first one is common to every painter who is born to what is called the West, and that is our great Western painting tradition from the caves to now. One had been a fellow-traveller in that tradition anyway (it is my host-language) but way back, even in the early sixties, I began to sense something Other. The Jewishness of that Other didn't speak clearly to me until about 1970 even though some of my earlier pictures were already gossiping Jewish themes. Jewish Otherness, by the way, has been identified as a prime cause of anti-Semitism as far back as the Book of Esther. I very quickly realised that there was no tradition of Jewish art to speak of – nothing that really moved me anyway. Everyone knows that the great modern artists often felt hungry for a spiritual Other. Picasso found it in Iberian and African art. Matisse found the Islamic Other in Munich and Morocco. Lesser painters like Klee and Dubuffet sought out the art of children and madmen. My precursor, Whistler had practised a brilliant, knowing Orientalism, and so on. Well, I was hungry too. My attention was on the Jews but their museums full of liturgical artefacts didn't keep me up all night. Then I arrived at the second force of destiny on my road... I would make up my own tradition out of what excited my passions in the here and now. I would do it myself as other modernist painters had done – within the Western tradition itself – that's when I started to draw again with a passion... Not only had the outstanding Jewish painters (there have been about a dozen) not identified with Jewishness (with the main exception of Chagall), but until recently they didn't draw very seriously either. In any case, the Other, my Tahiti, could only be located, I felt, on my own crude map of what Aby Warburg called Social Memory... one's particular felt experience as you put it. Of all the dozens of imaginative souls and visions I visited in art, in life, in books, the precursor I keep returning to the most, a kind of Columbus figure, has been the greatest Jewish artist, Kafka. It was the Kafka who famously 'eaves-dropped' on Jewish traditions which were no longer accessible to him, who would lead me to an *aggadah* (Jewish imaginative lore), however imperfect, which might deliver my painting to its natural home – the predicament I find myself in every day.

R.M. I take it that this predicament was what you would later formulate as Diasporism in the *Manifesto* you published in 1989. I know that you are unhappy with that book, but is Diasporism something you compare to the Other which, as you rightly say, appears as a force in modern art?

R.B.K. Yes, a romance had formed in my head and in my pictures, the romance of one Diaspora Jew, which seemed both natural and abnormal – a good romantic cliff from which to leap into the mist of art the unknown. Goethe had famously described Romanticism as a sickness, but Nietzsche defined art the way I really like it: 'the desire to be different, the desire to be elsewhere', and isn't one of the thousand meanings of romantic art that in its freedom it is subject to no agreed principles?

So, I set sail, as Gauguin had done for Samoa, into the storm of Jewish dispensation, which felt like forbidden excitement feels – that's how I knew it was true for my art, or at least akin to Kafka's 'rumour of true things'. The awakening of the Jews in the nineteenth century, after the Emancipation, their transforming modernisms, became wedded in the aesthetic growing in my system, to the painting from Manet to 1939 to which I was devoted. Both these modernist transformations happened during the same hundred years and encroached upon my own lifetime. Even the great anti-Dreyfusards, Cézanne and Degas, appear to me even now as all too human genius-cranks in a cosmopolitan Comedy which would become its well-known alter-ego which is called Tragedy.

If the vagaries of Jewish modernism itself became an artistic property for me, so would its tragedy, that tragedy which blocks the middle of the only century I've got. Early modern tragic-dramatists in Scandinavia seem to have been the first to stage the sense of diseased society as it affects ordinary people, as distinct from earlier tragedies with their kings and queens and princes. But the diseased events of 1940–5 not only took the breath away from life but away from *usual* art for some of us. This is what I thought when I plunged into study of those events and entered into a morbid period. A change came over me and a fearful sense that it could happen again – but one's predicament almost had a built-in

answer, or at least a weak resolve – if one's inner life had changed in a radical way then so would one's art.

R.M. Could it be the case that a reason why your work does not deal directly with very contemporary socio-political issues is that apart from drawing from life and paintings of your family and friends, it has always been heavily orientated towards the *past*?

R.B.K. I'm afraid I want a lot more for art than utterly news-worthy socio-political or for that matter, hot aesthetic issues (mine are hot enough)... One wants news that stays news, as Ezra Pound defined poetry. I know that sounds very grand and maybe I've never even once achieved it, but time will tell. As for the past... *Everything* is past! Everything sure as hell passes quickly into the past anyway and I don't see why events of ten minutes ago are any *better* for art than, say, wars that happened thirty years before Tolstoy was born, or crucifixions long past, etc. Someone said about Proust that sensation arrives after the event. And so I've never felt constrained as to how far into the past I steal myself in search of excitement, yesterday or a thousand years ago. All art is based on experience grasped from life and experience of other art – stored up past stuff... *Middlemarch*, maybe the best English novel, is set forty years before the date of its writing. Can there be an artist who does not respond to antiquity in some way or other, who does not answer, in his art, the voice of one's childhood, one's singular and collective past?

R.M. Second only to your central human theme – and, of course, inextricable from it – your subject is the culture itself in both the narrow and the broad sense. As it is unusual to find an artist who is engaged with this subject in ways at once so panoramic, so obsessive and so concerned with the patterns of interconnection, how isolated on these grounds do you feel among visual artists today?

R.B.K. Many years ago, my friend Isaiah Berlin distinguished artists and writers between those who, like the hedgehog, relate to a single central vision and those, like the fox, who pursue many ends, often contradictory and diffused. I guess I'm one of the little foxes but I don't feel too isolated because of one's 'innate idiosyncrasy', as Jung called it. He said that one's personality is an act of courage flung in the face of life but I don't feel too courageous either because my life is so damn privileged and either too lucky or too disturbed to be as marginal as I sometimes pretend. Nevertheless, one is marginal to the extent that one is obligated to one's idiosyncratic passions and, as you say, obsessions. Of course it's good fun to play the rebel – I've often said that I feel like I'm some well-paid misfit trudging down the Zeitgeist road and meeting all the art troops marching in the opposite direction (some of whom even wave genially to me).

Maybe at the heart of my cranky notion of art – what pisses a lot of people off about me – is my suspicion that art is not as obscenely visual as it's made out to be. Of course it is and it isn't... and both the is and the isn't thrill me to distraction. It is that distraction – call it cultural if you like – that I believe may help isolate me as you suggest because I'm afraid I do wander in a Diaspora of foxy ideas which come and go in my pictures including sexual ideas, American ideas, Jewish ideas, London ideas, bookish ideas and even a few art ideas. Panofsky (who has influenced my painting life since I was twenty), wrote a honey of a book called *Idea* about the eras when it was not as odd for a painter to wallow in ideas (and melancholia) as it is today. His great exemplars were Michelangelo (whose 'Last Judgement' is my absurdly favourite painting) and Dürer, who entertained a whole lot of ideas and wrote about them (as did Michelangelo in his poetry) when he wasn't painting them and drawing them. Ideas, for Dürer, ensured originality and *inexhaustibility* and they enabled him to create 'always something new' as he himself put it, from his mind into his art, things that never existed before, which Dürer called 'secret collected treasure of the heart'. He said that this art happens only when the artist 'filled his mind by much drawing from life'! It was for such 'ideas' that I was roundly damned some years back, as you well know, Richard, but maybe the Berlin Wall is not the only one that's tumbled down?

R.M. How important for you is the act of transmission (of an awareness of the past) that your works perform? Is there any sense in which transmitting things to the future is one of the mainsprings of your whole endeavour? This urge can be seen, for example, in the sense of commemoration and of warning given by your works on Jewish themes; in the eloquence of your own need to return to human themes and the act of drawing; and in the strong sense of inter-generational family continuity given by many of your works. More-over, your works give a greater sense than those of most of your contemporaries of the artist saying 'I was here, I did this, and my temperament and beliefs were this, this and this'. All art is an act of witness for the future, but for the reasons touched on here yours seems to be more so than most.

R.B.K. The act of transmission you ask about is something I think about every day because I am full of doubt about it and very unsure why we make paintings at all and why we all wish to show our damned paintings off in public self-assertion. I know there's a kind of false modesty in what I just said but one is forever stumbling upon the same senti-ments in the great and the good – just this morning I read much the same stuff in very late interviews with both Matisse and Camus – it sounds so familiar – Don't use me as a guide, they say, because of all my many shortcomings; I don't speak for anyone else, they say, because I scarcely know where I'm going myself and I know next to nothing anyway, etc, etc. Kafka, of course, instructed Max Brod to burn all his manu-scripts when he died and as the world knows, Max didn't do it. Like Dracula, this business of transmitting art to the future never seems to die. Walter Benjamin, in his great essay-letter to Scholem about Kafka, wrote: 'Kafka's real genius was that

he tried something entirely new: he sacrificed truth for the sake of clinging to transmissibility, to its aggadic element ... rumor about the true things (a sort of theology passed on by whispers)'. Kafka speaks to my painting like no one else and so one enables tradition by passing on one's own peculiar lore to a future. God knows why.

R.M. Can you say in a few words what are the essential aspects of your special engagement with the work of Degas and Cézanne?

R.B.K. Well, as I grow old, there are six or ten painters I stare at a lot who seem to be everlasting Prophets for me (from Giotto to Matisse) – every painter creates precursors, but yes, Cézanne and Degas are very special in my life, Cézanne the painter and Degas the draughtsman. I had lunch in London with my old UCLA friend Diebenkorn just before he died and we agreed (both grinning) that Cézanne was the best painter who ever lived. He was like Treasure Island for Matisse, Picasso and much of their succession, and every day when I wake up to art, he's like that for me too and I gaze at his map. Matisse wrote: 'If Cézanne is right, I am right.' Matisse meant something very particular, a stunning modern breakthrough which has not often been grasped, I think. Cézanne teaches me to try *harder* to follow the idiosyncratic temptations of my own nature when I'm at my easel. It sounds simple enough but it's the hardest thing to do really well... Matisse put it another way... He said he looked to Cézanne in moments of doubt, 'frightened sometimes by my discoveries'. This is both a key to Matisse and to the magic of the extreme which clasps me to the old isolate. I can't think about him in just these few words, but his lonely radicality seems as new to me today as it was for Picasso and Matisse almost a century ago. He's the Geist in my Zeit.

I believe Degas drew the human form better than anyone ever did and he lies closer to my own instincts than Michelangelo or Rembrandt, his greatest drawing rivals (both of whom I love to distraction). That Cézanne and Degas should appear at the same time and place can't be only a coincidence but I'm unwilling to detach myself from that coincidence because it feels so good and seems like last week to me. News that stays news.

R.M. In the work of many painters, the main theme of a painting is communicated very directly without need of explanation to understand what it is. Your work falls, on the whole, into a different category of art, in which, while the image has great power and emotional fullness and gives an immediate sense both of multiple suggestion and of its own particular emotion (and is therefore already very effective), added explanation may be needed in order to understand the full content of the work? Does it worry you that this explana-tion is needed?

R.B.K. Yes and no. I have worried over the elusive mean-ings and sometime obscurantism of many of my earlier pic-tures but we can't all be Vermeer or Lucian Freud can we? I would guess that half of my favourite paintings in history are quite elusive, from Giorgione's 'Tempesta' to Cézanne's last three 'Bathers', etc. I've always been attracted to what is called programme music – one of my favourites is the Fantastic Symphony, of which Berlioz wrote that he wanted to depict his passion for the actress Harriet Smithson. In fact my unease with this rather Symbolist predilection of mine led me many years ago to begin to do some straightforward pictures... less ratiocinative and sometimes quite as literal as my portraits and drawings of the naked form, which I continue to do, interleaved between painting my great American novels of time and the river unedited. I think that human natures are straight and bent in profound ways and that our Jekyll and Hyde selves both deserve an outing in pictures, explainable or not. And also, of course, I get a kick out of writing neo-Talmudic disquisitions about my pictures which turn out to explain away very little (in Talmudic doctrine there are forty-nine levels of meaning in every passage in the Torah). I'm just now reading van Gogh's letters again and thrilled to see his passion to explain his pictures in letter after letter, explaining his intentions, his symbolisms, his doubts, his art-historical ambitions for them, etc., and often at great length. I guess people got used to these running commentaries as long as the painter was safely dead and then three fat volumes of confessional literature about one's pictures becomes OK. By the way, my comrade Hockney has just published his second volume of commentary on his pictures, so the revolt against quietude proceeds. Modern art and problematic pictures are very often the same thing – in my experience, people rarely agree about what's what in art, just as they disagree in biblical and literary exegesis. Even Mondrian's rather clear-cut paintings have had an awful lot of explaining thrust upon them (not least from Mondrian himself), not to speak of the automatism of the classic School of New York which must have nearly as much exegesis as the Book of Genesis by now. I'm a sixty year old child of the great age of art books and museum catalogues and so are the best painters I know. That means that one has been imbibing a hell of a lot of interpretation and explanations (for better and worse) for half a century – of pictures one is often told need no explanation. Well, maybe they don't and maybe they do but I don't wish to beat around that tired old bush because, let's face it, everyone talks about pictures all the time and once in a while a holy fool of a painter will say his say and make his confession before the curtain comes down on the last act, whether or not anyone reads the programme.

R.M. Beyond achieving a distinctive late style, as such, what would you most like to go on to do in your art?

R.B.K. I'd like to retire. I'm not kidding. At the end of his life, Gide was asked what he would do differently if he could live over again and he said he would give in to even more temptations than he did. I've come to think that temptations are the same as what Cézanne called his little sensations. I'm convinced that giving in to temptation in painting is the stairway to heaven. I delude myself that if I can continue to retire from a lot of worldly stuff which doesn't tempt me anymore, to stand back from futility, I may get closer than I have to a kind of radical excess very few painters ever achieve. I'd love to start over again in old age almost from scratch. The blank canvas on the easel is, after all, the proverbial clean slate most people dream of if Thoreau was right (and I think he was), that most men lead lives of quiet desperation.

The end of my century is an age of societal/political miracles I never thought I'd see the like of and I sense something like a new aesthetic on the cards too (on *my* cards anyway). I've begun to turn with a passion to what I can only call the *subject*. I've got a gut instinct it's right for me and I don't feel in any danger of betraying a life of forms because I believe that attention to the power of subjects has met its moment now as attention to the power of forms did with a vengeance in, say, Cubism and its succession. Subjects are insistent occasions in the human comedy that I would expect to drive the life of forms after a century the other way round. I don't know where I'm going but I intend to give in to more subjective temptations, 'consubstantial with myself' as old Montaigne said about his essays done in retirement from the world.

Chronology

COMPILED BY JOANNE NORTHEY

Kitaj **Mother (Weeping)** 1983 (detail)
Charcoal on paper *The artist*

Kitaj **F.D.R.** 1992 Charcoal on paper
Marlborough Fine Art (London) Ltd

Kitaj **Dr Walter Kitaj** 1989 (detail)
Oil on canvas *Marlborough Fine Art (London) Ltd*

1932

Born in Cleveland, Ohio on 29 October to
Jeanne Brooks, American-born daughter of
Russian-Jewish immigrants, and Hungarian-
born Sigmund Benway. They soon divorced
and Benway left for California in 1934. Kitaj
never saw him again and he died in Los
Angeles in the late 1940s.

Roosevelt elected, 'Always a presence in
my life, I feel like a lifelong democrat and
Democrat largely because of him'. Hitler
attains power and 'casts his shadow on parts
of my life and art from year One'.

1936–42

During the Great Depression, his mother
worked as a secretary in a steel mill and
would later become a schoolteacher. His
movie obsession began, and his passion for
reading. Attended children's art classes at
the Cleveland Museum, 'which seemed like
paradise to me'. First experience of great
master painting and the practice of drawing,
often from sculpture. In 1941 his mother
married Dr Walter Kitaj, a Viennese refugee
research chemist, of whom he would grow
very fond. Imaginative drawings of the war,
'from far away, with fear in the air'.

1940–5

The murder of one-third of the Jews in the
world. 'Neither this nor what happened to
all the other victims of Nazism and Stalinism
would begin to stun me for many years,
except subliminally.'

1941–4

Family moved to Troy, NY. 'Smalltown life;
constant drawing, baseball and movies; por-
ing over art books and magazines like *Life*;
first book collecting which would grow into
a lifelong disease'.

1945–9

Death of Roosevelt, family mourning. War
ends.

Troy High School: 'Good friends, sports,
drawing. Ongoing mania for books, movies
and now, girls, almost untouchable girls.
Dread of family life, mowing the lawn and
summertime in general, including nature.
Longing to escape into the world, into art,
into sex, into big cities.' Arrival of Helene
Kitaj, Walter's mother, from her refuge in
Sweden. 'Most of her family murdered, she

Kitaj's identity card as a merchant seaman

Sydney Delevante, late 1940s

Kitaj outside the Louvre, Paris, 1951

will help change my life.' Birth of the state of Israel, 'which I hardly noticed at the time'. First sailed as a merchant seaman out of New York on *SS Corona*, a Norwegian cargo ship bound for Havana and Mexican ports. Virginity lost in a Havana brothel. 'I was an old hand upon docking at Vera Cruz and had a subsequent lifelong addiction to port life in big cities'.

1950

Arrived at the Cooper Union Institute. 'I was excited by Manhattan, my bright fellow students, memorable teachers, life in a Gorkyesque rooming house near Union Square and the delicious walk to Cooper down Fourth Avenue, the greatest bookshop street in America. It was the heyday of Action Painting which I watched out of the corner of my eye. First experience of life drawing, taught by a very neglected painter, Sydney Delevante (a student of George Luks and Robert Henri) who helped draw me into the Surrealist–Symbolist stream of modern art.' Kitaj first read Pound, Joyce, Eliot, Kafka and classic texts of modern art.

1951

Shipped out again, mostly on Standard Oil tankers to Caribbean and South American ports as an ordinary seaman. Arrived in Europe, glimpsed Paris and took the Orient Express to Vienna, during the Occupation, to study at the Akademie der Bildenden Künste in the class of Schiele's friend Paris von Gütersloh, a kind of Symbolist who had been a student of Maurice Denis. Spent the year mostly life drawing under Gütersloh and Fritz Wotruba. These drawings and also watercolours of bombed ruins are lost. He met Elsi Roessler, an American student at Vienna University, with whom he hiked in Austria and Yugoslavia, and was almost converted to Catholicism by Monsignor Leopold Ungar, who had been born a Jew. Discovered Klimt, Schiele and their circle.

1952

Returned to New York, shipped out again to South America and then attended Cooper Union for a second year, living with Elsi, who studied at the New School in 12th Street, where he sat in on her 'unforgettable night classes' with Harold Rosenberg, Hannah Arendt and Wallace Fowlie. At Cooper, his studio teachers were abstractionists John Ferren, Nicholas Marsicano and other painters of the School of New York. Delevante took him to visit his friends Isabel Bishop, Raphael Soyer and the unknown Louise Nevelson, 'who collected a dark houseful of wonderful early American modernist pictures by such as Louis Eilshemius'.

Began his friendship with Joe Kling, legendary old Greenwich Village bookseller,

Egon Schiele **Portrait of the Painter Paris von Gütersloh** 1918 (detail) Oil on canvas *The Minneapolis Institute of Arts. Gift of the P.D. McMillan Land Co., 1954*

Kitaj **Monsignor Ungar** ?1951 Oil on canvas *Whereabouts unknown*

Isabel Bishop, 1979 Photo: R.B. Kitaj

Ezra Pound, 1928 Photo: Bill Brandt *Collection R.B. Kitaj* © J.-P. Kernot

draughtsman and editor, who had first published Hart Crane, e.e. cummings and many early modernists. Kling encouraged Kitaj to read Hardy, Huneker, Peretz, D.H. Lawrence, Henry Miller, Babel, Svevo and many others, selling him their books.

1953

Joined the National Maritime Union and sailed on Moore-McCormack ships, on the 'Romance Run' (Rio, Santos, Montevideo and Buenos Aires), drawing shipmates and reading mostly Hemingway, Fitzgerald, Conrad, D.H. Lawrence and modern poetry. Kitaj and Elsi got married in the oldest Methodist church in New York. They returned to Vienna, then wandered Europe, North Africa and up through Spain, spending the winter at the port of Sant Feliu de Guixols in Catalonia, where Kitaj worked on a large allegorical painting (now mostly destroyed). He wrote to Ezra Pound, who answered: 'Pay more attention to external phenomena', and other responses 'to my oafish letter'. Met Josep Vicente Roma, a crucial friend.

1954–6

Death of Matisse, 'I look at his pictures every day, like psalms'.

Shipped out of New York for the last time as a sailor and after his last voyage he 'hung around Manhattan – reading Proust and seeing a movie a day on 42nd Street', until conscripted into the US army. Rather happy two years, first at Darmstadt in the occupation of Germany and then as an illustrator in Intelligence section of headquarters, Armed Forces Central Europe, at Fontainebleau, working (mainly at anti-Soviet war games) for General Philip Bethune in a wing of the great chateau. 'My wife and I lived in the Seine village of Thoméry near many Impressionist sites, driving into Paris most weekends. I don't think I did any art at all for two years (except an aborted mural) but I read a lot and we drove back to Vienna on leave.' First quick visit to England where he considered schools, including an interview at the Courtauld, but decided it would not be good for his painting. Discovered Cecil Court, Charing Cross Road and Blackwell's bookshop in their prime. Attracted about this time to Berenson's books, which led him to Sassetta, Lotto and the Venetians. First struck by Sickert, at the Tate, 'and I have never tired of him'.

1957–9

Upon discharge from the army, he drove to Oxford to study at the Ruskin School, University of Oxford, on the G.I. Bill, drawing and painting in the life room of the Ashmolean Museum almost every day. 'Stunned for life by the Raphael and Michelangelo drawings there.' Attended lectures by K.T.

Kitaj **Josep Vicente** 1972–unfinished
(detail) Oil on canvas *The artist*

Bernard Berenson

W.R. Sickert, 1942 Photo: Cecil Beaton
Collection R.B. Kitaj © Sotheby's, London

Edgar Wind in the garden of the Palais
Royal, Paris, 1960 Photo: Mrs Wind

Parker and by the Slade Professor, Douglas
Cooper, but above all by the spellbinding
Edgar Wind, who also invited him to teas
and to his seminars with Stuart Hampshire
at All Souls. His closest friends were three
American philosophers, the logician Dick Jef-
frey, Dan Bennett, John Searle (already a don
at Christ Church) and their wives. Searle
was the first person to buy a painting from
him. Discovering the Warburg milieu and
their version of art history, he bought the
entire set of *Warburg Journals*, from 1937 on,
and Fritz Saxl's Lectures, etc., which he still
uses. Percy Horton, the Ruskin Master,
helped fire his everlasting love of Cézanne
and encouraged Kitaj to sit the exam for
Horton's old Royal College of Art.

Birth of first son, Lem, in Oxford, 1958.

1959–62
After graduation and with money saved
from the army, he bought his first house, in
Dulwich village, South London, and arrived
at the Royal College of Art, 'where, in the
first week, I began my constant friendship
with the amazing Hockney'. Other lifelong
friendships formed, with the philosopher
Richard Wollheim, the architects Sandy Wilson and M.J. Long, and the poets Jonathan
Williams (who introduced him to post-Pound
poetry, especially his own Black Moun-
taineers Kitaj would meet later), Michael
Hamburger and Christopher Middleton. He
tended to do life-class work at the College
and his first ambitious paintings at home.
Teachers at the RCA included Carel Weight,
Roger de Grey and David Sylvester. The
many gifted students showed pictures at the
Young Contemporaries exhibitions. Worked on
two collage collaborations with Eduardo
Paolozzi. Summers at Sant Feliu. Graduation
(ARCA).

The Eichmann trial, 'which began to disturb something asleep in me', was closely
reported from Jerusalem at this time, especially by Hannah Arendt. 'This was exactly
the effect Ben-Gurion intended for young
Jews, I later learned'.

1962–5
First exhibition in 1963 (*Pictures with Commentary, Pictures without Commentary*) at
Marlborough Fine Art, London, who have
now been his dealers for over thirty years.
First met Francis Bacon, Lucian Freud,
Frank Auerbach, Michael Andrews, Henry
Moore and Leon Kossoff, who were all at the
same gallery. Made many visits to the
strange Russian-American painter, John Graham, who was dying in the Middlesex Hospital in Soho. First met Howard Hodgkin, Peter
Blake, Richard Hamilton and Tony Caro,
often at the house of Joe and Jos Tilson in
Argyll Road, Kensington, where he would
see Auerbach as well. Began casual teaching

Kitaj **Warburg as Maenad** 1961–2 (detail)
Oil on canvas *Kunstmuseum Düsseldorf im Ehrenhof*

Kitaj **Cézanne** *c.*1985 Charcoal on paper
Whereabouts unknown

Michael Powell directing Lem Kitaj in a film, 1973
Photo: R.B. Kitaj

Kitaj and David Hockney, 1970
Collection R.B. Kitaj

over the years, under Robert Medley at Camberwell and William Coldstream at the Slade among other places. Sandy Wilson invited him to speak at Cambridge and at the Institute of Contemporary Arts in London. First met Clement Greenberg, Andy Warhol, Claes Oldenburg 'and other American visiting firemen'. Kitaj and his wife adopted an Indian daughter, Dominie, born in 1964.

1965

Returned to America for the first time in nine years for first New York exhibition. 'Quite turned on by Manhattan again.' The newly opened Marlborough gallery, like New York itself, was a focus for artists and writers – he met Mark Rothko, David Smith, Frank O'Hara and Susan Sontag, among others – and he renewed old friendships and made new ones. Alfred Barr bought 'The Ohio Gang' (no.12) for the Museum of Modern Art, New York. 'Glorious period in Florida', drawing at the baseball spring training-camps for *Sports Illustrated* (met and drew Stengel, Berra, Spahn and others). Tearing himself away from Manhattan, he returned to London and set to work again, with mixed feelings about expatriation. Later that year, Maurice Tuchman curated Kitaj's first museum exhibition, a survey of seven years of work, at the Los Angeles County Museum of Art. With Jonathan Williams, visited Hugh MacDiarmid at his cottage in Scotland and drew him and other poets (Ed Dorn, Kenneth Koch, W.H. Auden) in London. Friendship with Robert Creeley began with the first of many drawings. First met Robert Lowell. First discovered Walter Benjamin, before his cult began, in a memoir by Gershom Scholem. Both Benjamin and Scholem would become inspirational sources for painting.

1966–8

Summers at Sant Feliu continue, sometimes staying with Josep Vicente. Collage print-making during this period continues with master printer Chris Prater, who had earlier been introduced by Paolozzi. Museum exhibitions at Stedelijk, Amsterdam, Kestner Gesellschaft, Hanover, and other places. Met Duchamp and Beuys at Richard Hamilton's house. Left London to teach at University of California, Berkeley (1967–8) for 'a happy–unhappy year rediscovering American life and poetry and baseball in the shadow of a fading marriage'. Met Rothko again, who taught the summer at Berkeley. Stayed in New Mexico with Creeley, who introduced Kitaj to Charles Olson and Allen Ginsberg at Berkeley and Kitaj would draw them. Start of friendship with the poet Robert Duncan and Jess, whose house in San Francisco became a second home. The bookseller, Peter Howard, fed him poetry and other books and he

Kitaj **Jonathan Williams** 1993 (detail) Charcoal on paper *The artist*

Kitaj **Study (Michael Hamburger)** 1969 Oil on canvas *Whereabouts unknown*

Kitaj **Christopher Middleton** 1993 (detail) Charcoal on paper *The artist*

Kitaj and his daughter Dominie, 1969 *Collection R.B. Kitaj*

Kitaj **Stanky and Berra at St Petersburg** 1965 Oil on canvas *Private collection*

Kitaj **Hugh MacDiarmid** 1965 (detail) Oil on canvas *The artist*

Robert Creeley and Kitaj, 1975 Photo: Sandra Fisher

Walter Benjamin (left): Gershom Scholem, 1927 (right)

would meet writers at Howard's Berkeley shop, including Wieners, Rexroth and McClure. Hockney and Peter Schlesinger stayed with Kitaj at Berkeley and he drew them. He loved his students and played league softball in Strawberry Canyon. Painted hardly at all, so fascinated was he by what he came to see as 'The spirit of '68 in Berkeley (as in Paris) – a bright, brief flowering among young people of an anarcho-Nietzschean sexual moment, one of those utopian stabs at delicious freedoms which seem to end quickly in sadness or madness'.

Robert Duncan and Jess, ?1968 Photo: R.B. Kitaj

Kitaj and Lee Friedlander, ?1975
Collection R.B. Kitaj

1969–70

Returned to England, to a house in Oxford and a flat in South Kensington, where 'Francis Bacon was a neighbour, strange acquaintance and florid inspiration'. Walked the city with another SW7 neighbour, the iconoclastic American writer Edward Dahlberg. Latenight suppers with Hockney at Peter Langan's first Odin's restaurant, exchanging pictures for food. Very unhappy period, hardly any work. Death of Kitaj's wife. He took his children to Emma Lake in the Canadian North Woods to try to recover, ostensibly to teach the summer art camp there. They arrived in Los Angeles where Kitaj would teach the year at UCLA.

Kitaj **Kenneth Rexroth and John Wieners** 1967
Oil on canvas *The artist*

Kitaj drawing David Hockney at Berkeley, 1967 Photo: Peter Schlesinger *Collection R.B. Kitaj*

1970–1

Rented a house in Hollywood overlooking Sunset Boulevard. Taught life drawing for a year at UCLA, making friendships there with Richard Diebenkorn and especially Lee Friedlander 'who has inspired my frail links with the practice of photography ever since'. Stayed with Creeley at Bolinas, Duncan and Jess in San Francisco. Kitaj painted very little that year, 'because my heart just wasn't in it', but preparing a large Hollywood painting (destroyed), he visited some of the great old directors, drawing them in their homes – Renoir, Wilder, Milestone, Hathaway, Cukor, Mamoulian, and especially John Ford on his deathbed. First met Sandra Fisher, the young American painter he would later marry.

Kitaj and Jean Renoir, 1970
Photo: Lem Kitaj *Collection R.B. Kitaj*

Kitaj drawing Rouben Mamoulian, 1970
Photo: Lem Kitaj *Collection R.B. Kitaj*

1972–5

Returned to London with his children, where they lived with Hockney in Powis Terrace for a few months while the newly bought house in Elm Park Road, Chelsea, was being renovated; it is still his home. Extraordinary chance meeting with Sandra Fisher again, who had arrived in London to paint. Kitaj, Fisher and his two children begin a new life there. They started to see Auerbach over regular suppers in town. Purchased house at Sant Feliu de Guixols and began to work there from time to time, studying Catalan. Josep Vicente became mayor of Sant Feliu. Stayed with Hockney in the Cour de Rohan on Paris visits. Start of friendship with John

Kitaj **Francis Bacon** 1969 Oil on canvas
Private collection

John Ford, 1970 Photo: R.B. Kitaj

Golding and James Joll. Death of Picasso in 1973, 'as my own affair with his art and with his Barcelona reached a peak'. Began serious collecting, mainly of his London contemporaries and prints by Manet and Cézanne.

1975

At the Petit Palais in Paris, Degas inspired Kitaj to work in pastel (encouraged also by Sandra Fisher's example) and he bought his first good pastels at Roché, as Degas had. Back in London he began using them to draw from life, which he had begun to do again in 1970. His Jewish interests had started to grow into a passion which 'I would translate as best I could into painting'. He began to read widely into Jewish culture and predicaments.

1976

Organised *The Human Clay*, a controversial exhibition of figurative drawings and paintings at the Hayward Gallery, having bought many of the works for the Arts Council of Great Britain during the previous year. In his introduction, Kitaj used the loose term School of London for the first time, to describe the thirty-four painters in the show and others in their wider London milieu whom he now regrets were not included. Very moved by the cave drawing at Altamira, stayed overnight at Guernica and drove across Navarre and Aragon back to Sant Feliu house.

1977

Third Alpine trip, staying at Sils Maria in the Lower Engadine, Giacometti's Stampa, and Lugano. Exhibition at Marlborough Gallery, Zurich. Began friendship with Isaiah Berlin at All Souls, Oxford.

1978-9

Returned to America as artist-in-residence at Dartmouth College 'for a very good winter period in New England again and intensive drawing'. Long summer at the Sant Feliu house, drawing in pastel, followed by a year in Greenwich Village, where Kitaj and Fisher took a flat in Ninth Street, drawing from models all year. Saw a lot of friends, including Lee and Maria Friedlander, Hockney, Avigdor Arikha (a great new friendship), Isabel Bishop, the novelist Frederic Tuten, Kitaj's childhood friend the actor Joel Grey, John Ashbery and others. Met Leland Bell, Louisa Matthiasdottír and also Meyer Schapiro, introduced to Kitaj by the painter, Irving Petlin, his neighbour in the Village. Friedlander drove Kitaj to Woodstock to meet Raoul Hague and Philip Guston in their studios. Exhibition of fifty pastels and drawings at Marlborough, New York. Returned to London.

Kitaj and Sandra Fisher, ?1975
Collection R.B. Kitaj

Sandra Fisher **Kitaj in his Library at the House in Sant Feliu** 1978 Oil on canvas
Collection R.B. Kitaj

Frank Auerbach, detail from Kitaj **Two London Painters (Frank Auerbach and Sandra Fisher)** 1979 Pastel and charcoal on paper *Michael and Dorothy Blankfort Collection*

Kitaj **Arikha Sketching** 1982 (detail) Charcoal on paper *The artist*

Kitaj **John Ashbery** 1978 (detail) Charcoal on paper *Private collection*

Hockney and Kitaj on the Pont des Arts, Paris, 1973 *Collection R.B. Kitaj*

Lee Friedlander and Philip Guston in Guston's studio, 1978 Photo: R.B. Kitaj

1980

Controversial exhibition of pastels and drawings at Marlborough, London – 'I had spent some years trying to improve my drawing (I still am), and that exhibition looked to some people like an eccentric or retrograde floating island drifting away from modernism, but in fact I felt that the better I could draw, the truer I would get to my own modern passions and obsessions, which I think is what counts.' Chose (and introduced in the catalogue) some of his favourite paintings at the National Gallery, London for *The Artist's Eye*, 'which was one of my best moments ... I held the Cézanne "Bathers" in my arms and kissed it when no one was looking'. Fisher and Kitaj made their first trip to Israel, seeing Arikha and his wife the poet Anne Atik and other friends every day in Jerusalem. Drove to Masada, the Negev, Acre, Galilee and the West Bank, very touched by it all. 'When people complain to me about Israel, I ask them what they expect from a country with four million Prime Ministers.' First visit to Rome 'I think Michelangelo's Last Judgement wall is the best painting I've ever seen.'

1981-2

Retrospective exhibition initiated by Joe Shannon at the Hirshhorn Museum, Washington and toured to the Cleveland Museum and Kunsthalle, Düsseldorf. Moved to Paris for a year, to a studio in an ancient house in the rue Galande. Kitaj and Fisher saw the Arikhas every few days and Kitaj worked once a week with the master etcher, Aldo Crommelynck. Duncan stayed for a month and Kitaj drew him each day. He introduced Kitaj to Edmund Jabès, whose books Kitaj had admired. Many friends visited that year. 'This was the happiest year of my life for a hundred crazy reasons. I felt hidden away in time and romance and I found or invented some of the lost Paris which people said was gone – the Paris of Henry Miller and René Clair. I should have just stayed put in that dreamworld I stumbled into'.

1982

Elected to the American Academy of Arts and Letters. Honorary Doctorate, University of London. Visited van Gogh's grave at Auvers. Visited Drancy with Anne Atik. They would later collaborate on a book about that visit.

Death of Dr Walter Kitaj.

1983

After twelve years together, Kitaj and Sandra Fisher married at the ancient Sephardic Synagogue of Bevis Marks in London, with Hockney as best man and Auerbach, Freud and Kossoff as part of the orthodox minyan (ten Jewish men).

Exhibition poster reproducing detail of Degas, 'The Young Spartans' 1860 *Reproduced by courtesy of the Trustees of the National Gallery, London*

Sandra Fisher and Avigdor Arikha drawing the Israeli curator Yona Fisher in Kitaj's studio in Paris, 1982 Photo: R.B. Kitaj

Graves of Vincent van Gogh and his brother Theo, Auvers-sur-Oise, 1982 Photo: R.B. Kitaj

Kitaj and Sandra Fisher at their wedding, 1983 Photo: David Hockney

Kitaj **Anne on Drancy Station** 1985 (detail) Charcoal on paper *Whereabouts unknown*

Kitaj **The Poet, Eyes Closed (Robert Duncan)** 1982 Charcoal on paper *Private collection*

Wedding of Kitaj and Sandra Fisher, 1983 (left to right: Lucian Freud, Dominie Kitaj, Frank Auerbach, Lem Kitaj, David Hockney)

1984
Birth of second son, Max, in November.

1985
Friendship began with Philip Roth, who with his wife Claire Bloom, were neighbours in London.

Elected to the Royal Academy, the only American since Benjamin West in the eighteenth century and J.S. Sargent in the nineteenth century.

Continued to meet up with Isaiah Berlin: 'Isaiah has been one of the central figures in my Jewish self-education, suggesting what to read and who I should talk to. He remains an abiding master of the strange phenomenon sometimes loosely called "identity" which I have wished to paint as if it were a tree'.

1986–9
This was a period of growing reclusion, which had begun in Paris. Kitaj withdrew into his family life and 'grew more and more unsure of what I could do in painting – I felt I had no method and I was driven nearly mad, experimenting with more painterly painting and feeling I was going nowhere'.

1989
Published *First Diasporist Manifesto*, 'This was meant as a Summing Up of my erratic Jewish obsessions, but I came to regret its hasty publication. It seems to me like an unfinished, unresolved painting which should not have left the studio when it did, during a very difficult period. Although there are passages which seem OK, I should like to revise it and change it. Maybe I'll get around to a Second one'. Kitaj had a mild heart attack in April – his cardiologist prescribed fast walking, which he does early each morning for some miles in the London

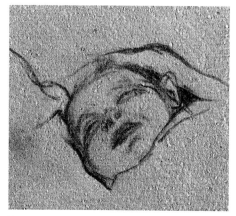

Kitaj **Max, 10 Minutes Old** 1984
Charcoal on paper *The artist*

Kitaj **Mother** 1990 (detail) Charcoal on paper
The artist

streets: 'I always hated exercise, but these walks are now delicious events when I concentrate mainly on the picture back on my easel.' Slowly he began to regain some measure of confidence: 'I would often dwell on Cézanne. I read that Matisse never met Cézanne but did speak to his widow, who told Matisse that Cézanne had no idea how to finish a painting and somehow that helped me – the famous *doubt* of Cézanne'.

1990
Large exhibition of Jewish art at the Barbican, London, entitled *From Chagall to Kitaj*. Philip Roth introduced Kitaj to Aharon Appelfeld, whose novels Kitaj admired, and they became fast friends. Continued to visit Los Angeles, where his mother and elder son had settled, often staying with Hockney, with whom he continues their thirty year dialogue on art and expatriation.

1991–3
Honorary Doctorate, Royal College of Art, London.

Began to make lithographs with master printer Stanley Jones, mainly biblical portraits inspired by Adin Steinsaltz.

Regular trips to Amsterdam: 'I've grown very fond of the place and some egalitarian, lenient quality in Dutch society – I spend a lot of time in the van Gogh Museum which has many of the seventy paintings he did in his last seventy days. He seems more and more Dutch to me.' The years since 1990 have been 'more intense painting years than ever ... I feel I've had to take my pictures into some dangerous places for art. Some people call it the biographical fallacy, but I believe that what is best in modern art has been predicated on danger, not unlike this most dangerous of centuries which has spawned modernism.'

Kitaj **Philip Roth** 1991 (detail)
Charcoal on canvas *The artist*

Kitaj **Isaiah Berlin** 1992
Charcoal on canvas *The artist*

Kitaj **Aharon Appelfeld** 1991 (detail)
Oil on canvas *The Israel Museum, Jerusalem*

Colour Plates
with Prefaces by R.B. Kitaj

About the Prefaces

> I only offer some remarks, notes made in the course of my lifetime as a painter. I ask that one read them in the indulgent spirit generally accorded the writings of a painter.
>
> Henri Matisse

I have always loved the tradition of the new, which is I believe a very old tradition. I know that many people have been brought up to believe that gentlemen don't explain – especially modern art gentlemen and gentlewomen, except that everyone and his brother and sister usually comment on paintings in our time except the painter himself. But if the following writings of a painter, reflecting the twists in the course of a lifetime, can be indulged within the tradition of the new or unusual, by the kindness of strangers, perhaps a modern art will be fleetingly served, as if by magic. In any case, these are *not* explanations of the paintings, whose chastity and autonomy remain, if not pure as driven snow, then only somewhat shopworn like people are in real life. I only offer some remarks about some of my paintings because we all talk about real life all the time and I hope my paintings are little imitations of my life. Some paintings have resisted my advances so far and their quietude persists. When a painting says no, I assume she means no.

Miss Ivy Cavendish (Oxford)
1958 (detail)
Pencil on paper
53.3 × 41.6 (21 × 16⅜)
The artist
(no.3)

Oxford Woman *c*.1958 (detail)
Charcoal pencil on paper
35.5 × 30.5 (14 × 12)
The artist
(no.5)

Erasmus Variations 1958

This was the first modern art I committed. Everything before had been smaller fragments, even more frightened (in the face of past art) and lost, the way so much youthful art is either bluff or consoles itself hidden away within schoolwork. This was bluff too of course, but it was the first synthesis of some of the ideated strands that would probably never leave me or my art: Symbolism-Surrealism, the spectres in books, and the woman question, among others. One of the first books I read in Oxford was Huizinga's *Erasmus* in the delicious little Phaidon series of classic gems Bela Horowitz used to publish along with his incomparable art books. The pretext for my painting was a page of doodles Erasmus had drawn in the margins of a manuscript. They looked like the surrealist automatic art I had been digesting unquietly for years. De Kooning's surreal-automatic 'Women' were my favourite action paintings of the School of New York, a recalcitrant or truant of which I had been during my Manhattan years, and so I adapted something of that mode here; Double Dutch (Erasmus and de Kooning, both of Rotterdam). But hark, these masks were but fanciful fronts for sweet secrets from my nether or surreal life. In a spirit of serious play, where one summons up forbidden pleasure In Praise of Folly, I assigned each disguised visage in this picture to a Woman I had known in fleeting encounters – quite real ones, which are described in my journals. Even though I was already given to a passion (roundly cursed then, as this present writing will be) for confessional exegesis in my first exhibition in 1962, I dared not ascribe these images openly at the time for fear of wrecking my first marriage, which I wrecked later. This picture leads to the next painting I made at Oxford, over which hovers another American's unhappy London marriage.

Oil on canvas 104.2 × 84.2 (41 × 33⅛)
Private collection
(no.1)

Tarot Variations 1958

> I am not familiar with the exact constitution of the Tarot pack of cards, from which I have obviously departed to suit my own convenience.
>
> T.S. Eliot (Notes on *The Waste Land*)

Besotted since teenage with Eliot and Pound and *The Waste Land*, I believed I had truly found myself in their violet American airs (in their cracks and reforms and bursts), in an England which would never be real home because I would never, like the Luftmensch, be at home anywhere. Eliot inspired me, first in a tentative way in this painting and then more plainly and awkwardly in a few others, to place images abreast (and later annotated), as if they were poetic lines on a page. Some few early modernist poets had arranged words to resemble pictures or designs and I began to think I could do the reverse for art: to lay down pictures as if they were poems to look at. And, oh, those inspired notes! *The Waste Land* seemed as revolutionary to me, then and now, as it did in 1922 when Malcolm Cowley said all the poets felt like giving up upon its publication. When I got to the Royal College of Art a year or two later, I bought the first appearance of that mighty poem in Eliot's own Criterion and proceeded to blandly incorporate notes into paintings for the first time, as a rash act I thought.

My journal entries for this painting are lost and I can't remember what exactly stands for what, but Eliot claimed that characters and genders melt into each other in his poem, and anyway I have obviously departed to suit my own convenience.

Oil on canvas 109.2 × 86 (43 × 33⅞)
High Museum of Art, Atlanta, Georgia. Purchase with J.J. Haverty Memorial Fund, 68.7
(no.2)

Nietzsche's Moustache 1962
Oil on canvas
122 × 122 (48 × 48)
Private collection, London
(no.8)

Ashmolean Drawing (Oxford) IV
1958 (detail)
Pencil on paper
53.3 × 41.6 (21 × 16⅜)
The artist
(no.4)

Reflections on Violence 1962

> His writings remained episodic, unorganised, unfinished, fragmentary ... the expression of a singular temperament ... His ideas, which beat like hailstones against all accepted doctrines and institutions ... do so still not only because of their intrinsic quality and power, but because what in his day was confined to small coteries of intellectuals has now grown to world-wide proportions.
>
> Isaiah Berlin on Sorel

This is just about my first London painting, aside from lifeclass work, and maybe the first where I pressed down notes among the pictographs and ideograms. When I arrived in London, one thing I did was to seek out Vorticism and its milieu at the Tate because I'd been reading Wyndham Lewis and his anti-liberal friends. Very soon they would bore me, but from that circle, it was T.E. Hulme's translation of *Reflections on Violence* by Georges Sorel that caused this picture to happen. Sorel is one of those lesser iconoclasts (not a genius poet like Nietzsche) one stumbles upon when young, whose furious insights induce a shock of recognition. When I was an excitable kid, I was outraged by this and that. I'm still outraged at decrepit sixty, but not by the same things – or, if some of the things are the same, my outrages are very much more odd, conditional and frazzled, as befits funny older age.

Isaiah Berlin, in his classic essay on Sorel (which I didn't read until many years after my painting), calls him an outsider of outsiders who prized only total independence and who still has the power to upset. Sounds like red meat for a hungry young painter for whom such books were as trees for a landscapist. Sorel was called a lot of names: romantic, pessimist, erratic, muddlehead (Lenin called him that), all of which I call myself. Leafing through Sorel again after more than thirty years, he attracts me and repels me in equal daubs, as does this painting of mine whenever I see it on my trips to Hamburg. His proto-surrealist emphasis on the power of the irrational in human thought and action sparked my late surrealist reflections on canvas in a little terrace house in south London called Oban.

Oil and collage on canvas 152.4 × 152.4 (60 × 60)
Hamburger Kunsthalle, Hamburg
(no.10)

Apotheosis of Groundlessness 1964
(Two Men who Should Never Have Met)

Children love illustrations to stories. This short story is an illustration to my painting in which the antagonists are not shown. Once there was a rich and talented man named Bob Maillart who had just moved into an empty warehouse he was fixing up to live in. The warehouse was in the great and splendid city of Paris, hidden away in an ancient alley on the Left Bank, with lots of mist and other atmosphere for which the Latin Quarter is world renowned. A man named M. Bill phoned who wanted to meet Bob, who asked Bill to come over. These two men should never have met because they made each other too nervous and anxious almost from the start, which was a shame because they shared so many interests, but both men were somewhat ill in body and mind when they met and they irritated each other, at first in subtle ways but then increasing toward savage drama. Bill was also very gifted and had quite a good job but he yearned for the kind of freedom money can buy and would come to feel that Bob wronged him and that he fell into a trap by asking to meet and talk. Bob realised after some minutes that destiny had sucked out any future for them and that he had made a big mistake asking Bill to come, even though he had looked forward to meeting Bill. They were countrymen, and Bob offered to show Bill his new home and so he walked Bill around the colourful early modernistic warehouse (see picture), telling Bill all about its sordid history, anecdotes about the romantic neighbourhood and its denizens, where (in the warehouse) he intended to keep his books and pictures, how he wanted only very few chairs and maybe a table aside from the bed, which was just about the only thing there – you can't see the bed in my painting because I haven't painted it in yet. Bob got carried away as he gestured here and there and bragged of the beautiful women from the ancient streets who would come to his warehouse if he recovered his health. Bob was a very sensitive man, quick to see that Bill, who was just as sensitive, was reacting poorly to what he was hearing and what he saw, the warehouse as you can see it yourself, its infinite levels and perspectives, spaces and corners, pastel colours subtly judged and that heartbreaking Paris light spreading into Bob's new home from the turn-of-the century skylights, making everything look like a storybook picture. Bill began to hate Bob slowly and surely. Bob knew he had talked too much, said all the wrong things as usual and had upset Bill, but it was too late. They were both sick and exhausted and humiliated. Bill killed Bob and went to prison and then to hell.

Oil on canvas 153 × 213.4 (60¼ × 84)
Cincinnati Art Museum. The Edwin and Virginia Irwin Memorial
(no.11)

Kennst du das Land? 1962
(for Josep Vicente)

> Know'st thou the land where lemon-trees do bloom ...?
> from Goethe, *Wilhelm Meister*

Goethe meant Italy of course in his famous lines, but my picture is about Spain, because I had fallen in love with Catalonia since my first wife and I spent the winter of 1953 in the port of Sant Feliu de Guixols, where I would buy a house twenty years later. What I loved even more than Catalonia was my friendship with Josep, just about the purest heart I've ever known, and this painting, begun in his house high over the sea is really about what he called 'our war' which tore his Spain apart and burned its way into the souls of so many people I've known. Hommage to Catalonia and to the Spanish Republic is not unusual in my lifetime. This painting of mine is just another little altarpiece among those many journeyman shrines which mark the graveyards of fascism. I make no special claims for it except to remember a remark by Martin Buber, someone I try to listen to from time to time. Buber said (in the year I was born) that no matter how brilliant, the human intellect that wishes to keep to a plane above the events of the day is not really alive.

Julián Ríos suggests that my collaged images above the snowy battle (of Teruel?), including various granadas (grenades/pomegranates), my drawn transcription of Goya's whore (and even the dumb lemons?), remind him of the convention in Spanish art called *santo y seña* (picture saint and sign). I've kept this sign painting many years. It swings in my attic, creaking nostalgia, and reminds me that fascism is not dead after all (as if one needs reminding). The picture recalls a lost period in my life, a loss I regret. I haven't gone back to Sant Feliu or the Aragon Retreats for about fifteen years because of my acedia, but I'm about to return to see Josep again.

Oil and collage on canvas 122 × 122 (48 × 48)
The artist
(no.9)

**Specimen Musings of
a Democrat** 1961

Oil and collage on canvas
102 × 127.5 (40¼ × 50¼)
Colin St John Wilson
(no.7)

**Grandmother Kitaj,
aged 102** 1983

Charcoal on paper
19.7 × 14.6 (7¾ × 5¾)
The artist
(no.62)

The Murder of Rosa Luxemburg 1960

This was one of the last pictures where I collaged notes onto the surface to help tell or interpret a story-painting. I had no Jewish education and I was only darkly aware of those exegetical traditions of explanation and interpretation which often appeared as notation inscribed in the margins of texts. Could the force of that lineage have somehow got to me through the ether just in time to further irritate my antagonists? There is also an exegetical strain among Jewish modernists like Kafka, Scholem and Benjamin, novelist, historian and critic, according to Robert Alter who says that those three cast themselves in that role. But I only came across the wonderful Scholem/Benjamin letters being geniuses together many years after this painting. I did, however, know Kafka's *Penal Colony*. Who could forget the machine he invented that inscribes the condemned man's sentence on his body with needles, re-enacting the exegetical role within his art? In my painting, Rosa is 'inscribed' by the pointed shapes and her murder is inscribed in notation on the body of her picture.

Rosa was a student work begun at the Royal College of Art. It looks naive and graceless to me now. It arose out of meditation upon two of my grandmothers (there had been a third). It is about an historic murder, but it is really about murdering Jews, which is what brought all my grandmothers to America (fifty years apart). Grandma Rose is given as her veiled wraith, upper left, but it is grandmother Helene (whose two sisters, like Kafka's three sisters and four of Freud's five sisters were murdered in the same camps by the Germans/Austrians), who really prefigures Rosa L. (in my life). My grandmother was not political, but Helene and Rosa L. looked alike, dressed alike (Helene wore those long black skirts and boots in America until she died at 103), and came from the same cultivated milieu whose brilliance and disaster are now legend. Helene was born in Vienna the same year as Picasso, the year Disraeli died, when Dreyfus was an obscure captain on the French General Staff. I didn't paint Rosa because I was attracted to her revolution. That God never failed me because I never worshipped in his church, but this painting has always seemed failed to me, although I do ponder its terms now and again as if those terms have some breath left in them... I would never quite be free of what is called the lachrymose view of Jewish history.

note: The more elaborate programme of this painting is in the Archive of the Tate Gallery

Oil and collage on canvas 153 × 152.4 (60¼ × 60)
Tate Gallery. Purchased 1980
(no.6)

The Murder of Rosa Luxemburg

The Ohio Gang 1964

This (very) late Surrealist picture was a freely associated depictive abstraction, and its consciousness (or mine) is still streaming. The yellow ribbon signifies that the young woman pledges herself, like in Ford's great movie, without divulging to which of two men. The suitors in my painting, imprecating her, were painted in the images of two very disparate friends: Robert Creeley (standing), whose love poetry I'd just discovered and whom I would draw through a lifetime ... and Jack Wandell, an actor I knew in the late forties when we lived in the same rooming house near Union Square. Where are you Jack? I haven't seen you (except in this picture) for over forty years! Remember when we did that scene from *Of Mice and Men* in an acting class and you played big Lenny to my George? The woman is naked for the men, as in Manet's 'Déjeuner', and attended like his 'Olympia', by a black maid. The Black Maid is an American tragedy which struck me as a child in Ohio and never ends. She deserves a memorial of her own as big as Lincoln's. I was still under the Warburg spell in those early sixties and the Maenad-Nanny at the right is a memory of those pre-Christian wraiths the Warburgers detected at the base of crucifixions in art. She is pushing a homunculus-manikin because I'd just bought a pram for a second child, who died at birth as I began this painting. The little apelike figure escalating away is an ancient symbol of vice and lust. The ape also became associated with the art of painting because of his imitative skills. There was no rational plan for this picture, no programme to speak of. The irrational title doesn't refer to the Ohio Gang of Mark Hanna etc. but to my own cast of characters associated here in free verse or as in early Buñuel.

Oil and graphite on canvas 183.1 × 183.5 (72⅛ × 72¼)
The Museum of Modern Art, New York. Philip Johnson Fund, 1965
(no.12)

Erie Shore 1966

Oil on canvas
2 panels: each 183 × 152.4 (72 × 60)
Staatliche Museen zu Berlin, Nationalgalerie
(no.16)

Walter Lippmann 1966

Every day since I was in high school I read political criticism of many stripes. In the beginning was the word, and a columnist I often read said that the picture was not far behind.

Although this painting is a little too oblique for my taste, it's one of my few favourites among my early pictures partly because I'm so pleased with the configurational debt it expresses to this type of journalism I read each day, that I fancy some of the pleasure I've had from columnists, like the pleasure another painter may get from trees or ancient ornament, has translated into the painted correspondences I've collected here. Now, people like Lippmann, Max Lerner, Conor Cruise O'Brien, George Will and almost all the guys at the *New Republic*, write clear prose for their millions of readers, but perhaps I can be forgiven the difficulty of the stream-of-consciousness into which the parts of my picture flow if only because the eventful world those editorialists try to explain doesn't really come to order very often either. So, in my own practice, some art is fairly straight and some need not be, just like news, and, like stale news and ancient art, some of the original meanings in this picture are lost.

W.L., at stage right, is the voyeur and explainer of complex events he was in my youth. I took the liberty of embroidering those serious events in terms of romance, intrigue, spies and alpine idyll, like movies did in those days, often made by refugees, themselves escaping from serious events. When movies were first shown, the form was so new and unusual that most people found it difficult to understand what was happening, so they were helped by a narrator who stood beside the piano.

Oil on canvas 183 × 213.4 (72 × 84)
Albright-Knox Art Gallery, Buffalo, New York. Gift of Seymour H. Knox, 1967
(no.15)

Juan de la Cruz 1967

This is the only picture I did about Vietnam (partly), and since then, heresies and orthodoxies about that war have changed places many times, just as they do in art and just as the line between heresy and orthodoxy in St Juan's time was very fine indeed. I used to spend my summers in Franco's Spain and I became very interested in Juan who spent forty-nine years in and out of the claws of the Inquisition. He was born to an underclass, like my Sgt Cross, torn between devotion to his calling and tradition on the one hand and St Teresa's Reform on the other, like the American Black soldier must have been in Vietnam. Traditions and Reforms and Inquisitions are not strangers in our art histories, so I believe such things may be as proper a study in a painting itself as, say, subjects in nature. During my sojourn in Catalonia, I read the small body of poems written by St John of the Cross (mainly when he was in prison). Mystics are said to discover a new world, very different from our familiar one and that is very much one of the things I hope a painting can do in its unlikely correspondences and citations based on sensation. The Mystic enjoins a new kind of love, remote from hot sensual love, after a sort of death which purges, so it is said (like war?). My poor and maybe tasteless couple to the right of Juan celebrate a blasphemous mystical union. Bridegroom and Bride are St Juan's own symbolic forms for this union. St Teresa, whose protégé was St John of the Cross, is made to walk the plank by Inquisitors.

Juan's poems express Christian mystery, and wars are most awful expressions of political mystery, so I meant my painting as a mystery-picture. The very mysterious origins of St Teresa and her Juan began to intrigue me because Teresa was of proven Jewish (Marrano) descent through her grandfather, accused by the Inquisition of having relapsed into Judaism. St Juan's possible Jewish descent is unproven. I was just beginning, when I made this picture, to become fascinated with secret Judaisers and such worldly mysteries. With hindsight, this painting was a timid early step for me toward a strange mystical light of my own, which grew brighter and curiouser.

Oil on canvas 183 × 152.4 (72 × 60)
Astrup Fearnley Museum of Modern Art, Oslo
(no.17)

Dominie (Dartmouth) 1978

Pastel and charcoal on paper
56 × 38.1 (22 × 15)
The artist
(no.38)

Lem (Sant Feliu) 1978

Pastel and charcoal on paper
76.8 × 56 (30¼ × 22)
The artist
(no.39)

The Autumn of Central Paris (after Walter Benjamin) 1972–3

Dear Benjamin is now a truly chewed-over cultural spectre, not least in art writing. I started to chew on him myself in the late sixties after having fallen upon him, before the deluge, in a publication of the Leo Baeck Institute. His wonderful and difficult montage, pressing together quickening tableaux from texts and from a disjunct world, were called citations by a disciple of his who also conceded that the picture-puzzle distinguished everything he wrote. His personality began to speak to the painter in me – the adventure of his addiction to fragment-life, the allusive and incomplete nature of his work (Gestapo at his heels) had slowly formed up into one of those heterodox legacies upon which I like to stake my own dubious art claims – against better judgements of how one is permitted to burden the crazy drama of painting. When I first showed this picture, a reviewer even began his attack by choking on the title, which he said I'd stolen from a sociological treatise having nothing to do with Benjamin. The critic was dead right. Benjamin thrills me in no small measure because he does not cohere, and beautifully. He was one of those lonely few who lived out Flaubert's instruction: 'Not to resemble one's neighbour; that is everything.' A lot of people, a whole lot of artists would wish for that, I think, but it eludes us more than we imagine it does. His angry neighbours drove him to kill himself in that very autumn of 1940 which saw the Fall of France and in which I've set this picture, some of my working notes for which are published elsewhere. I feel I ought to apologise for this type of painting because it's such a rouged and puerile reflection upon such vivid personeity, but maybe I won't (apologise); maybe a painter who snips off a length of picture from the flawed scroll which is ever depicting the train of his interest, as Benjamin did, may put a daemon spirit like Benjamin in the picture.

Oil on canvas 152.4 × 152.4 (60 × 60)
Mr and Mrs Francis Lloyd
(no.19)

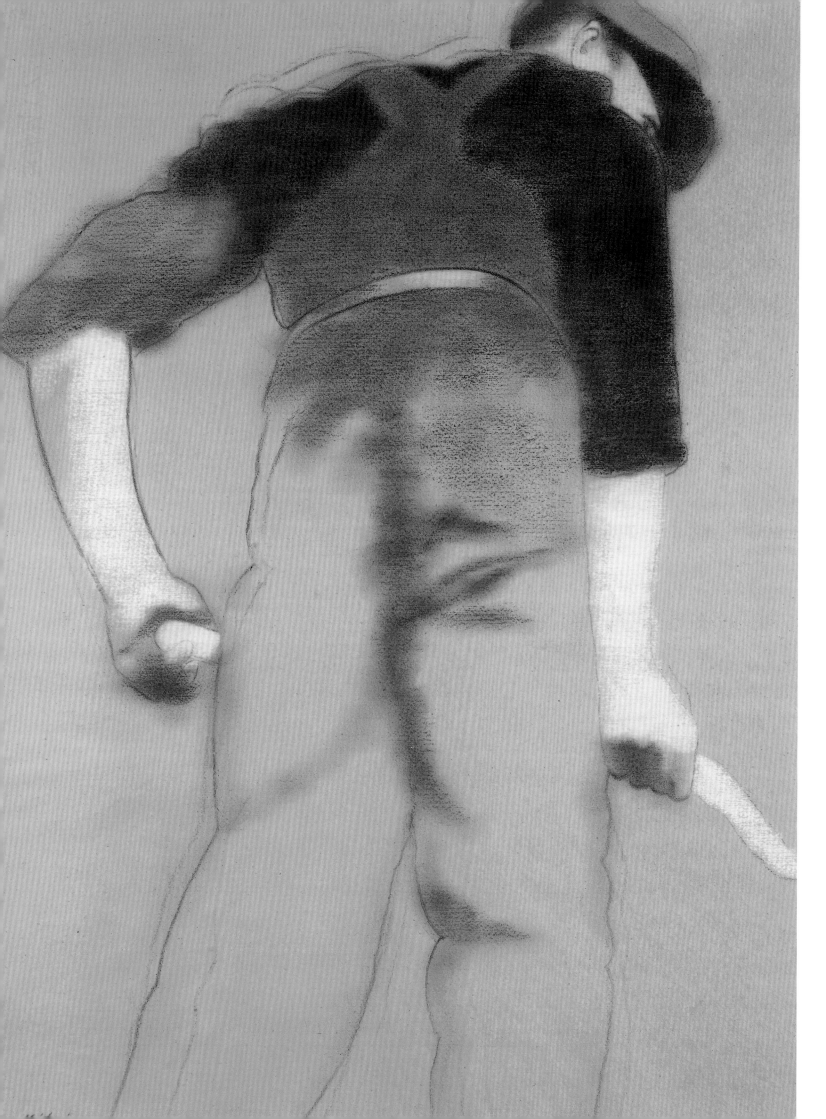

Sculpture 1974
Pastel on paper
76.2 × 50.8 (30 × 20)
Achim Moeller Fine Art, New York
(no.24)

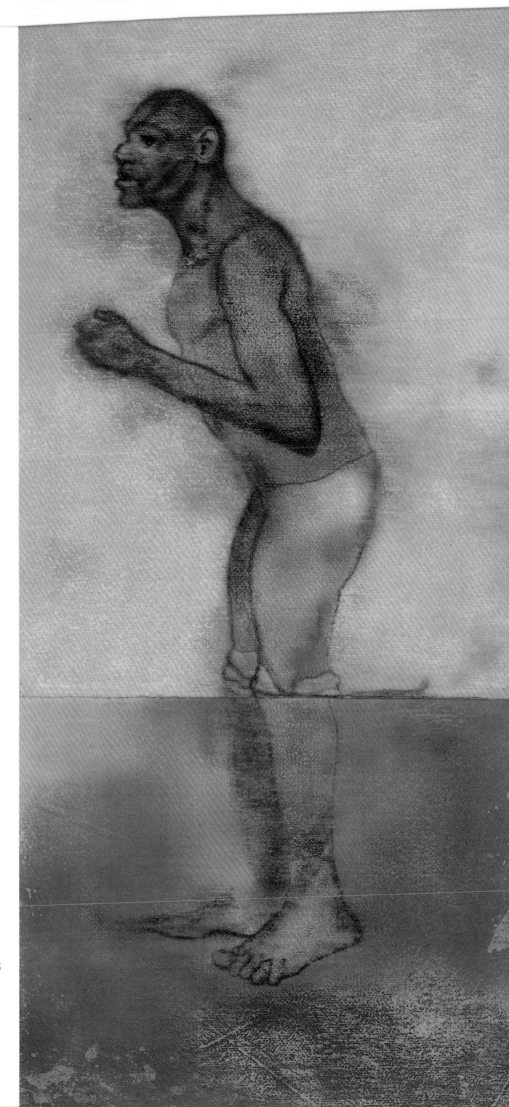

Bather (Wading) 1978
Pastel on paper
123.8 × 56.8 (48¾ × 22⅜)
Private collection
(no.41)

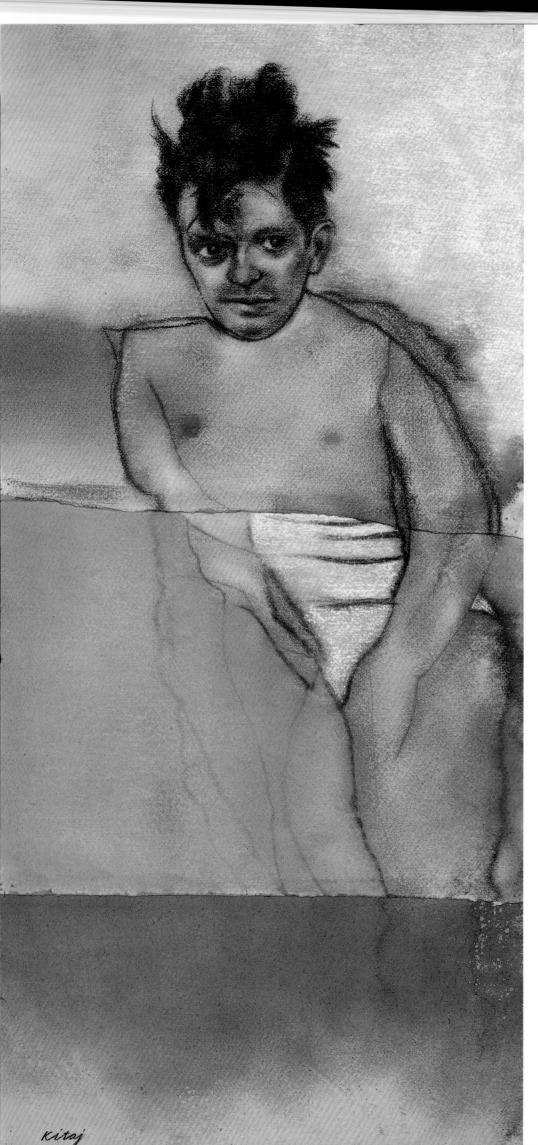

Bather (Tousled Hair) 1978
Pastel on paper
121.3 × 56.8 (47¾ × 22⅜)
Private collection
(no.40)

Bather (Torsion) 1978 (detail)
Pastel on paper
137.8 × 56.8 (54¼ × 22⅜)
Diane L. Ackerman
(no.42)

Bather (Psychotic Boy) 1980

Pastel and charcoal on paper
134 × 57.2 (52¾ × 22½)
*Astrup Fearnley Museum of
Modern Art, Oslo*
(no.56)

Dismantling the Red Tent 1964
Oil on canvas, including an original
etching by Alphonse Legros
122 × 122 (48 × 48)
Michael and Dorothy Blankfort Collection
(no.14)

Where the Railroad Leaves the Sea 1964

The single-gauge railroad left the sea at a small port town on the Catalan coast which I used to know and like in the fifties when I was married to an unhappy, disappointed man who died of a broken heart as I was about to begin the next part of my life with the painter of this picture.

My painter, who is also now dead, had lived all his life in the town and I moved into his little bachelor house just near the old railroad station, the station of the painting, in which he painted us kissing as you can see. The railroad, the small district station and those marriages are all defunct. By chance, they died as Franco died. I now live in London with this painting. Like the Toonerville Trolley of my girlhood, the little train would chug up the coast from Barcelona, stopping at all the bittersweet resort villages until it came to our port, where the old engine sat on a turntable as it had to be faced away from the sunny afternoon sea to begin on its way inland to the provincial capital, Girona.

My painter, Eusebio, had never lived with a woman before, except for his mother who died a year before I came to him, and then a funny thing happened. Almost overnight he stopped painting the small touristic, albeit intelligent, townscapes for which he was known in Catalonia (he was about fifty by then) and began to paint technicolour, whimsical pictures about me and about us, like this one, in a new style, in fact many new styles which, I'm afraid, discouraged the few people who used to buy his paintings. Aside from painting me, Eusebio kept to his lifelong habits. Every Friday, he would kiss me goodbye in the tiled waiting room at the station and take the little train back along the sea to Barcelona where he would spend the weekend, mainly in the lesser brothels. I don't know why he painted me bare-breasted and I never asked him. Nor do I understand the cursive flourish in the way he drew the contours of his own head, like a signature. But he was rather a dandy within his limited means, a smalltown *flâneur*, even in those drab backstreets where we lived, and this kind of fantasy art or whatever you want to call it became his fancy way of addressing a larger world which would never get to hear of him anyway. But even if Eusebio would have prospered on account of such paintings as this, I truly believe that worldly success could not have comforted him more than the eloquence of the regime one only knew in those forgotten lanes and damp terraces, an excruciating eloquence now that it is lost to me. Can you not see my rapture, how happy I look in the painting?

Oil on canvas 122 × 152.4 (48 × 60)
The artist
(no.13)

Land of Lakes 1975–7

Oil on canvas
152.4 × 152.4 (60 × 60)
Private collection
(no.32)

Study for the World's Body 1974

Pastel on paper
76.2 × 50.8 (30 × 20)
Private collection
(no.25)

Desk Murder (formerly The Third Department (A Teste Study)) 1970–84

The subject of this picture turns out to be hate. It was only upon reading the obituaries of Herr Walter Rauff that I knew my painting was finished. I hadn't touched it for many years, in its metaphysical desuetude, but the last stroke would be to give it this final title. Fourteen years before, I'd called it 'Teste Study', after Valéry's mindful Monsieur (based on Degas), who had so entranced my youth. Then, for a while, it was 'The Third Department' (political police; getting warmer). I think the new title is just right because the terms of the picture fit so well.

Herr Rauff, *Schreibtischtaeter* (Desk-Murderer), was dead, but I could now float this office picture out, with just a wee bit more confidence, into the same world in which his pals are still alive, including those who gave the Hitler-salute at his grave in Chile. Some people will laugh at my ignorance of the proper powers of the painting art (as if one *could* express an historical unhappiness), but I'll tell you, it makes *me* feel a little keener to get a painting to 'work' in my own way, and so there may be a very small art lesson in it. Let me go on:

Incredibly, there used to be a naval officer in my painting until I took him out years ago. Rauff, I just learned, had been a failed naval officer who turned to the SS after he was kicked out of the navy. At some point in the life of this picture, I stuck on a fragment of canvas and drew on it what looks like a contraption of some sort, emitting fume. Rauff was the guy who designed the mobile gas vans used by *Einsatzgruppen* in Eastern Europe before the German killing-centres became operational. At last I knew what my odd device was. I had even obliged fate by draping my composition in mourning black and sketching in an unlaid ghost. The murder office is empty and my banal picture of evil, like Rauff, is finished, its purpose, as Helen Gardner said of *The Waste Land*, altered in fulfilment.

Oil on canvas 76.2 × 122 (30 × 48)
The artist
(no.63)

The Rise of Fascism 1979–80
Pastel, charcoal and oil on paper
85.1 × 158.4 (33½ × 62⅜)
Tate Gallery. Purchased 1980
(no.51)

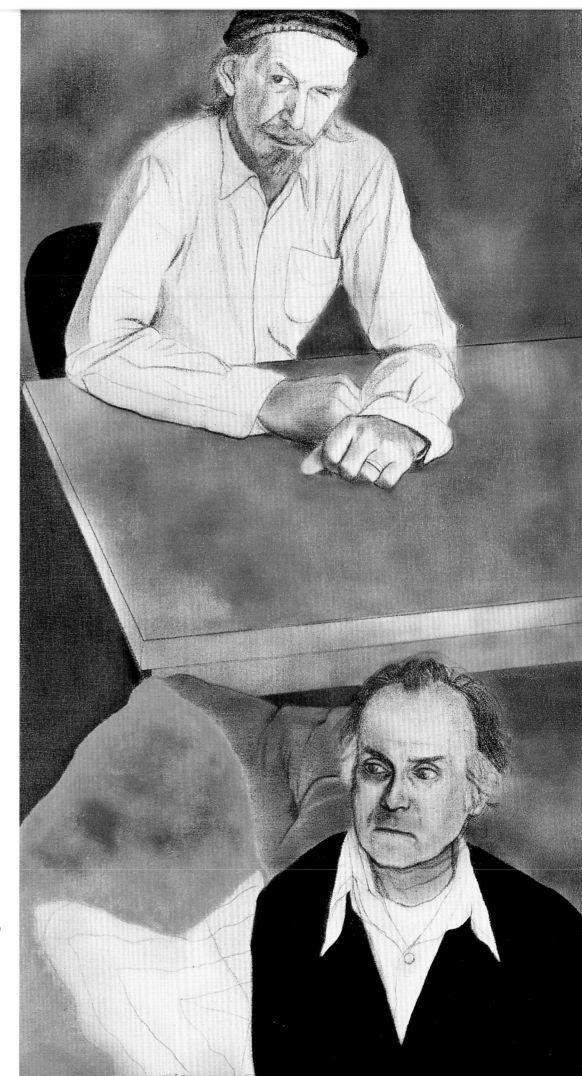

A Visit to London (Robert Creeley and Robert Duncan) 1977–9 (detail)

Oil and charcoal on canvas
183 × 61 (72 × 24)
*Fundación Colección
Thyssen-Bornemisza, Madrid*
(no.45)

To Live in Peace (The Singers) 1973–4
Oil on canvas
77.5 × 214.5 (30½ × 84½)
Marlborough International Fine Art
(no.23)

Unity Mitford 1968
Oil on canvas
25.4 × 20.3 (10 × 8)
The artist
(no.18)

The Orientalist 1976–7
Oil on canvas
243.8 × 76.8 (96 × 30¼)
Tate Gallery. Purchased 1977
(no.33)

The Arabist 1975–6
Oil on canvas
243.8 × 76.2 (96 × 30)
*Museum Boymans-van
Beuningen, Rotterdam*
(no.30)

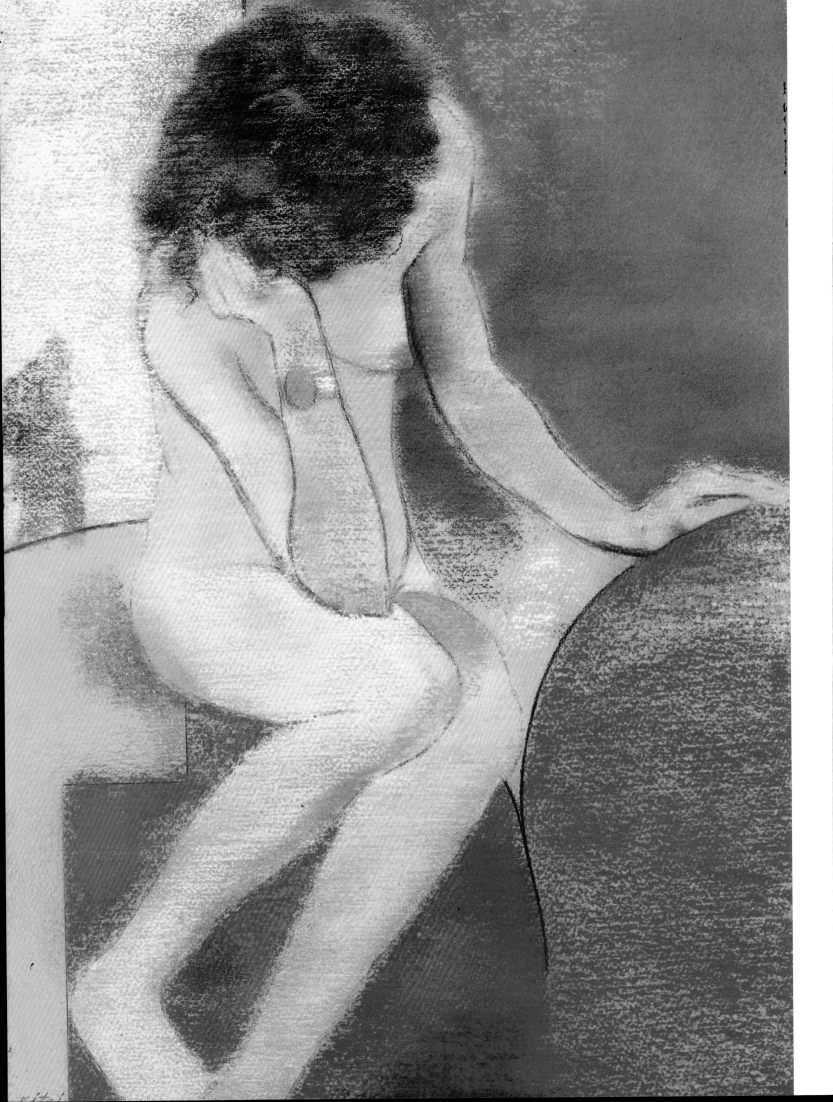

Kitaj

My Cat and Her Husband 1977
Pastel and charcoal on paper
38.1 × 56 (15 × 22)
Dominie Kitaj
(no.35)

Waiting 1975
Pastel on paper
78.5 × 56.5 (30⅞ × 22¼)
Private collection
(no.27)

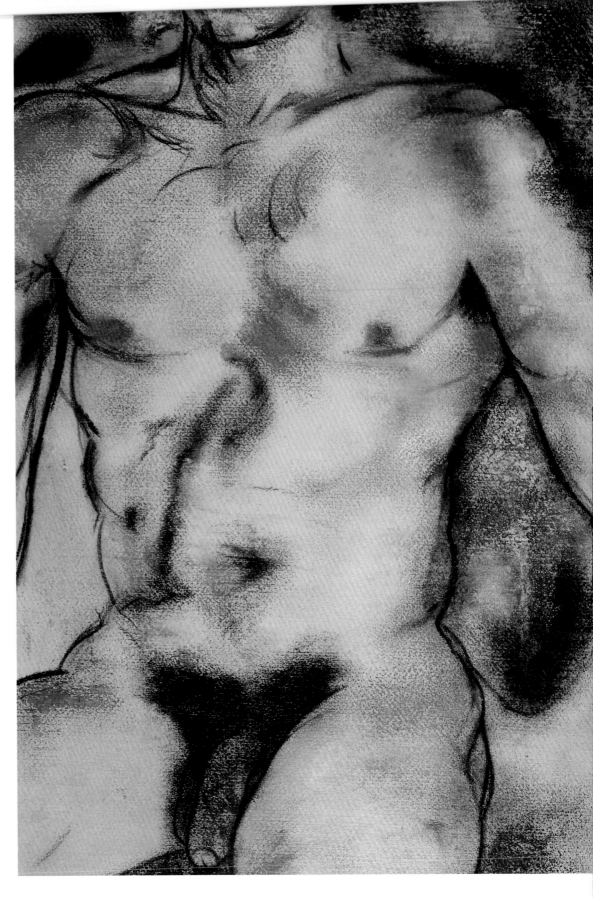

His New Freedom 1978
Pastel and charcoal on paper
76.8 × 56 (30¼ × 22)
The artist
(no.44)

Actor (Richard) 1979
Pastel and charcoal on paper
76.8 × 49.2 (30¼ × 19⅜)
*Scottish National Gallery of
Modern Art. Edinburgh*
(no.49)

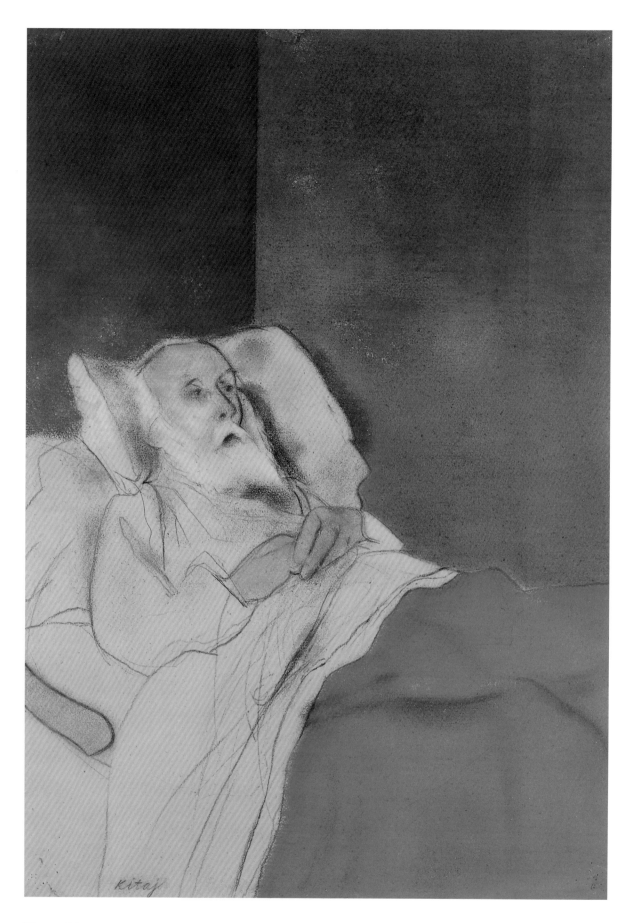

Degas 1980
Pastel and charcoal on paper
73 × 50.8 (28¾ × 20)
The artist
(no.52)

Marynka Smoking 1980
Pastel and charcoal on paper
90.8 × 56.5 (35¾ × 22¼)
The artist
(no.53)

If Not, Not 1975–6

Two main strands come together in the picture. One is a certain allegiance to Eliot's *Waste Land* and its (largely unexplained) family of loose assemblage. Eliot used, in his turn, Conrad's *Heart of Darkness*, and the dying figures among the trees to the right of my canvas make similar use of Conrad's bodies strewn along the riverbank.

Eliot said of his poem, 'To me it was only the relief of a personal and wholly insignificant grouse against life; it is just a piece of rhythmical grumbling'. So is my picture... but the grouse here has to do with what Winston Churchill called 'the greatest and most horrible crime ever committed in the whole history of the world'... the murder of the European Jews. That is the second main theme, presided over by the Auschwitz gatehouse. This theme coincides with that view of the Waste Land as an antechamber to hell. There are (disputed) passages in the poem where drowning, 'Death by Water', is associated with either the death of someone close to the poet or the death of a Jew... like most of the poem, these passages are fraught with innuendo.

The man in the bed with a child is a self-portrait detail in the waste-like middle ground which also shows scattered fragments (such as the broken Matisse bust) being sucked up as if in a sea of mud. This sense of strewn and abandoned things and people was suggested by a Bassano painting, of which I had a detail, showing a ground after a battle. Love survives broken life 'amid the craters', as someone said of the poem.

The general look of the picture was inspired by my first look at Giorgione's 'Tempesta' on a visit to Venice, of which the little pool at the heart of my canvas is a reminder. However, water, which often symbolises renewed life, is here stagnant in the shadow of a horror... also not unlike Eliot's treatment of water. My journal for this painting reports a train journey someone took from Budapest to Auschwitz to get a sense of what the doomed could see through the slats of their cattle cars ('beautiful, simply beautiful countryside')... I don't know who said it. Since then, I've read that Buchenwald was constructed on the very hill where Goethe often walked with Eckermann.

Oil on canvas 152.4 × 152.4 (60 × 60)
Scottish National Gallery of Modern Art, Edinburgh
(no.29)

Mary-Ann 1980
Pastel and charcoal on paper
77.5 × 56 (30½ × 22)
Private collection
(no.54)

His Hour 1975
Pastel and charcoal on paper
77.5 × 57.2 (30½ × 22½)
Nan and Gene Corman
(no.26)

Marynka Pregnant II 1981
Pastel and charcoal on paper
56.5 × 77.2 (22¼ × 30⅜)
The artist
(no.60)

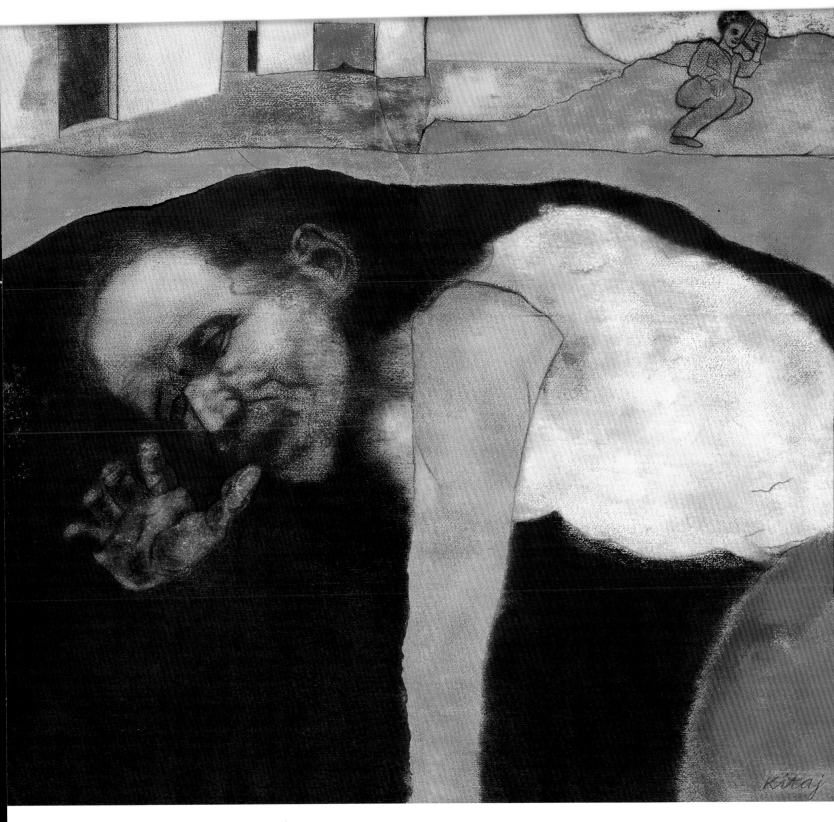

The Listener (Joe Singer in Hiding) 1980
Pastel and charcoal on paper
103.2 × 108.2 (40⅝ × 42⅝)
Whereabouts unknown
(no.55)

The Sensualist 1973–84

Cézanne! He was my one and only master!

Picasso

In modern art, it is undoubtedly to Cézanne that I owe the most.

Matisse

Cézanne is my favourite painter too. This picture belongs some to one of my hobbies: trying to figure him, trying to figure his little and big sensations all over again. Pete Rose said: 'Nobody's got a book on me.'* Cézanne could have said it. Maybe that's why he draws so many of us to him.

This (canvas) began life the other way round, as a woman. You can still see her pink head upside down at the bottom. I don't remember who she was but I think she represents the real woman in the Sensualist's life in the repainted picture. This studio picture was not painted from life. First, I painted over the woman a kind of copy of the famous Cézanne male 'Bather' of 1885 (itself painted after a photo). Then, the Titian 'Marsyas' came to the Royal Academy and blew everyone's mind. I'd put a postcard of it upside down on my wall and meanwhile Kossoff, who'd been drawing from the 'Marsyas', gave us one of those drawings as a wedding present. The drawing was lying on the floor, again upside down, looking like a man walking, so I painted from that over my bather, which became the final version. All too artful, so I wrote ART over the mean street doorway, for Art's sake. In the end oneself is the making of it; not after life but about life, I think Pound said. Titian came to exploit what has been called the victory of the subjective principle, then only recently prepared. The depiction of human proportions would always now turn on the mystery of subjective styles – never more so before or since Cézanne's bathers, bemused as they often are by a torsion like that in the dangling Marsyas, though not in the frontal magic of the great New York Male Bather whose (implied) quadri-facial stance I grafted onto my tall canvas at first. I left his right hand on his hip as you can see, as an action between the crises of the torsion. In the end, the muscularity comprises frontal breast, three-quarter hips and profile legs, the transition or joining of which Titian seems to have beautifully fudged, for the sake of, I suppose, an animality.

* Pete Rose was one of the greatest hitters in baseball. The meaning of his saying is that no one could predict or anticipate how he would hit the ball.

Oil on canvas 246.4 × 77.2 (97 × 30⅜)
The Foundation FOR ART and The National Museum of Contemporary Art, Oslo
(no.64)

The Hispanist (Nissa Torrents) 1977–8
Oil on canvas
243.8 × 76.2 (96 × 30)
Astrup Fearnley Museum of Modern Art, Oslo
(no.36)

His Last Painting 1987
Oil on canvas
99.7 × 62.9 (39¼ × 24¾)
Private collection
(no.80)

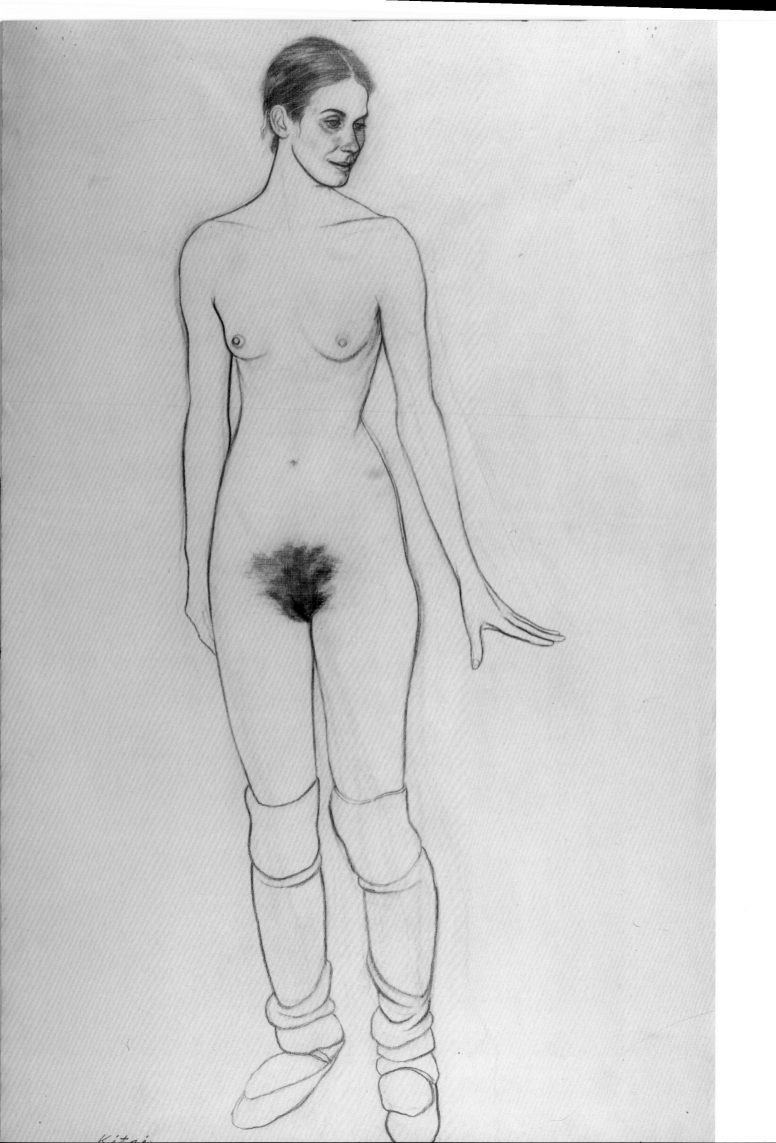

Kitaj

The Dancer (Margaret) 1978

Pencil on paper
100 × 64.8 (39⅜ × 25½)
Mrs Edwin Bergman
(no.37)

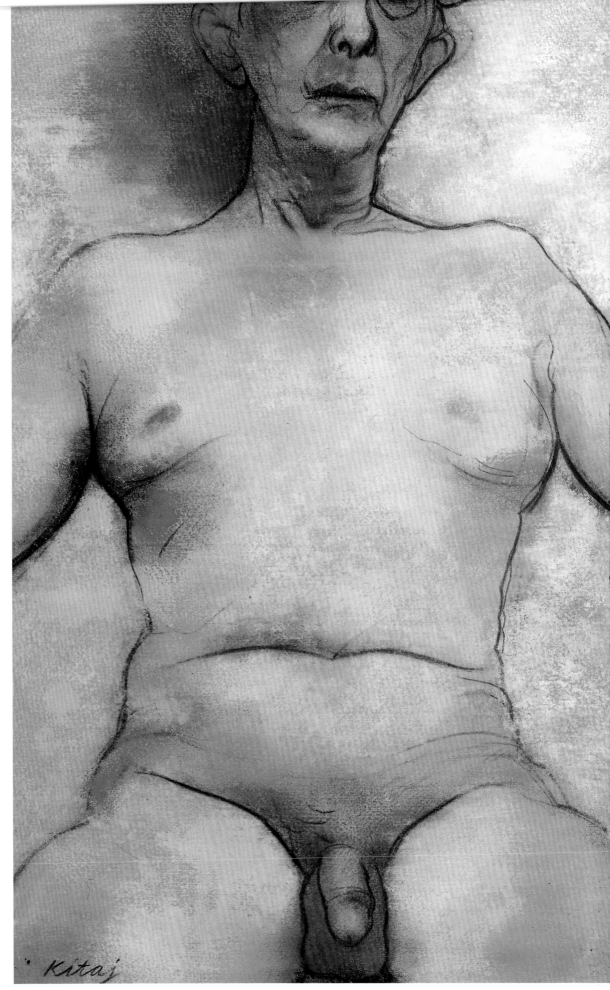

Quentin 1979

Pastel and charcoal on paper
65.4 × 40 (25¾ × 15¾)
The artist
(no.50)

The Jew Etc. 1976–unfinished

> I have long since resolved to be a Jew ... I regard that as more important than my art.
>
> Schönberg

I've seen people wince at this title; sophisticated art people, who think it's better not to use the word Jew. Kafka, my greatest Jewish artist, never utters the word once in his fiction, so I thought I would. This name-sickness, which many Jews will recognise and understand in different ways, is so touching to me, that I've also given my Jew a secret name: Joe Singer. Now it's not secret anymore.

In this picture, I intend Joe, my emblematic Jew, to be the unfinished subject of an aesthetic of entrapment and escape, an endless, tainted Galut-Passage, wherein he acts out his own unfinish. All painters are familiar with the forces of destiny embedded in happy accident and other revelations and failures which inform one's painting days. In that way, I'd like to expose Joe, in his representation here, to a painted fate not unlike the unpredictable case of one's own dispersion in the everyday world. For instance, before long I may name Joe's fellow passengers, those you can't see unless I paint them in, even though there's not much room left. In fact, I've begun to people this train compartment in my journal. One of Joe Singer's jobs relates to a tradition of our exile, which influences this picture, whereby living messengers are trained up, who take the place of books, in order to preserve a freshness of teaching, not endangered by date or dogma. Joe is the messenger-invention of my own peculiar dispersion (Galut), about which I learn more every day. His depiction on his expiatory pilgrimage presides over my sense of that changeful exilic condition and its uncertain art habits and futures, as in these beautiful lines about the Jews by the Catholic Péguy: 'Being elsewhere, the great vice of this race, the great secret virtue, the great vocation of this people.'

Oil and charcoal on canvas 152.4 × 122 (60 × 48)
The artist
(no.31)

**The Man of the Woods and
the Cat of the Mountains** 1973

Oil on canvas
152.4 × 152.4 (60 × 60)
*Tate Gallery. Presented by the
Friends of the Tate Gallery 1974*
(no.22)

Smyrna Greek (Nikos)
1976–7 (detail)
Oil on canvas
243.8 × 76.2 (96 × 30)
Fundación Colección
Thyssen-Bornemisza, Madrid
(no.34)

**Pacific Coast Highway
(Across the Pacific)** 1973

Oil on canvas
2 panels: 152.4 × 243.8;
152.4 × 152.4 (60 × 96; 60 × 60)
Colin St John Wilson
(no.20)

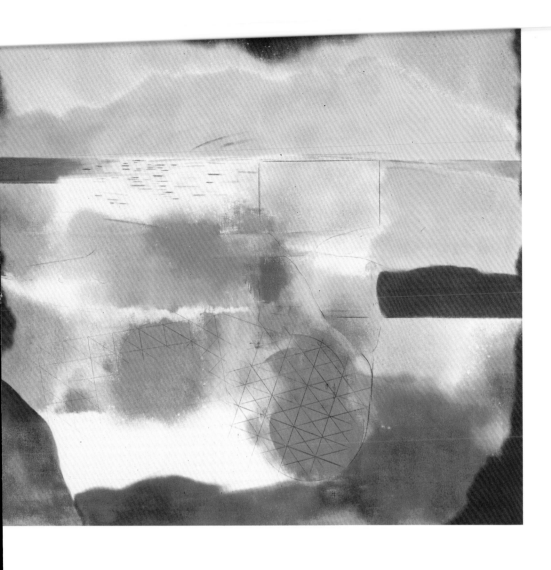

**Kenneth Anger and
Michael Powell** 1973

Oil on canvas
243.8 × 152.4 (96 × 60)
*Ludwig Museum Koblenz
Deutschherrenhaus*
(no.21)

The Jewish School (Drawing a Golem) 1980

This is the first oil painting I made to attempt to cut through the vexing and, to me at least, fascinating questions and arguments swirling around the notion of Jewish art. During my years of discovery before I made the picture and in the years of selective learning since it was painted, it never occurred to me to *prove* that there's such a thing as Jewish art, any more or less than one could prove anything much about any art at all. Very roughly speaking, I now feel that there has been no tradition of Jewish art (in the discernible sense of Islamic or Japanese or Egyptian art for instance). And so, the Jewishness of a painting such as this one may have to depend on the various diasporist 'Jewish' attentions I sought to lavish upon it. Among my Warburg publications is a study by Isaiah Schachar of the savage, anti-Semitic *Judensau* motif in visual 'art' through the ages, in which I fell upon a nineteenth-century German watercolor caricature called 'Die Judenschule' by one G.E. Opitz, the source for my painting. The original picture supposed to show typical chaos in a Jewish schoolroom over which the hapless rabbi can't exert order, the visual implication being to instruct decent Aryan Germans about the plague of alien *Ostjuden* in their midst, just like pictures in Streicher's *Der Stürmer* would do in our time with murder (of children) as an endgame. I don't wish to inscribe a plot for my painting in stone, but in a plausible drama the teacher, with experience of the notorious blood-libel (see inkwell spilling blood), fears he can't save the children, one of whom will resist his fate by attacking a brick wall (suggested by a parable in Breugel) and maybe even escaping. The middle boy represents the incredible tradition of Jewish learning which will survive even if the boy doesn't. The third child wants to be emancipated as an artist and draws a Golem on the blackboard (instead of the vile *Judensau* in Opitz). His Golem begins to come alive but not in time because the painting concludes at that moment. The sequence of Matisse 'Back' sculptures at the Tate, done after intervals in his life, tempt me now to paint a sequel or two, revisiting the figures in my picture after almost fifteen years have gone by. One idea I have for a sequel would be to try to paint into Martin Buber's formulation of the 'Eclipse of God' (He is sometimes hidden and sometimes revealed). I've never tried to paint God before, so I've been looking at William Blake and the early Italians a lot.

Oil on canvas 152.4 × 152.4 (60 × 60)
Private collection
(no.57)

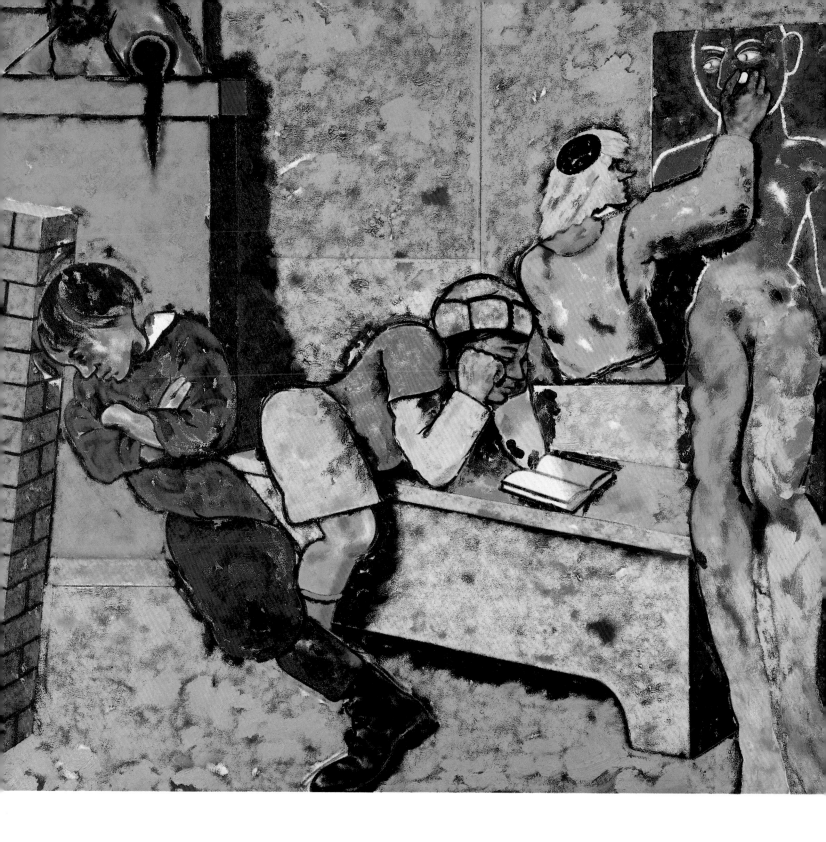

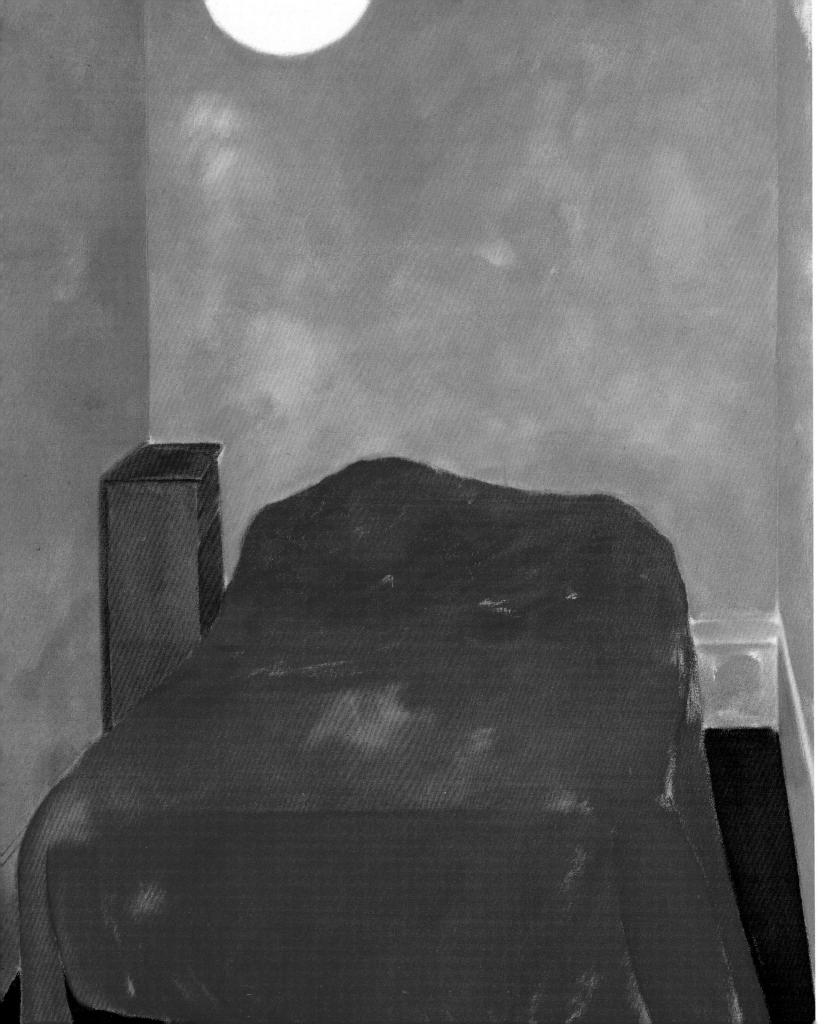

The Room (Rue St Denis)
1982–3
Oil on canvas
122 × 91.4 (48 × 36)
Mrs David G. Kangesser
(no.61)

The Sniper 1987
Oil on canvas
305 × 91.4 (120 × 36)
Saatchi Collection, London
(no.79)

**From London (James Joll
and John Golding)** 1975–6

Oil on canvas
152.4 × 243.8 (60 × 96)
Private collection
(no.28)

The Garden 1981
Oil on canvas
122 × 122 (48 × 48)
The Cleveland Museum of Art
(no.58)

Self-portrait as a Woman 1984

My name is Hedwig Bacher and I'm still alive, more's the pity. When the author of this painting was a nineteen year old art student in Vienna in 1951, I was his landlady and for about six months, we were also lovers. I was thirty-seven and I rented him the garden room in my flat in the 18th District, just off the Währingerstrasse. He was a skinny American boy with acne and an Eisenhower jacket. I had a regular boyfriend, a cultivated and caustic brewer, then in his sixties, who had looked after me since I was sixteen and would remain constant to the day he died in 1969 no matter how much I slept around, which he did too. And that's what got me in trouble during the Nazi years. I slept with a Jew and got caught, so these thugs stripped me and I had to march naked through the streets of the suburb of Währing wearing this placard and yelling out that I'd slept with a Jew. You can read about such nice incidents in histories of the period. They did no further harm to me because my brewer knew the right people. The next Jew I slept with was Ronald, my young lodger. In order to save on heating, Ronald and I used to bathe together and one Sunday, in the bathtub, I told him the story of my little ordeal as we were clasped together in the tepid water. What a great idea for a painting, he said, and would I take him through those very streets where they had marched me. So I did, and he made some drawings in his sketchbook of the quaint buildings and the Annakirche. In the spring, Ronald took up with a neighbour girl who used to come to his room through the garden and we stopped sleeping together more or less. When I saw this painting of his in a book forty years later, I wrote to him in London saying I had no idea he felt close enough to my humiliation to have put himself in my place as it were, to have put himself into the picture.

Oil on canvas 246.4 × 77.2 (97 × 30⅜)
Astrup Fearnley Museum of Modern Art, Oslo
(no.69)

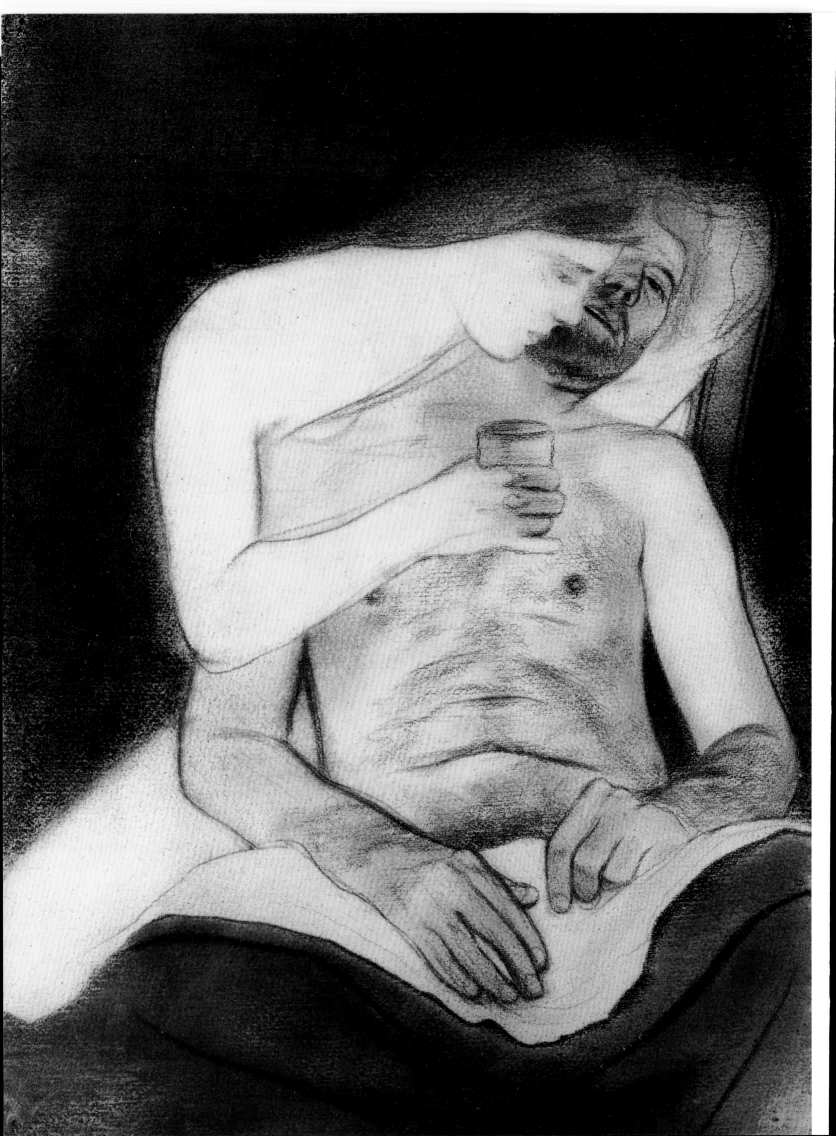

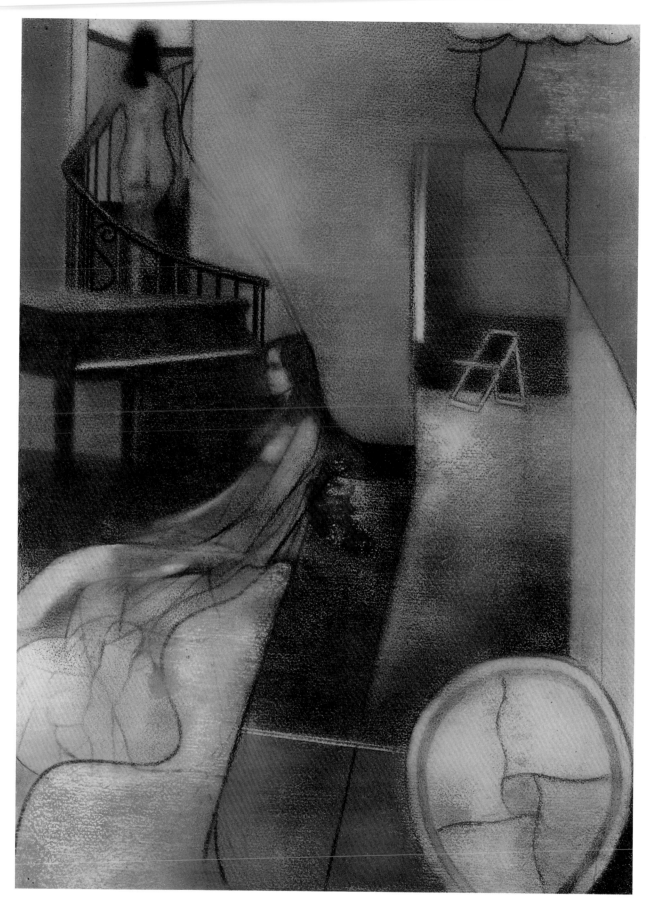

The Green Blanket 1978
Pastel and charcoal on paper
76.8 × 56 (30¼ × 22)
Private collection
(no.43)

The Philosopher-Queen 1978–9
Pastel and charcoal on paper
76.8 × 56 (30¼ × 22)
The artist
(no.46)

John Ford on his Deathbed 1983–4

Ford has always been my favourite director. Even as a boy, he brought tears to my eyes and resolution to my heart. An old mutual friend phoned him for me and asked him if I could sketch him for a Hollywood painting I wanted to make (in Hollywood where we were living) in 1970. Ford said OK and so I took my eldest son Lem, who even then, aged about eleven, wanted to direct, in the path of the master. Ford lived near UCLA, where I was teaching, in an old-fashioned house full of mementos – Academy awards, Will Rogers' lasso, signed photos everywhere 'to Jack' from Ike, from Bull Halsey, from Mark Clark etc. We nearly died because we were told John Wayne had just left. Ford was in bed, like my painting shows, wearing what I thought at first was a baseball cap, but turned out to be an admiral's bridge cap. I think he was made an admiral for filming the battle of Midway. He looked like a dying man as I sketched him. He had a bowl to spit into. I've painted a picture above his head that wasn't there, near where his rosary beads were hanging. It's a still from his favourite among his own films – *The Sun Shines Bright*, a marvellous post-war tearjerker about Judge Priest. At the foot of his bed sit Charlie Grapewin and Elisabeth Patterson, as if on their front porch in *Tobacco Road*, being directed by Ford in his prime at the lower left. There's a kind of dance going on, as in so many Ford movies, and Victor McLaglen looms as Quincannon of the Cavalry Trilogy at the top left. I got the idea for all these corny ghosts from that wonderful last scene in Huston's *Moulin Rouge*, when all his past characters reappear at Lautrec's deathbed. Ford's Irish rebel, anti-British chat was memorable, but I noticed he kept *Burke's Peerage* on his bookshelf. He told Lem not to go to film school because it's a waste of time, advice which Lem took because if John Ford tells you not to go to film school, you don't go. That year, I also sketched Renoir, Cukor, Milestone, Mamoulian, Hathaway and Wilder out there, but in the end I lost heart for a Hollywood *Gesamtkunstwerk*. It took me fifteen years to get around to my Ford painting.

Oil on canvas 152.4 × 152.4 (60 × 60)
The Metropolitan Museum of Art, New York. Purchase, Lila Acheson Wallace Gift, 1986
(no.66)

Baseball 1983–4

> The day Custer lost at the Little Big Horn, the Chicago White Sox beat the Cincinnati Red Legs, 3–2
>
> Charles O. Finley

From time to time I have to make a baseball painting to express a deep national love. By national I mean where you come from, grow up, get formed, national pride, etc., etc. What can it be if not a national feeling translated into painting? This is the most serious one so far. I've lived most of my life far away from the Summer Game of my childhood. I was never any good at it but it is rarely out of my thoughts and I still follow baseball every day like some kind of moveable feast. Red Smith and Bill James ('a first-rate mind wasting itself on baseball', someone said) are right up there on my bookshelves, next to Kafka and Dürer. And it was Kafka's *Amerika* which inspired me to set all those little players in a Nature-Theatre not unlike the fields of my otherwise boring boyhood in Ohio and upstate New York, where one toiled in ecstasy at the blessed game. The great Velázquez fieldscape of the Boar Hunt at London reminded me of the low hills of home which often framed the theatres where we played and that picture is paraphrased here in mine. I look to baseball lives, as to the characters in great novels, for some little help, not only to get through each day, but to persist at painting pictures. As I grow older and amazing baseball records are broken by some few aged players who stay at it through decades, or baseball lives are regained and renewed by men given up for lost in particular American circumstances ... I feel their breath on my neck and I try not to look back at my own failures too much because 'something may be gaining on you', as Satchel Paige said. He thrilled me to tears when Bill Veeck brought him up to Cleveland from the Negro League in old age. Find him in this painting if you can. Max Brod recalled what Kafka felt about his unfinished novel, *Amerika*, and I want to cite it as an attention for this 'Baseball' picture: 'In enigmatic language Kafka used to hint smilingly, that within this 'almost limitless' theater his young hero was going to find again a profession, a stand-by, his freedom, even his old home and his parents, as if by some celestial witchery.'

Oil on canvas 152.4 × 152.4 (60 × 60)
Private collection
(no.67)

Kitaj

Rock Garden (The Nation) 1981
Oil on canvas
122 × 122 (48 × 48)
Private collection
(no.59)

Philip Roth 1985
Charcoal on paper
77.8 × 57.2 (30⅝ × 22½)
The artist
(no.74)

Germania (The Tunnel) 1985
Oil on canvas
183.2 × 214 (72⅛ × 84¼)
Private collection
(no.73)

Germania (The Engine Room) 1983–6
Oil on canvas
122 × 122 (48 × 48)
Private collection
(no.75)

The Neo-Cubist 1976–87

Oil on canvas
177.8 × 132.1 (70 × 52)
Private collection
(no.78)

The Jewish Rider 1984–5

Oil on canvas
152.4 × 152.4 (60 × 60)
*Astrup Fearnley Museum of
Modern Art, Oslo*
(no.71)

Cecil Court, London WC2 (The Refugees) 1983–4

> I consider myself no longer a German. I prefer to call myself a Jew.
>
> Sigmund Freud

I have very little experience of water lilies or ballet dancers or jazz or wine or loneliness. Among some other things, I think I have a lot of experience of refugees from the Germans, and that's how this painting came about. My dad and grandmother Kitaj and quite a few people dear to me just barely escaped. One of the first friends to see this painting (a seventy-five year old refugee) said the people in it looked meshuga. They were largely cast from the beautiful craziness of Yiddish Theatre, which I only knew at second hand from my maternal grandparents, but fell upon in Kafka, who gives over a hundred loving pages of his diaries to a grand passion for these shabby troupes, despised by aesthetes and Hebraists, who were revolted by them. Painters are in the business of 'baking' (a plot device from Yiddish Theatre) pictures whose perpetration may be sparked by unlikely agents of conversion, which in Kafka's case really caused his art to turn when he met these players. Excited, according to my own habits, I began (in Paris, California, New York, Jerusalem and London), to collect scarce books and pictures about this shadow world, the trail of which has not quite grown cold in my past life. I would stage some of the syntactical strategies and mysteries and lunacies of Yiddish Theatre in a London Refuge, Cecil Court, the book alley I'd prowled all my life in England, which fed so much into my dubious pictures from its shops and their refugee booksellers, especially the late Mr Seligmann (holding flowers at left) who sold me many art books and prints. Another day I'll tell who the other people in the painting are supposed to be, whether aesthetes find such midrashic gloss and emendation revolting or not. For now, I must confess that I wish I could paint the shop signs in the spirit of a distinction made by my favourite anti-Semite, Pound, who said that symbols quickly exhaust their references, while signs renew theirs.

Oil on canvas 183 × 183 (72 × 72)
Tate Gallery. Purchased 1985
(no.65)

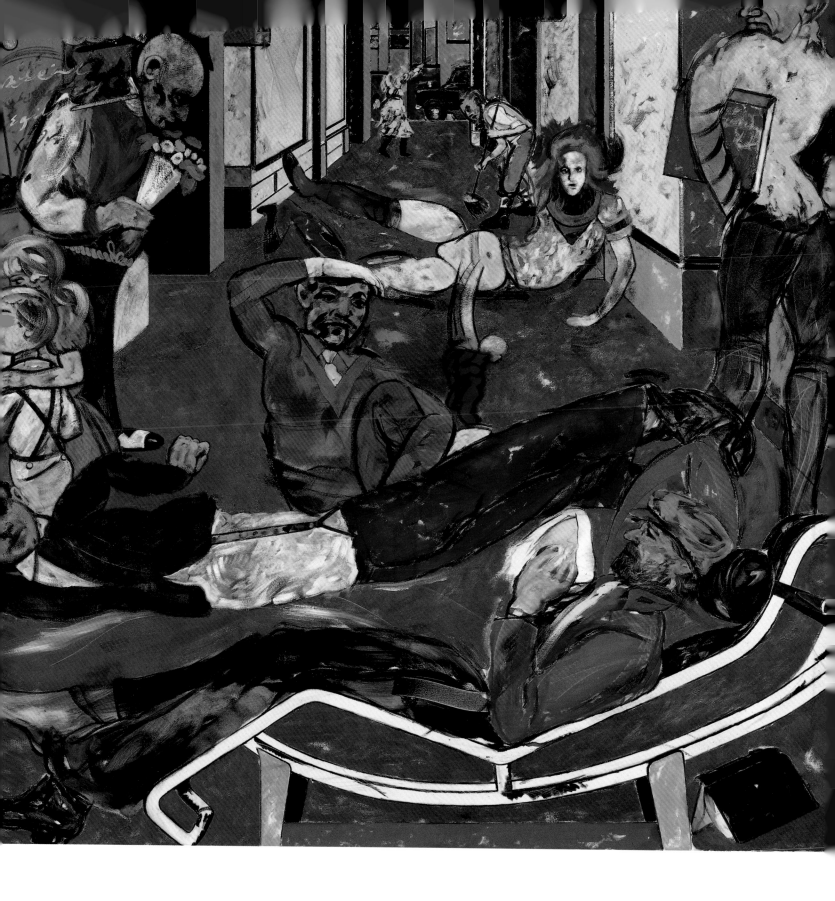

Kitaj

Drancy 1984–6
Pastel and charcoal on paper
100.3 × 78.1 (39½ × 30¾)
Fondation du Judaisme Français, Paris
(no.76)

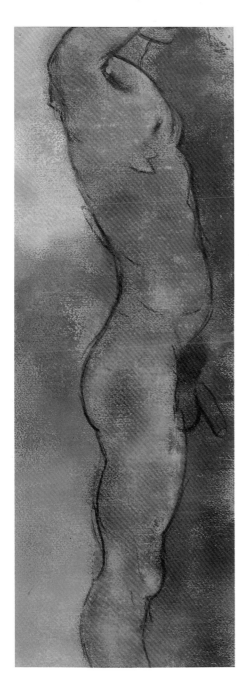
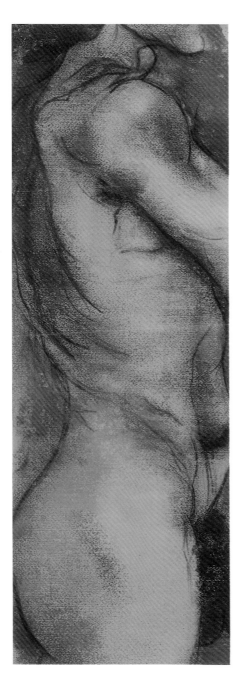

Sides 1979
Pastel and charcoal on paper
3 panels each: 77.5 × 28.2 (30½ × 11⅛)
Trustees of the British Museum, London
(no.48)

Jack My Hedgehog 1991

Oil on canvas
122 × 122 (48 × 48)
Marlborough Fine Art (London) Ltd
(no.87)

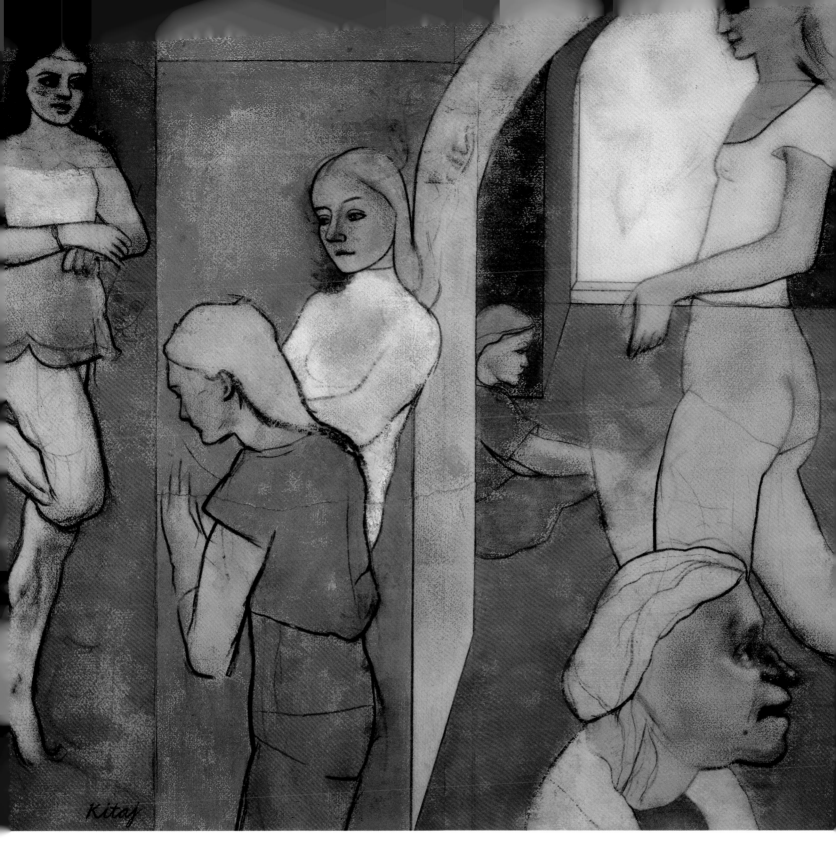

Sighs from Hell 1979
Pastel and charcoal on paper
97.8 × 100.3 (38½ × 39½)
Mrs Edwin Bergman
(no.47)

Sir Ernst Gombrich 1986

Pastel and charcoal on paper
67.3 × 56.8 (26½ × 22⅜)
National Portrait Gallery, London
(no.77)

Ellen's Back 1984

Pastel and charcoal on paper
78.1 × 56.8 (30¾ × 22⅜)
Whitney Museum of American Art, New York. Gift of
Edward L. Gardner in honour of Flora Biddle and the 60th
Anniversary of the Whitney Museum of American Art
(no.68)

Heart Attack 1990

Oil on canvas
122.5 × 122.5 (48¼ × 48¼)
Private collection, Switzerland
(no.81)

Redemption through Sin 1990–3
Charcoal on canvas
152.4 × 153 (60 × 60¼)
Marlborough Fine Art (London) Ltd
(no.103)

Whistler vs. Ruskin (Novella in Terre Verte, Yellow and Red) 1992

Anyone who doesn't know about the famous and absurd Whistler–Ruskin trial a century ago should look it up because it's lots of fun even though it ruined both of them. Whistler was bankrupted and Ruskin entered his final madness. The issues, aesthetics and dramas are still quite electric today, at least to me, but cockeyed and complicated by many of the subsequent heavyweight brawls in modernist history which overturn the Whistler–Ruskin decision time and again as, for instance, the theory called art for art's sake gets sanctified, damned, reborn, etc. until hell freezes over. My subtitle above means to say that the literary stigma in modernism is no more of a blasphemy than the musical analogy introduced by Whistler and perfected by some abstraction. The painting is based mainly on my fellow Ohioan, Bellows, of course. Not on the picture I grew up with at the Cleveland Museum (Stag at Sharkey's), but the more wooden Dempsey and Firpo, at the Whitney. Henry McBride, an art critic I liked in my youth, found the likenesses disappointing. What a fight that must have been – even Babe Ruth was there for the whole four minutes it lasted. I've followed boxing all my life and I've taken liberties with some of the strange events of those four minutes (it was Dempsey, the eventual winner, who was knocked out of the ring), but even though Whistler won his case, we're not sure he did, are we? Anyway, this painting is also about London American coxcombs getting our chops in, and about the way painting may be said to extend its aesthetic reach or punch beyond the sacred picture plane, into time, historical stream and vivid lineage or bloodline: the Ruskin figure is based on the amazing torso (which I've upended) of a Rembrandt Christ (the Munich 'Descent From The Cross'); which itself is based on a famous picture by *his* fellow Lowlander, Rubens. Rembrandt comments on this transcription of his. He wrote that he wanted to express the 'deepest inward emotion'. I think I projected my deepest emotion into the referee, which is a self-portrait, by an old boy of the drawing school Ruskin founded at Oxford.

Oil on canvas 152.4 × 152.4 (60 × 60)
Marlborough Fine Art (London) Ltd
(no.92)

Against Slander 1990–1

> Who desires life and loves to see good days?
> Keep your tongue from evil, keep your lips from deceit.
>   from the 34th Psalm

Painters have often been inspired by sainthood. This painting was inspired by a Jewish saint, which may or may not be unusual in art... I don't know. The Hafetz Hayim (1837–1933) is always called a saint. At the very moment Cézanne was showing in the first Impressionist exhibition, the Hafetz Hayim, across Europe, published (anonymously) his first book (translated as *Hold your Tongue*), a three hundred page tract against slander (*lashon hara*), evil speech and defamation – all of which Cézanne was suffering. After some false starts and discarded pictures, trying to paint this unpaintable *lashon hara* over a few years, I almost gave up. But then I received an affecting slander and the blow sent me reeling. I began to read the Hafetz Hayim again – about When It Is Difficult To Remain Silent, Backbiting, Belittling A Craftsman, Insults, etc. I became drawn into the kindly aura of this saint and I resolved to really try not to speak evil of anyone. At the time, I was painting a great oak tree I can see from my studio window and I thought that slander and trees are both good subjects, both very present in all our lives. For thirty years I'd kept a reproduction of a detail of a small relief by Donatello which became the main source for my composition. The picture took about two months to paint and when it was finished I read Pope-Hennessy on the Donatello relief. His vivid description of it seemed weirdly in accord with my own intention. He writes of the complex, difficult and varied patterning and of the anxiety, confusion and disorientation expressed by the figures in an emotional event taking place in an atmosphere of charged excitement... just what I wanted. The little sage of Radun has changed my life. I now have a funnier attitude and a painting as well. If only I could hold my tongue.

Oil on canvas 152.4 × 152.4 (60 × 60)
Mr and Mrs Francis Lloyd
(no.84)

The Waiter 1991

Oil on canvas
122.5 × 122.5 (48¼ × 48¼)
Private collection, London
(no.89)

My Mother Dancing 1992
Oil on canvas
92.1 × 92.1 (36¼ × 36¼)
The artist
(no.91)

Rousseau 1990

> I have resolved on an enterprise which has no precedent, and which, once complete, will have no imitator. My purpose is to display to my kind a portrait in every way true to nature, and the man I shall portray will be myself ... I am made unlike any one I have ever met; I will even venture to say that I am like no one in the whole world. I may be no better, but at least I am different.
>
> Jean-Jacques Rousseau, *The Confessions*

When Rousseau began his last book, *Reveries of the Solitary Walker*, in the stirring year 1776, he had just emerged from one of the darkest passages of his life, and so had I in early 1990 when I read the slim Penguin edition. There is something truly mad (a terminal paranoia), about this beautiful little book which uncorked some of my own demons and terrors and it will always stand for me, as people say Rousseau himself does, as a manic prelude to Romanticism. Not being at all done with Romanticism (the modernist art I love best is its true flowering in my mind), I set out to celebrate this strange man of feeling and by the way, in a specific tradition of confessional celebrants, to chase the Black Dog deeper into the shadows of one's life (I want to get my picture back so I can paint the BD retreating into the foreground enclosure). I didn't have to look farther than the cover of the paperback I was reading. Reproduced there is a painting of Rousseau meditating in a park, by one Alexandre-Hyacinthe Dunouy, in the Musée Marmottan, which I guess is overlooked when we go there for the Monets. Anyway, I painted mainly from this source and finished my first eighteenth-century post-depression costume pastoral during the hottest London days this century. Rousseau's central theme may have been the conflict between solitude and society which I believe lies at the very heart of the painter's everyday life in a profound way. He thought we die without serving either ourselves or other people and that our natural state is solitude. Self-love and its vanity seem to me so much what painting is about that one must consider Rousseau's theory that a social deformation may have replaced our more natural selves when we press our absurd pictures on society.

Oil on canvas 152.4 × 152.7 (60 × 60⅛)
Private collection, Switzerland
(no.83)

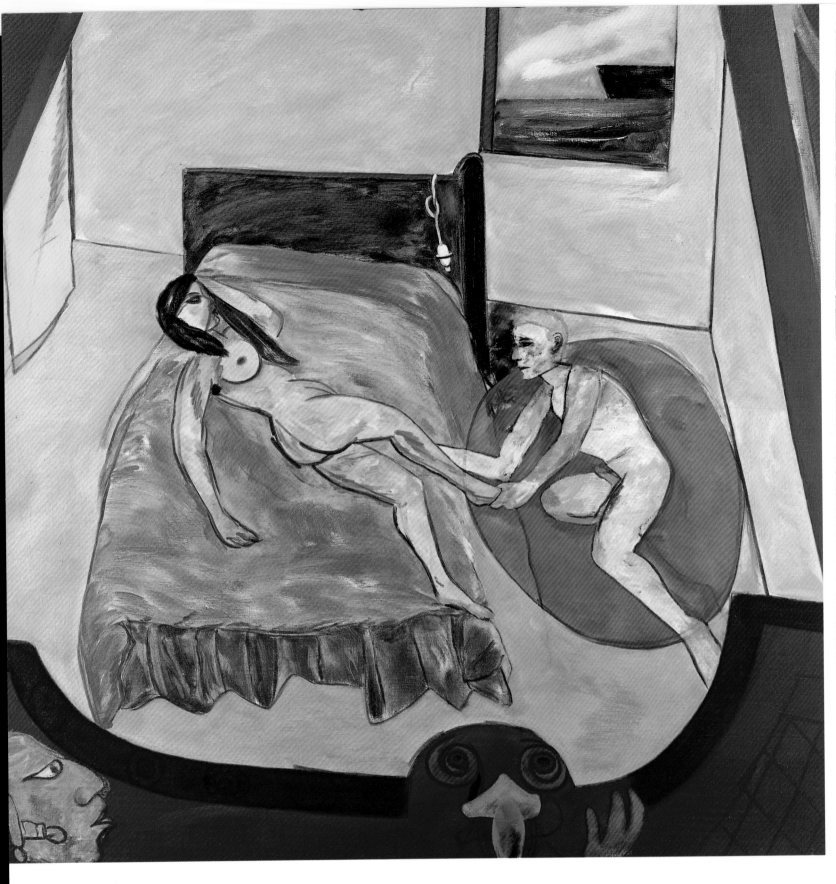

The Second Time (Vera Cruz, 1949)
A Tale of the Maritime Boulevards 1990

Oil on canvas 153 × 153 (60¼ × 60¼)
Private collection, USA
(no.82)

The Education of Henry Adams 1991–3
Oil on canvas 122.5 × 122.5 (48¼ × 48¼)
Marlborough Fine Art (London) Ltd
(no.106)

The Sculptor 1992

This is a painting of a sculptor I know who is dying. When his wife died a few
years ago, he fell into utter depression. Angry, he refused to contemplate that
their life together had ended just like that, because their marriage had been so
very good as marriages go – yes, happy even, in spite of what is considered his
finest sculpture: 'Who Can Be Happy and Free?'. He borrowed that title from
me, from a painting I'm still working on. His grief was so profound that I was
shocked into delight when he began to work on a larger than life sculpture of
his wife in order to recall, if not to relive, their marriage. It took me a while to
see what he was up to... he wanted to keep the sculpture in a state of unfinish
till the end of his own days. It is, perhaps, an original concept, to treat one's
art as something which not only replaces the inertia of despair, which may be
common enough, but to press art into a fiction which sustains an undying
love. And then it was discovered he had a cancer, whereupon a transformation came upon him... he would continue to spend his days caressing his wife
into art as it were, but now he wanted to live long enough to finish his act, to
climax one last time. He submitted to chemotherapy and other measures –
that's why his hair is sparse and his skin looks flushed in my painting.

The Sculptor is in a hurry now. His wife, impatient with her replica and
eager for him to join her whether the damn thing is finished or not, appears at
the enormous doorway to his studio, calling to him (so he tells me and as I've
shown), just like she used to call him to put his tools down, wash up and get
ready for the evening movie they would watch on television. Should he come
to her in death as she insists? She is a spectre after all... or will he linger with
her unfinished daemon, cleaving to what she was, or something like it in my
painting?

Oil on canvas 122.9 × 122.9 (48⅜ × 48⅜)
Marlborough Fine Art (London) Ltd
(no.93)

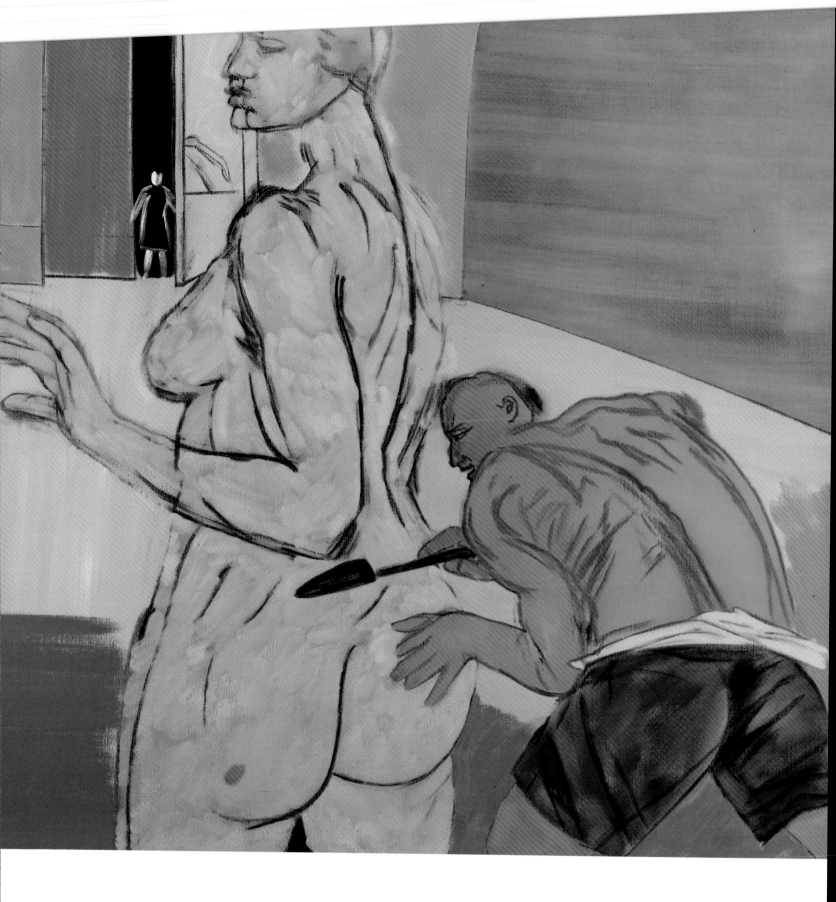

Women and Men 1991–3

This painting was inspired by my second favourite painting in London, 'The Young Spartans' by Degas, which I had in my *Artist's Eye* exhibition at the National Gallery. I can't think of a sexier painting in my own experience of art and I can't think of another oil painting done before it which is so supremely drawing that it manages to suggest an exciting art form not tried out until then. Surely Matisse was encouraged by any number of Degas oil paintings in which drawing (as drawing) becomes at least as decisive as the thin painterly painting. For me, Matisse would bring this new kind of painting-drawing to an apotheosis of sorts in a picture like his 'Violinist at the Window' of 1918, a painting I adore, which I try to visit every time I go to Paris.

I guess these are the two main themes in 'Women and Men', sexual drama and the idea of painting-drawing, both themes provoking each other, not unlike the provocation between the Spartan girls and boys. I prefer that each person makes up her/his own fantasy-story as to what's going on in my picture, if anyone's interested enough. But I will just say that as I enter my nightmare of sexual decline, I've noticed that I get a little less depressed as I take up sexual questions in my art with a new passion. I'm fascinated by all the furious sexual debates swirling around like crazy at the end of my century and I think that the hubbub maybe ought to take into account something I've noticed about our late modern art. It occurs to me that men and woman are rarely seen together in paintings anymore, at least they are not depicted together in heterosexual relationship in the work of the dozen or so very well-known painters I most admire. One must go back to late Picasso and early Balthus for this all too human stuff. Has our art been too exhausted by sophistication? Women and men will never be stale news in art. Women and men, as a subject in painting, can help bring beauty and good cheer and erotic pleasure back from wherever those things have gone. Amen and Women.

Oil on canvas 153.3 × 153.3 (60⅜ × 60⅜)
Marlborough Fine Art (London) Ltd
(no.108)

The Flag 1991–3
Oil on canvas
122.5 × 122.5 (48¼ × 48¼)
Marlborough Fine Art (London) Ltd
(no.107)

Lucian Freud 1990–1
Charcoal and pastel on paper
77.5 × 57.2 (30½ × 22½)
The Metropolitan Museum of Art, New York.
Gift of the artist, 1992
(no.85)

[182]

The Immoralist 1991

Oil on canvas
122.3 × 122.3 (48⅛ × 48⅛)
Dr and Mrs Jerry Sherman
(no.88)

The Oak Tree 1991
Oil on canvas
152.7 × 152.4 (60⅛ × 60)
Mr and Mrs Francis Lloyd
(no.86)

Tempesta (River Thames) 1992–3

I only saw Giorgione's 'Tempesta' once, on one of my rare visits to Venice, and ever since it's been one of my favourite paintings. It's just so beautiful, and nobody knows what it means although many people have tried to interpret it, including my old professor, Edgar Wind, who suggests it's a pastoral allegory, as against Kenneth Clark who calls it a free fantasy without intended theme. Vasari pretended to be stumped. I got a canvas the same size and painted my own Tempesta and here's a very short story to illustrate it, sort of...

The young man with a permanently bemused look (unless I change it) just got out of the army, while the getting was good, after deciding he wasn't cut out to be a soldier. To the young woman sitting in the foreground of the land-scape, crying, he says: 'Why are you unhappy and why are you naked, or nude?' 'Well, I'm not a Gypsy, as scholars have rumoured. In this painting, I'm the Girl Next Door', she replies through her fingers, upon which she's sob-bing. 'What's a nice girl like you...' 'I'm pregnant I think', she interrupts, 'and not that nice'. 'Who did this with you or to you?', asks the ex-soldier. 'That Bather* you can see cavorting gleefully in the middle distance if only you could turn your head', she says. 'Look,' says the steadfast ex-soldier, 'I've fall-en in love with you at first sight. I'd like to settle down with a wife after stand-ing around in this pastoral allegory long enough. I've saved a little money from the army, enough for a downpayment on one of those cottages in Bat-tersea across the Thames over there, where all the antiquarian bookshops, bordellos, cafés, and museums face out bravely upon the mighty river over which a storm is rising, said by the ancients to represent fortune, so if you're really pregnant, I'd like you to stop crying, get an abortion and marry me. I don't want another man's child. What do you say?' 'OK', she says almost inaudibly, even though she hardly knows him in spite of being in the same picture, and what will her mother say?

* X-rays have shown a third figure under Giorgione's Tempesta, identified as a bather, which Wind compares to the man discovered under Gainsborough's Blue Boy. I had no idea that another figure existed under the Tempesta when I painted in my little bather, which just goes to show you something but I don't know what.

Oil on canvas 78.1 × 72.3 (30¾ × 28½)
Richard Wookey, Toronto, Canada
(no.109)

**My Cities (An Experimental
Drama)** 1990–3
Oil on canvas
183.2 × 183.2 (72⅛ × 72⅛)
Marlborough Fine Art (London) Ltd
(no.104)

The Novelist (My Neighbor, Anita Brookner) 1993

Oil on canvas
101.6 × 50.8 (40 × 20)
Sandra Fisher
(no.113)

In the Sea 1993

Oil on canvas
183 × 183 (72 × 72)
Marlborough Fine Art (London) Ltd
(no.112)

The Flat 1993
Oil on canvas
122.2 × 122.2 (48⅛ × 48⅛)
Private collection
(no.111)

The End of Communism 1992

When Communism ended, I began to paint again. The self-portrait you can
see here (before my diet) is the only painting I've finished and the only one I
ever intend to show anyone. It had been very many years since I last practiced
painting, which I had abandoned because I wanted to do something more
unusual with my life, something more difficult to approach and unlike anyone
else's life, and I thought, well, millions of people paint pictures and they all try
to show off their pictures so I would turn elsewhere, I would concentrate each
moment on escape from the ways of the world. The story of that superficial
escape, which, like most things, had its ups and downs, is, well, another story
– in fact, the theme of another, much more elaborate painting I began four
years ago and expect to work on until I die, because its subject – that other life
I led for so long – still attracts my interest and I think it may be an unusual
subject for painting.

I never met my grandfather, who was a painter of disturbing originality, so
they say, one of those reckless ones who couldn't keep his mouth shut and dis-
appeared during the Communist years, into the wastes of the living dead.
Upon the end of Communism, my grandmother returned to their old house,
which had been kept in her absence by her brother. She stayed a few weeks
and brought some of my grandfather's things back to London, where she and
I had been living together. All his paintings had been confiscated, but she gave
me my grandfather's portable easel, his brushes and colours and she urged me
to paint again now that I had nothing better to do anymore, since I had tired
of my chosen privations and adventures and I wasn't getting any younger, as
you can see in the painting. So that's what I'm doing in this picture, with a
happy sense of relief because it seemed so unusual to be painting the only picture I would ever show anyone, come what may. It may not sound altruistic,
but I want from now on to paint for myself alone, not for anyone else.

Oil on canvas 96.5 × 96.5 (38 × 38)
Private collection
(no.90)

Painting 1983–5

When the Old Vic asked me to do their safety curtain, they lent me a pile of books about the history of that theatre. In one of these books there is a plate of a seated man painting stage scenery. I read that his name was Wilfred Walter and that the great Lilian Baylis had hired him as an actor just after he was demobbed in 1919. It was discovered that he could paint and so, aside from acting, he was asked to resuscitate neglected scenery. He found this an enormous relief to his spirit after four years of war, so I painted my actor painting as if he was enjoying himself. Since he's an actor, I wanted to give him a new face or disguise for this new role in 'Painting'. Looking for a new face, I came across a plate in the same Meyerhold book I used twelve years before when I made the pastel called 'His Hour'. At first I thought it was another picture of Meyerhold himself, as an actor, like the film-frame source for the pastel, but the new face turned out to be another actor (looking like Meyerhold) named Sergei Martinson in a comic scene from a play called *The Warrant* (1925). This satirical fantasy by N. Erdman, said to be in the style of Gogol, was produced by Meyerhold, who regarded it as the first true Soviet comedy, and Stanislavsky was much impressed with it. I decided to use other details from the costume and posture of Meyerhold's actor, like his scarf ... but I was most taken with an acting device with traditional antecedents in Japanese and Chinese Theatre which Meyerhold sought to introduce into this play and others, called 'pre-acting'. It is a mimetic action and expression the actor begins to adopt even before he speaks, which in Meyerhold's words 'prepares the spectator's perception in such a way that he comprehends the scenic situation fully resolved in advance and so has no need to make any effort to grasp the underlying message of the scene ... When the actor–tribune lifts the mask of the character to reveal his true nature to the spectator he does not merely speak the lines furnished by the dramatist, he uncovers the roots from which he has sprung.' The actor–painter is poised in an act of dramatic preparation before his next stroke – a commonplace very familiar to painters. Meyerhold's own life of the mind in art can also be seen, I like to pretend, as pre-acting his own death at the hands of the Soviets he tried to serve – another commonplace drama.

Oil on canvas 105.4 × 105.4 (41½ × 41½)
Nan and Gene Corman
(no.70)

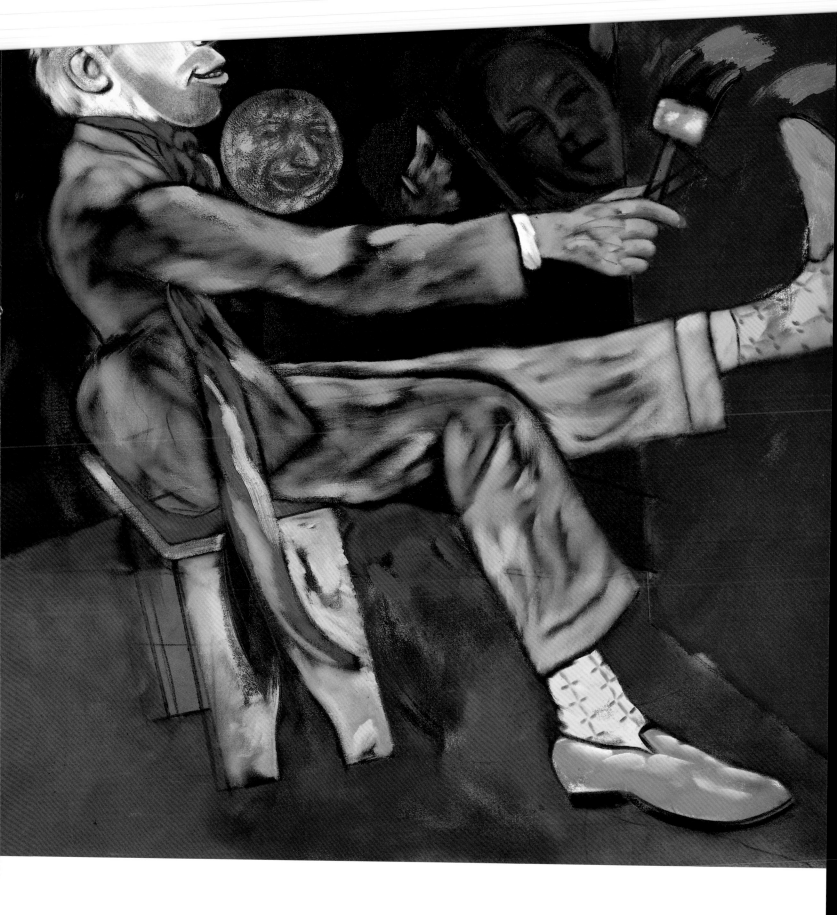

Bad Back 1990–2

Oil on canvas
61.2 × 51.1 (24⅛ × 20⅛)
Marlborough Fine Art (London) Ltd
(no.94)

Ronald

Bad Eyes 1990–2
Oil on canvas
61.2 × 51.1 (24⅛ × 20⅛)
Marlborough Fine Art (London) Ltd
(no.95)

Bad Foot 1990–2

Oil on canvas
61.2 × 51.1 (24⅛ × 20⅛)
Marlborough Fine Art (London) Ltd
(no.96)

Bad Thoughts 1990–2
Oil on canvas
61.2 × 51.1 (24⅛ × 20⅛)
Marlborough Fine Art (London) Ltd
(no.97)

Bad Sinus 1990–2

Oil on canvas
61.2 × 51.1 (24⅛ × 20⅛)
Marlborough Fine Art (London) Ltd
(no.98)

[200]

Bad Knee 1990–2
Oil on canvas
61.2 × 51.1 (24⅛ × 20⅛)
Marlborough Fine Art (London) Ltd
(no.99)

Bad Heart 1990–3

Oil on canvas
61.2 × 51.1 (24⅛ × 20⅛)
Marlborough Fine Art (London) Ltd
(no.100)

Bad Character 1990–3

Oil on canvas
61.2 × 51.1 (24⅛ × 20⅛)
Marlborough Fine Art (London) Ltd
(no.101)

Greenwich Village 1990–3

Auden, who lived in the Village, said that every poem he writes involves his whole past. How could it be otherwise when one paints a picture? Greenwich Village was where my grown-up art life began when I was seventeen and where I have tended to land during Manhattan periods ever since.

I first read Hart Crane in the Village, pressed into my hands by the Eighth Street bookseller Joe Kling, whose remembered visage appears on the old gent at the lower right with handkerchief sticking out of his pocket. Joe, who deserves a book or picture to himself, was the first to publish the teenage Harold Crane, fresh from Chagrin Falls, Ohio, which I used to give as my birthplace when I was young because I thought it sounded more poetic than Cleveland. At Joe's last shop in Greenwich Avenue, I used to turn the pages, washing my hands first, of the Black Sun edition of Crane's masterwork *The Bridge*, which I could not afford to buy until many years later when I became a rich artist. It was in the spirit of that other wide-eyed symbolist ode to New York by another Ohio boy that I conceived this picture. At the top is a cursory sign of the arch where Fifth Avenue begins, and that's me sleeping on a park bench (which I did a few nights between ships) and also me later in uniform, on weekend pass from Fort Dix, hanging upon the dry fountain at Washington Square, trying without luck to meet girls. At other Village moments in time during the picture, I would be luckier as you can see... earlier, as an art student, I would draw girlfriends there (lower left) and later in life I would love there and suffer love there.

At first, the whole central composition was based on the two receding ark walls of Uccello's great 'Flood', but after almost a year I decided on less fearful symmetry and only the left-hand indigo wall remains, to which Village memories cling, still, mood indigo.

Oil on canvas 182.6 × 183.2 (71⅞ × 72⅛)
Private collection
(no.105)

Western Bathers 1993–4

This is my first real Western. After sixty years of fumbling, I've become a fast gun, a regular shootist, and I did the damn thing within a one month shooting schedule. Western movies are among the happiest things in my life. In fact I owe quite a few narrow escapes from boredom and desperation to their familiar intimacies, graces and subtexts, so I thought I'd better direct a Western picture or two before I ride into the sunset. My favourite painting in London is Cézanne's very late, absurd 'Bathers' in the National Gallery. Sitting in front of it one day, the crazy figures looked like they were grouped around a campfire and so I got the idea for my first Western. I got a canvas the same size, in order to do my picture in the highest Western tradition and also the more specific genre which Matisse brought to a climax in his tremendous Chicago 'Bathers by a River' and which Picasso pursued into the 1970s. I thought I'd try to get it up again, which is hard to do when you get to be sixty. Cézanne's Bathers are works of imagination, the opposite (in a sense) of his mode of observation, but I had to start somewhere, so I began to look at filmframes of Budd Boetticher's *Ride Lonesome* (1959) starring Randolph Scott and the heavenly Karen Steele. That got me going and then I adopted the techniques I love in Ford and Peckinpah of using a dependable stock-company to act the character roles. My own regulars are drawn mostly from figures and images in past art which tend to stay with me always – not unlike a habitual method of Cézanne and many painters from Michelangelo to Picasso. You want loyal friends around your campfire as a man grows older.

Oil on canvas 127.3 × 195.9 (50⅛ × 77⅛)
Marlborough Fine Art (London) Ltd
(no.114)

London Landscape 1993

Oil on canvas 153 × 152.7 (60¼ × 60⅛)
Marlborough Fine Art (London) Ltd
(no.110)

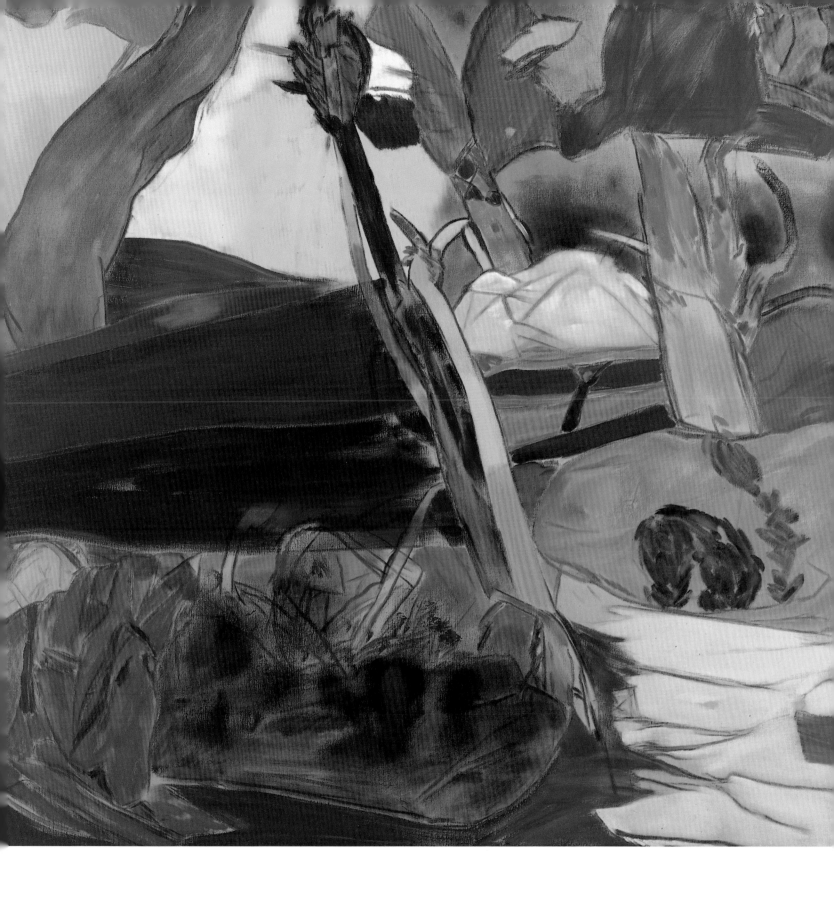

The Wedding 1989–93
Oil on canvas 183 × 183 (72 × 72)
Tate Gallery. Presented by the artist 1993
(no.102)

The Wedding 1989–93
(detail)

**Father Reading Tom Sawyer
to his Son** 1994
Oil on canvas
122 × 152.4 (48 × 60)
Marlborough Fine Art (London) Ltd
(no.115)

The Painter (Cross and Chimney)
1984–5 (detail)
Charcoal and pastel on paper
78.1 × 111.1 (30¾ × 43¾)
Marlborough Fine Art (London) Ltd
(no.72)

Kitaj, 1984
Photo: Lee Friedlander

Catalogue

Dimensions are given in centimetres, converted from inches given in brackets; height before width. Cross-references refer to Prefaces which appear in the plates section.

1   **Erasmus Variations** 1958
Oil on canvas
104.2 × 84.2 (41 × 33⅛)
Private collection
See p.68; illustrated on p.69

2   **Tarot Variations** 1958
Oil on canvas
109.2 × 86 (43 × 33⅞)
High Museum of Art, Atlanta, Georgia. Purchase with J.J. Haverty Memorial Fund, 68.7
See p.70; illustrated on p.71

3   **Miss Ivy Cavendish (Oxford)** 1958
Pencil on paper
53.3 × 41.6 (21 × 16⅜)
The artist
Detail illustrated on p.66

4   **Ashmolean Drawing (Oxford) IV**
1958
Pencil on paper
53.3 × 41.6 (21 × 16⅜)
The artist
Detail illustrated on p.72

5   **Oxford Woman** c.1958
Charcoal pencil on paper
35.5 × 30.5 (14 × 12)
The artist
Detail illustrated on p.67

6   **The Murder of Rosa Luxemburg** 1960
Oil and collage on canvas
153 × 152.4 (60¼ × 60)
Tate Gallery. Purchased 1980
See p.82; illustrated on p.83

7   **Specimen Musings of a Democrat**
1961
Oil and collage on canvas
102 × 127.5 (40¼ × 50¼)
Colin St John Wilson
Illustrated on p.80

One of the joys of the *Warburg Journal* in my youth was stumbling into vast and inaccessible countries of art and ideas about art as an explorer might do. Such was the impact, for instance, of the papers of Frances Yates on the Art of Ramon Lull, the great thirteenth-century Catalan mystic. As a student of Surrealism and Dada, I was drawn both to the outlandish imagery of such Warburg nonsense-visions as Lull's diagrammatic 'Art' and to his absurdist claims to demonstrate infallible truth in all spheres through his art. This collage painting was suggested by the type of crazy chart by Lull which had been treated with contempt by previous scholars as useless speculation, not unlike the way Cabbalism was treated until our own time. Lullism and Cabbalism (which may have influenced each other) were both born around the same time in the Catalan province of Girona, where I spent some of my sunniest hours among Catalan anarchist friends who fed me, the Democrat, some of the useless Surreal musings and correspondences which found their way into this student work long ago.

8   **Nietzsche's Moustache** 1962
Oil on canvas 122 × 122 (48 × 48)
Private collection, London
Illustrated on p.73

In their reaction against Hitler's authoritarianism, German universities since the war are given to punctilious observation of democratic procedures; and during the past years the faculty of one great university after another had to reject by solemn vote an offer for the sale of – Nietzsche's moustache, allegedly severed from the corpse before burial.
from 'Nietzsche and the Seven Sirens'
by Walter Kaufmann. Partisan Review,
May – June 1952

9   **Kennst du das Land?** 1962
Oil and collage on canvas
122 × 122 (48 × 48)
The artist
See p.78; illustrated on p.79

10 **Reflections on Violence** 1962
Oil and collage on canvas
152.4 × 152.4 (60 × 60)
Hamburger Kunsthalle, Hamburg
See p.74; illustrated on p.75

11 **Apotheosis of Groundlessness** 1964
Oil on canvas
153 × 213.4 (60¼ × 84)
Cincinnati Art Museum. The Edwin and Virginia Irwin Memorial
See p.76; illustrated on p.77

12 **The Ohio Gang** 1964
Oil and graphite on canvas
183.1 × 183.5 (72⅛ × 72¼)
The Museum of Modern Art, New York. Philip Johnson Fund, 1965
See p.84; illustrated on p.85

13 **Where the Railroad Leaves the Sea** 1964
Oil on canvas
122 × 152.4 (48 × 60)
The artist
See p.102; illustrated on p.103

14 **Dismantling the Red Tent** 1964
Oil on canvas, including an original etching by Alphonse Legros
122 × 122 (48 × 48)
Michael and Dorothy Blankfort Collection
[Exhibited Los Angeles only]
Illustrated on p.101

Mean something! You and I, mean
something! Ah,
that's a good one!
Samuel Beckett

Kennedy had just been killed and I meant 'The Red Tent' to paraphrase the surprising longevity of an American democracy which works pretty well and which belongs to a quite rare species: government by consent. The Red Tent was a beacon used by polar explorers in the wastes. Men could return to it in some hope and I designed a nice Red Tent to come home to. Coming in to warm from the cold I take to be one of the meanings of art, and the political men in my picture (some hollow, some not) hover about the Red Tent for warmth after a regicide, a perpetual play of governance by consent in what Hannah Arendt called 'the public space'. Thirty years later, I wish this little mystery-picture had been more profoundly painted, because I like its terms even more deeply now than I understood then.

15 **Walter Lippmann** 1966
Oil on canvas 183 × 213.4 (72 × 84)
Albright-Knox Art Gallery, Buffalo, New York. Gift of Seymour H. Knox, 1967
See p.88; illustrated on p.89

16 **Erie Shore** 1966
Oil on canvas 2 panels:
each 183 × 152.4 (72 × 60)
Staatliche Museen zu Berlin, Nationalgalerie
Illustrated on p.86–7

17 **Juan de la Cruz** 1967
Oil on canvas 183 × 152.4 (72 × 60)
Astrup Fearnley Museum of Modern Art, Oslo
See p.90; illustrated on p.91

18 **Unity Mitford** 1968
Oil on canvas 25.4 × 20.3 (10 × 8)
The artist
Illustrated on p.111

Hitler's English Rose, done from a snapshot. Cyril Connolly told me my tiny picture didn't look much like her.

19 **The Autumn of Central Paris (after Walter Benjamin)** 1972–3
Oil on canvas
152.4 × 152.4 (60 × 60)
Mr and Mrs Francis Lloyd
See p.94; illustrated on p.95

20 **Pacific Coast Highway (Across the Pacific)** 1973
Oil on canvas 2 panels:
152.4 × 243.8; 152.4 × 152.4
(60 × 96; 60 × 60)
Colin St John Wilson
Illustrated on p.136–7

21 **Kenneth Anger and Michael Powell** 1973
Oil on canvas
243.8 × 152.4 (96 × 60)
Ludwig Museum Koblenz Deutschherren-haus
[Not exhibited]
Illustrated on p.137

22 **The Man of the Woods and the Cat of the Mountains** 1973
Oil on canvas
152.4 × 152.4 (60 × 60)
Tate Gallery. Presented by the Friends of the Tate Gallery 1974
Illustrated on p.134

This composition is based on an engraving in the British Museum attributed to one Thomas Lane and dated 1821, satirising the final stages of a boring Royal Marriage you can look up yourself if you've nothing better to do. The subject was unknown to me until someone wrote me about it. All I had was a small reproduction from which I cooked up my composition. Since I knew nothing about the theme of the original engraving, I like to think some people may be interested in my picture without knowing anything about it. I thought that the man should be telling the cat that there is a better life out in the world beyond the room; I remember wanting to make a magical composition. The Tate catalogue compiler detected a South American air, which must have been correct, because while I was painting the picture (first six months of 1973) I was deeply reading Waterton and Burton and mainly Humboldt's travel in the Orinoco... I must have been touched some by the wonderful plates you find in those books.

23 **To Live in Peace (The Singers)** 1973–4
Oil on canvas
77.5 × 214.5 (30½ × 84½)
Marlborough International Fine Art
Illustrated on p.110

Watching the Catalans, this family of friends, emerge from under fascism to live in peace during the years I had a house there, played strange tricks on me because I would eat at the table you see in the painting year after year and envy their, what shall I call it? – their elective affinity for what they deemed to be their own... and I took heart and I raised myself up, said a grateful goodbye to Catalonia and went in search of my own elective affinities.

24 **Sculpture** 1974
Pastel on paper 76.2 × 50.8 (30 × 20)
Achim Moeller Fine Art, New York
Illustrated on p.96

25 **Study for the World's Body** 1974
Pastel on paper 76.2 × 50.8 (30 × 20)
Private collection
[Not exhibited]
Illustrated on p.104

26 **His Hour** 1975
Pastel and charcoal on paper
77.5 × 57.2 (30½ × 22½)
Nan and Gene Corman
Illustrated on p.123

27 **Waiting** 1975
Pastel on paper
78.5 × 56.5 (30⅞ × 22¼)
Private collection
Illustrated on p.114

28 **From London (James Joll and John Golding)** 1975–6
Oil on canvas
152.4 × 243.8 (60 × 96)
Private collection
Illustrated on p.142

29 **If Not, Not** 1975–6
Oil on canvas
152.4 × 152.4 (60 × 60)
Scottish National Gallery of Modern Art, Edinburgh
See p.120; illustrated on p.121

30 **The Arabist** 1975–6
Oil on canvas 243.8 × 76.2 (96 × 30)
Museum Boymans-van Beuningen, Rotterdam
Illustrated on p.113

31 **The Jew Etc.** 1976–unfinished
Oil and charcoal on canvas
152.4 × 122 (60 × 48)
The artist
See p.132; illustrated on p.133

32 **Land of Lakes** 1975–7
Oil on canvas
152.4 × 152.4 (60 × 60)
Private collection
[Exhibited London only]
Illustrated on p.105

An optimistic scenic view inspired by a detail of Lorenzetti's 'Effects of Good Government' fresco at Siena, said to be the first landscape of its kind to have survived, and only incidentally alluding to reds and whites supposed to be burying the hatchet in Italy (see red flag and cross), which was in the news when my picture was made.

33 **The Orientalist** 1976–7
Oil on canvas
243.8 × 76.8 (96 × 30¼)
Tate Gallery. Purchased 1977
Illustrated on p.112

I did not come to England as a refugee, nor did I emigrate here as so many did to America, but I stayed on, and it became a habit. Some people live out their lives in places they don't come from, assigning themselves to a strange race and an alien sense of land and city. Who is to say why they do what they do with their lives, or for that matter, why painters do what they do with their painting lives? This picture belongs to such questions. Getting dressed up in another culture is no more a mug's game, I guess, than dressing our pictures in the borrowings, trickery and deceit we all affect, which Degas likened to the perpetration of a crime. Speaking of tricksters, my Orientalist relates to Trevor-Roper's amazing book about Edmund Backhouse, *The Hermit of Peking*. The setting was inspired by Whistler's Peacock Room in Freer's Detroit house. The real subject here is un-at-homeness.

34 **Smyrna Greek (Nikos)** 1976–7
Oil on canvas 243.8 × 76.2 (96 × 30)
Fundación Colección Thyssen-Bornemisza, Madrid
Detail illustrated on p.135

This portrait of my friend Nikos Stangos was inspired by his fellow Greek poet Cavafy, who described his daily walk past the brothels in the port of Alexandria. I had just returned to London from my only trip to Greece, which lasted very few days and while he posed for me in that walking position, I told Nikos about my bizarre and unconsummated wander down the port of Piraeus, as if in imitation of C.P. Cavafy. So the painting is about the two poets and me.

35 **My Cat and Her Husband** 1977
Pastel and charcoal on paper
38.1 × 56 (15 × 22)
Dominie Kitaj
Illustrated on p.115

36 **The Hispanist (Nissa Torrents)** 1977–8
Oil on canvas 243.8 × 76.2 (96 × 30)
Astrup Fearnley Museum of Modern Art, Oslo
Illustrated on p.128

37 **The Dancer (Margaret)** 1978
Pencil on paper
100 × 64.8 (39⅜ × 25½)
Mrs Edwin Bergman
Illustrated on p.130

34

38 **Dominie (Dartmouth)** 1978
Pastel and charcoal on paper
56 × 38.1 (22 × 15)
The artist
Illustrated on p.92

39 **Lem (Sant Feliu)** 1978
Pastel and charcoal on paper
76.8 × 56 (30¼ × 22)
The artist
Illustrated on p.93

40 **Bather (Tousled Hair)** 1978
Pastel on paper
121.3 × 56.8 (47¾ × 22⅜)
Private collection
Illustrated on p.98

41 **Bather (Wading)** 1978
Pastel on paper
123.8 × 56.8 (48¾ × 22⅜)
Private collection
Illustrated on p.97

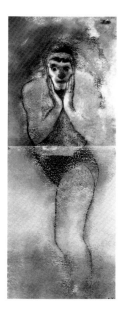

42 Bather (Torsion) 1978
Pastel on paper
137.8 × 56.8 (54¼ × 22⅜)
Diane L. Ackerman
Detail illustrated on p.99

43 The Green Blanket 1978
Pastel and charcoal on paper
76.8 × 56 (30¼ × 22)
Private collection
[Not exhibited]
Illustrated on p.146

When I was sick in bed once in my house in Catalonia, this pastel was inspired by Goya's self-portrait, being attended by Dr Arrieta, for whom I substituted Sandra.

44 His New Freedom 1978
Pastel and charcoal on paper
76.8 × 56 (30¼ × 22)
The artist
Illustrated on p.116

45 A Visit to London (Robert Creeley and Robert Duncan) 1977–9
Oil and charcoal on canvas
183 × 61 (72 × 24)
Fundación Colección Thyssen-Bornemisza, Madrid
[Not exhibited]
Detail illustrated on p.109

46 The Philosopher-Queen 1978–9
Pastel and charcoal on paper
76.8 × 56 (30¼ × 22)
The artist
Illustrated on p.147

The year we lived in Greenwich Village, Sandra had to be very philosophical and queenly about some personal stuff and so I represented her twice in this pastel done in the almost empty flat in Ninth Street.

47 Sighs from Hell 1979
Pastel and charcoal on paper
97.8 × 100.3 (38½ × 39½)
Mrs Edwin Bergman
[Exhibited London only]
Illustrated on p.163

48 Sides 1979
Pastel and charcoal on paper 3 panels
each: 77.5 × 28.2 (30½ × 11⅛)
Trustees of the British Museum, London
Illustrated on p.161

49 Actor (Richard) 1979
Pastel and charcoal on paper
76.8 × 49.2 (30¼ × 19⅜)
Scottish National Gallery of Modern Art, Edinburgh
[Exhibited London only]
Illustrated on p.117

45

50 Quentin 1979
Pastel and charcoal on paper
65.4 × 40 (25¾ × 15¾)
The artist
Illustrated on p.131

Quentin Crisp, who posed in the London art schools in my youth, lived in a room near my house for forty years. One day I bumped into him in my street and he told me he was going to New York forever, because 'Everyone there has a big window overlooking the park'. So I asked him to pose for a pastel before he left for good.

51 The Rise of Fascism 1979–80
Pastel, charcoal and oil on paper
85.1 × 158.4 (33½ × 62⅜)
Tate Gallery. Purchased 1980
Illustrated on p.108

The bather on the left is the beautiful victim, the figure of Fascism is in the middle and the seated bather is everyone else. The black cat is bad luck and the bomber coming over the water is hope.

52 Degas 1980
Pastel and charcoal on paper
73 × 50.8 (28¾ × 20)
The artist
Illustrated on p.118

53 Marynka Smoking 1980
Pastel and charcoal on paper
90.8 × 56.5 (35¾ × 22¼)
The artist
Illustrated on p.119

54 Mary-Ann 1980
Pastel and charcoal on paper
77.5 × 56 (30½ × 22)
Private collection
Illustrated on p.122

55 The Listener (Joe Singer in Hiding) 1980
Pastel and charcoal on paper
103.2 × 108.2 (40⅝ × 42⅝)
Whereabouts unknown
[Not exhibited]
Illustrated on p.125

56 Bather (Psychotic Boy) 1980
Pastel and charcoal on paper
134 × 57.2 (52¾ × 22½)
Astrup Fearnley Museum of Modern Art, Oslo
Illustrated on p.100

57 **The Jewish School (Drawing a Golem)**
1980
Oil on canvas
152.4 × 152.4 (60 × 60)
Private collection
See p.138; illustrated on p.139

58 **The Garden** 1981
Oil on canvas 122 × 122 (48 × 48)
The Cleveland Museum of Art
Illustrated on p.143

59 **Rock Garden (The Nation)** 1981
Oil on canvas 122 × 122 (48 × 48)
Private collection
Illustrated on p.153

I was inspired by the large heads which revolutionaries had knocked off sculpture on Notre Dame that I used to see at the Cluny Museum in Paris and I wanted to do some sculpture to populate a nation in my London garden with made-up characters, so I painted this picture to remind me, but I haven't gotten around to sculpture yet.

60 **Marynka Pregnant II** 1981
Pastel and charcoal on paper
56.5 × 77.2 (22¼ × 30⅜)
The artist
Illustrated on p.124

61 **The Room (Rue St Denis)** 1982–3
Oil on canvas 122 × 91.4 (48 × 36)
Mrs David G. Kangesser
Illustrated on p.140

The year I lived in Paris, I painted this room which is in the mile-long street I have haunted since I was eighteen, a street Picasso also loved but I don't know if he ever painted it or its small rooms.

62 **Grandmother Kitaj, aged 102** 1983
Charcoal on paper
19.7 × 14.6 (7¾ × 5¾)
The artist
Illustrated on p.81

63 **Desk Murder (formerly The Third Department (A Teste Study))**
1970–84
Oil on canvas 76.2 × 122 (30 × 48)
The artist
See p.106; illustrated on p.107

64 **The Sensualist** 1973–84
Oil on canvas
246.4 × 77.2 (97 × 30⅜)
The Foundation FOR ART and The National Museum of Contemporary Art, Oslo
See p.126; illustrated on p.127

65 **Cecil Court, London WC2 (The Refugees)** 1983–4
Oil on canvas 183 × 183 (72 × 72)
Tate Gallery. Purchased 1985
See p.158; illustrated on p.159

66 **John Ford on his Deathbed** 1983–4
Oil on canvas
152.4 × 152.4 (60 × 60)
The Metropolitan Museum of Art, New York. Purchase, Lila Acheson Wallace Gift, 1986
See p.148; illustrated on p.149

67 **Baseball** 1983–4
Oil on canvas
152.4 × 152.4 (60 × 60)
Private collection
[Exhibited London and New York only]
See p.150; illustrated on p.151

68 **Ellen's Back** 1984
Pastel and charcoal on paper
78.1 × 56.8 (30¾ × 22⅜)
Whitney Museum of American Art, New York. Gift of Edward L. Gardner in honour of Flora Biddle and the 60th Anniversary of the Whitney Museum of American Art
Illustrated on p.165

69 **Self-portrait as a Woman** 1984
Oil on canvas
246.4 × 77.2 (97 × 30⅜)
Astrup Fearnley Museum of Modern Art, Oslo
See p.144; illustrated on p.145

70 **Painting** 1983–5
Oil on canvas
105.4 × 105.4 (41½ × 41½)
Nan and Gene Corman
[Exhibited Los Angeles only]
See p.194; illustrated on p.195

71 **The Jewish Rider** 1984–5
Oil on canvas
152.4 × 152.4 (60 × 60)
Astrup Fearnley Museum of Modern Art, Oslo
Illustrated on p.157

My friend Michael Podro posed for this Diasporist painting, which is loosely based on Rembrandt's 'Polish Rider', ghosts of which lie beneath my picture.

72 **The Painter (Cross and Chimney)**
1984–5
Charcoal and pastel on paper
78.1 × 111.1 (30¾ × 43¾)
Marlborough Fine Art (London) Ltd
Detail illustrated on p.212

73 **Germania (The Tunnel)** 1985
Oil on canvas
183.2 × 214 (72⅛ × 84¼)
Private collection
Illustrated on p.154

This may be my most difficult painting. The most difficult thing about it for me is that I have forsworn depictions of events during the Shoah, for all the usual reasons. That makes the right-hand side of my picture unusual. I think I was overwhelmed by having a young wife and new baby and so I dared an iconic depiction of a young mother and child entering the tunnel leading to the gas. Also, I think it was Tolstoy who said don't be afraid to make a fool of yourself. It is a mere monochrome sketch: a shadow of a ghost. The central tunnel is, of course, taken from the van Gogh madhouse gouache. Two insane passageways connected across the foreground corridor where the halt and ageing painter, maimed by books and constricted by art, tries to keep up with his new son, divine *sefirot* or intelligences flashing between them. The painter also 'belongs' to the historical madhouse. Philip Roth had just given me a terrifying Penguin book he'd edited, called *This Way for the Gas, Ladies and Gentlemen* by

Tadeusz Borowski.* It was van Gogh's transcription of Doré's prison courtyard that influenced me to transcribe van Gogh here.

* The 'way' to the gas has been given several names. I believe I saw 'Tunnel' recorded somewhere. But subsequently, in Lanzmann's great film, *Shoah*, he presses an SS officer from Treblinka: 'Can you describe this "funnel" precisely? What was it like? How wide? How was it for the people in this "funnel"?'

74   Philip Roth 1985
Charcoal on paper
77.8 × 57.2 (30⅝ × 22½)
The artist
Illustrated on p.152

75   Germania (The Engine Room) 1983–6
Oil on canvas 122 × 122 (48 × 48)
Private collection
Illustrated on p.155

76   Drancy 1984–6
Pastel and charcoal on paper
100.3 × 78.1 (39½ × 30¾)
Fondation du Judaisme Français, Paris
Illustrated on p.160

When I lived for a year in Paris, my friend Anne Atik, the American poet, and I took a suburban train to Drancy to see the place where the Jews of Paris were collected by their hosts for their trip to oblivion. This unmemorable little sheet was drawn back in gay Paris, from memory and curdled imagination after reading about the scared and sick children, some of whom were lucky (like Max Jacob) and never got to leave Drancy alive for the east. I keep promising myself to leave this lachrymose perspectivism behind (in art anyway) because life is so short, but as someone said, our moral seriousness is measured by our attention span, and that reminds me of trying to do serious art.

77   Sir Ernst Gombrich 1986
Pastel and charcoal on paper
67.3 × 56.8 (26½ × 22⅜)
National Portrait Gallery, London
[Not exhibited]
Illustrated on p.164

78   The Neo-Cubist 1976–87
Oil on canvas
177.8 × 132.1 (70 × 52)
Private collection
Illustrated on p.156

A rather literal painting I had abandoned, of a naked Hockney, lay in storage for more than a decade until David's new obsession with what one might call his modern after-thoughts about Cubist spatial theory began in earnest and we would talk about that and exchange letters about his obsessions and my own obsessions. So I took the canvas up again to rework it in a later mood of simultaneity, within the kind of grey ellipse of classic Cubism. I've always felt like a Symbolist myself, and when Hockney told me in some detail about the death in a sublime old-age of his friend Isherwood (whom I used to see over many years only with David), I painted in the symbolical Christopher, head drooped in death across to the left, as a simultaneous *memento mori*. The flowers of evil are symbols of the AIDS deaths which had also begun to enter David's conversation and earthly paradise.

79   The Sniper 1987
Oil on canvas 305 × 91.4 (120 × 36)
Saatchi Collection, London
Illustrated on p.141

There are snipers about, firing from apartments at strangers they don't like. This picture-parable is a reminder not to throw stones from glass houses. If the sniper is surprised to be taken so seriously, he or she may be lacking in imagination, which may be the reason to have become a sniper in the first place. When I was a boy, during the Second World War, I liked to draw battle scenes full of crisscross, zinging shots exchanged by Americans and their enemies. This composition is a stagey reversion to that. The pedestrian victim becomes a Doppelgänger, reacting to phases of his wounds. In his instant of wish-fulfillment, he, or an ally, has clambered up gaily decorated dream steps to shoot back at the sniper, hitting the sniper's head. I like to think my tall stage could be cleared away for a second act, the farce removed so that a new street scene might be enacted. Maybe a more tragic version of 'The Sniper', for which the present events are only a comic rehearsal.

80   His Last Painting 1987
Oil on canvas
99.7 × 62.9 (39¼ × 24¾)
Private collection
Illustrated on p.129

Bonnard is working on his last painting, 'L'Amandier en fleur', in 1946... My painting is after a famous photo by Cartier-Bresson, but it touched my heart, perhaps the way Bacon was touched by Vincent on his way to paint. I painted my Bonnard over a failed painting about the Canadian North Woods.

81   Heart Attack 1990
Oil on canvas
122.5 × 122.5 (48¼ × 48¼)
Private collection, Switzerland
Illustrated on p.166

After my heart attack I got very interested in heart attacks, so I painted this one which was suggested by a man shot in the eye with an arrow, depicted by Mantegna.

**82   The Second Time (Vera Cruz, 1949)
A Tale of the Maritime Boulevards**
1990
Oil on canvas
153 × 153 (60¼ × 60¼)
Private collection, USA
Illustrated on p.176

I've been possessed by a very occasional semi-secret life, not at all uncommon to judge only by erotic art and literature of many cultures, and its bittersweet addictions have fascinated me since my First Time in Havana forty-five years ago (Flaubert says 'He has not lived' who has not been drawn into and shamed by this ill-famed addiction), but when I think that a rare beauty has transpired in my secret life, not unlike any other experience of nature which one tries to commit to canvas, I feel it may belong to painting, even when I suspect that the bitter undertaste of the sensual port and its streets of shame may be unknowable to many people, and so it seems to me that if I can recall some sense of sexual drama, as in this *bildungsroman* about my lost youth, the singular tense in art may be faintly heard and one's youth may even seem regained.

83   Rousseau 1990
Oil on canvas
152.4 × 152.7 (60 × 60⅛)
Private collection, Switzerland
See p.174; illustrated on p.175

84   Against Slander 1990–1
Oil on canvas
152.4 × 152.4 (60 × 60)
Mr and Mrs Francis Lloyd
See p.170; illustrated on p.171

85   Lucian Freud 1990–1
Charcoal and pastel on paper
77.5 × 57.2 (30½ × 22½)
The Metropolitan Museum of Art, New York. Gift of the artist, 1992
Illustrated on p.183

The Oak Tree 1991
Oil on canvas
152.7 × 152.4 (60⅛ × 60)
Mr and Mrs Francis Lloyd
Illustrated on p.185

I see this huge oak tree every day from my studio window but not in Technicolor like this painting sees it.

87 **Jack My Hedgehog** 1991
Oil on canvas 122 × 122 (48 × 48)
Marlborough Fine Art (London) Ltd
[Not exhibited]
Illustrated on p.162

88 **The Immoralist** 1991
Oil on canvas
122.3 × 122.3 (48⅛ × 48⅛)
Dr and Mrs Jerry Sherman
Illustrated on p.184

89 **The Waiter** 1991
Oil on canvas
122.5 × 122.5 (48¼ × 48¼)
Private collection, London
Illustrated on p.172

90 **The End of Communism** 1992
Oil on canvas 96.5 × 96.5 (38 × 38)
Private collection
See p.192; illustrated on p.193

91 **My Mother Dancing** 1992
Oil on canvas
92.1 × 92.1 (36¼ × 36¼)
The artist
Illustrated on p.173

92 **Whistler vs. Ruskin (Novella in Terre Verte, Yellow and Red)** 1992
Oil on canvas
152.4 × 152.4 (60 × 60)
Marlborough Fine Art (London) Ltd
See p.168; illustrated on p.169

93 **The Sculptor** 1992
Oil on canvas
122.9 × 122.9 (48⅜ × 48⅜)
Marlborough Fine Art (London) Ltd
See p.178; illustrated on p.179

94 **Bad Back** 1990–2
Oil on canvas
61.2 × 51.1 (24⅛ × 20⅛)
Marlborough Fine Art (London) Ltd
Illustrated on p.196

When I started to notice all the things going wrong with my body and mind as I grow old, I realised these were endless subjects for pictures which may also keep track of my decline in case I forget something bad. I never liked the name Ronald and never used it before but I figured if Vincent could sign Vincent, I could sign Ronald. *(Work in progress.)*

95 **Bad Eyes** 1990–2
Oil on canvas
61.2 × 51.1 (24⅛ × 20⅛)
Marlborough Fine Art (London) Ltd
Illustrated on p.197

96 **Bad Foot** 1990–2
Oil on canvas
61.2 × 51.1 (24⅛ × 20⅛)
Marlborough Fine Art (London) Ltd
Illustrated on p.198

97 **Bad Thoughts** 1990–2
Oil on canvas
61.2 × 51.1 (24⅛ × 20⅛)
Marlborough Fine Art (London) Ltd
Illustrated on p.199

98 **Bad Sinus** 1990–2
Oil on canvas
61.2 × 51.1 (24⅛ × 20⅛)
Marlborough Fine Art (London) Ltd
Illustrated on p.200

99 **Bad Knee** 1990–2
Oil on canvas
61.2 × 51.1 (24⅛ × 20⅛)
Marlborough Fine Art (London) Ltd
Illustrated on p.201

100 **Bad Heart** 1990–3
Oil on canvas
61.2 × 51.1 (24⅛ × 20⅛)
Marlborough Fine Art (London) Ltd
Illustrated on p.202

101 **Bad Character** 1990–3
Oil on canvas
61.2 × 51.1 (24⅛ × 20⅛)
Marlborough Fine Art (London) Ltd
Illustrated on p.203

To be continued.

102 **The Wedding** 1989–93
Oil on canvas 183 × 183 (72 × 72)
Tate Gallery. Presented by the artist 1993
Illustrated on p.211

Sandra and I were married in the beautiful old Sephardic Synagogue founded in London by Rembrandt's friend, Menasseh ben Israel. Under the *chupa* (canopy), aside from my children and the Rabbi in top hat, Freud is on the left, Auerbach in the middle, then Sandra and me, and Hockney (best man) is to the right of us. Kossoff appears at the far right, transcribed from a drawing by John Lessore. I worked on the painting for years and never learned how to finish it even though painter friends, including most of those in the picture, gave me good advice about it which I took up and changed things all the time. In the end, instead of finishing it, I finished with it and gave it away to a deserving old friend.

103 **Redemption through Sin** 1990–3
Charcoal on canvas
152.4 × 153 (60 × 60¼)
Marlborough Fine Art (London) Ltd
Illustrated on p.167

104 **My Cities (An Experimental Drama)** 1990–3
Oil on canvas
183.2 × 183.2 (72⅛ × 72⅛)
Marlborough Fine Art (London) Ltd
Illustrated on p.188

The three main actors represent myself in youth, middle age and old age. Behind them is a drop-curtain inscribed with historiated capital letters of cities where I've lived or loved. Over the course of a few years these capital letters (inspired by William Blake and the paintings of Victor Hugo) have been sublimated by white paint for the most part because they got too emphatic, so now they're not too easy to read or even see, some of them representing faded (whitened) memories anyway. The idea for the painting comes from a page I've kept as long as I can remember, torn from a copy of the old American magazine *Theater Arts*, showing a scene from what is described as 'an experimental drama', 'A Happy Journey to Trenton and Camden' by Thornton Wilder. The catwalk stage upon which the figures tread and stumble through life becomes the roof of a baseball dugout in which I've tried half-heartedly to draw some of my demons (Don't Ask!), colourless spectres only thinly isolated from the three leading players above as in a predella.

105 **Greenwich Village** 1990–3
Oil on canvas
182.6 × 183.2 (71⅞ × 72⅛)
Private collection
See p.204; illustrated on p.205

106 **The Education of Henry Adams**
1991–3
Oil on canvas
122.5 × 122.5 (48¼ × 48¼)
Marlborough Fine Art (London) Ltd
Illustrated on p.177

My friend Leon Wieseltier sent me a recent paperback of *The Education of Henry Adams*, for which he had written a new introduction, and a flood of memories came back to me because I'd first read this autobiography when I was nineteen or twenty on a train back to my art academy in Vienna, stopping a few days in the Austrian mountains at the fairytale village of St Wolfgang to see the great wooden altarpiece by Michael Pacher... So, I guess that's why the painting turned out looking like a fairytale with wooden figures. I've illustrated the part where recalcitrant little Henry gets dragged down the country road to school by his grandfather, John Quincy Adams, the sixth President.

107 **The Flag** 1991–3
Oil on canvas
122.5 × 122.5 (48¼ × 48¼)
Marlborough Fine Art (London) Ltd
Illustrated on p.182

In a letter to his best friend Max Brod, Kafka described their strange predicament on the new frontier between the past of their fathers and free modernism, using striking terms only Kafka would invent, and these phrases of his caused me to paint this allegorical picture of a predicament which I think some people still feel today. Kafka wrote that with one's posterior legs one is still glued to the world of the father and with one's waving anterior legs one is searching for new ground. As I write these lines, I'm still trying to work out the terms of this painting for myself but when I began it a few years ago, I'd already cast the drama upon a flag which one could continue to colour and inscribe with drawing and the flagpole would be the father, planted at the dawn of something new.

108 **Women and Men** 1991–3
Oil on canvas
153.3 × 153.3 (60⅜ × 60⅜)
Marlborough Fine Art (London) Ltd
See p.180; illustrated on p.181

109 **Tempesta (River Thames)** 1992–3
Oil on canvas
78.1 × 72.3 (30¾ × 28½)
Richard Wookey, Toronto, Canada
See p.186; illustrated on p.187

110 **London Landscape** 1993
Oil on canvas
153 × 152.7 (60¼ × 60⅛)
Marlborough Fine Art (London) Ltd
Illustrated on p.209

This is my only landscape so far (I think), the only picture I ever intended as just landscape – an alien genre to me because I spend as little time in landscapes as possible and so, even this one has been corrupted by the Pathetic Fallacy, invented by Ruskin to derogate the ascription of human feelings to the inanimate in nature, a very old and evergreen tradition which he thought went against the 'true appearances of things to us'. It seems the great man didn't believe in 'extraordinary, or false appearances, when we are under the influence of emotion or contemplative fancy', all of which untrue appearance I do believe in.

111 **The Flat** 1993
Oil on canvas
122.2 × 122.2 (48⅛ × 48⅛)
Private collection
Illustrated on p.191

112 **In the Sea** 1993
Oil on canvas 183 × 183 (72 × 72)
Marlborough Fine Art (London) Ltd
Illustrated on p.190

113 **The Novelist (My Neighbor, Anita Brookner)** 1993
Oil on canvas 101.6 × 50.8 (40 × 20)
Sandra Fisher
Illustrated on p.189

114 **Western Bathers** 1993–4
Oil on canvas
127.3 × 195.9 (50⅛ × 77⅛)
Marlborough Fine Art (London) Ltd
See p.206; illustrated on p.207

115 **Father Reading Tom Sawyer to his Son** 1994
Oil on canvas
122 × 152.4 (48 × 60)
Marlborough Fine Art (London) Ltd
[Not exhibited]
Illustrated on p.213

This selective bibliography has been compiled by Krzysztof Z. Cieszkowski of the Tate Gallery Library, in consultation with the artist.

The compiler gratefully acknowledges the use made of earlier bibliographies, particularly that by Anna Brooke in the 1981 Hirshhorn catalogue, and those in Marco Livingstone's unpublished 1976 Courtauld thesis and in his 1985 Phaidon monograph on Kitaj.

The bibliography is divided into six sections:

1 Writings by R.B. Kitaj
2 Interviews
3 Books on R.B. Kitaj
4 Writings on R.B. Kitaj
5 Solo exhibition catalogues
6 Group exhibition catalogues

In each section, entries are listed in chronological order. Items marked with a dagger (†) have not been seen by the compiler, and the bibliographical data for these derives from secondary sources. Annotations are introduced where the title of an item does not in itself indicate the nature of the content.

The section of *Interviews* consists of abbreviated references to articles and other texts incorporating interviews with Kitaj: Kitaj has always given written interviews, and so the items in this section in fact contain original and considered written material by him, occasioned by questions put to him in writing.

In the section of *Writings on R.B. Kitaj*, items marked with an asterisk (*) are those which, in the opinion of the compiler, are of greatest interest, originality and substance.

The section of *Solo exhibition catalogues* is as complete as possible; it also includes catalogues of exhibitions selected and/or curated by Kitaj, whether these included works by him or not.

A more extensive version of this bibliography is located in the Tate Gallery Library.

1 Writings by R.B. Kitaj

Kokoschka [review of exhibition in Künstlerhaus, Vienna, 19 May – 13 July 1958]. *Art News and Review*, 16 Aug. 1958, vol.10, no.15, p.5.

Two paintings with notes, in *Gazette* (London), [Feb.] 1961, no.2, p.3.

[introductory notes and commentary], in *R.B. Kitaj: pictures with commentary, pictures without commentary*. London: Marlborough Fine Art, 1963 (catalogue of exhib.), pp.3–13 [in his commentary R.B.K. quotes extensively from Fritz Saxl's lecture on Aby Warburg, A.R. Orage's essay on Sorel's 'Reflections on violence', and other texts].

De los textos parafrasis, comentarios, listas, notas y otro material manuscrito o impreso asociados con los cuadros, in *Premio Internacional de Pintura, Instituto Torcuato Di Tella, 1963*. Buenos Aires: Museo de Artes Visuales del Instituto Torcuato Di Tella, 1963 (catalogue of exhib.), p.24.

On associating texts with paintings [described as 'a fragment of a projected paper']. *Cambridge Opinion*, [Jan. 1964], no.37 (issue title: *Modern art in Britain*, ed. Michael Peppiatt), pp.22–3; section repr. in Andrew Brighton, Lynda Morris (eds.), *Towards another picture: an anthology of writings by artists working in Britain 1945–1970*. Nottingham: Midland Group, 1977, p.97; German trans., 'Über die Verbindung vom Texten und Bildern (Fragment eines geplanten Vortrags...)', publ. in *R.B. Kitaj: In our time – Mappenwerke und Grafik aus den Jahren 1969–1973*. Berlin: Amerika Haus, 1973 (catalogue of exhib.), p.2.

Excerpts from an after-dinner speech delivered at London and entitled: This museum shows all kinds social disease and self abuse, young boys need it special. Second part: (Mainly about using photos; re: the prints). in *R.B. Kitaj*. Berkeley: University of California, 1967 (catalogue of exhib.), pp.[3–12]. 2nd section (i.e. 'Mainly about using photos; re: the prints') repr. in *Art and Artists*, Nov. 1969, vol.4, no.8, p.25; in catalogue of 1969 Berlin exhib., pp.[9–10]; catalogue of 1970 Hanover exhib., pp.[14–15]; catalogue of 1970 Rotterdam exhib., pp.[18–19]; and in catalogue of 1976 Ljubljana exhib., with Slovene translation, 'Predvsem o uporati fotografij; zadera: grafike'.

re: The Mahler prints / A celebration and a crutch, in *R.B. Kitaj*. Hanover: Kestner-Gesellschaft, 1970 (catalogue of exhib.), p.[15].

[extract from letter by R.B.K., dated July 1968], in *Contemporary art 1942–72: collection of the Albright-Knox Art Gallery*. New York: Praeger; Buffalo NY: Albright-Knox Art Gallery, 1972, p.149.

[statement], in *European painting in the Seventies: new work by sixteen artists*. Los Angeles: Los Angeles County Museum of Art, 1975 (catalogue of exhib.), p.73.

[extract from letter by R.B.K. dated 7 May 1974], in [Anne Seymour], R.B. Kitaj: 'The Man of the Woods and the Cat of the Mountains', 1973. *The Tate Gallery 1972–4: biennial report and illustrated catalogue of acquisitions*. London: Tate Gallery, 1975. pp.181–3.

[introductory text], in *The human clay: an exhibition selected by R.B. Kitaj*. London: Arts Council of Great Britain, 1976 (catalogue of exhib. in Hayward Gallery, London, 1976, then touring), pp.[5–8].

[text], in *Arte inglese oggi 1960–76*. Milan: Electa Editrice, 1976 (catalogue of exhib. in Palazzo Reale, Milan; organised by Commune di Milano and British Council), p.128 [English text with Italian translation].

R.B. Kitaj and David Hockney discuss the case for a return to figuration [dialogue]. *New Review* (London), Jan.–Feb. 1977, vol.3, nos.34/5, pp.75–7; section repr. in Andrew Brighton, Lynda Morris (eds.), *Towards another picture: an anthology of writings by artists working in Britain 1945–1970*. Nottingham: Midland Group, 1977, pp.98–100.

[text], in Word and image [responses to questionnaire on books on art which have made the strongest impression on a number of contemporary artists]. *Times Literary Supplement*, 18 March 1977, no.3014, p.306.

[foreword], in *Open photography 1978* [catalogue of exhib. selected by John Szarkowski and R.B.K.]. Nottingham: Midland Group, 1978 (exhib. travelling to Serpentine Gallery, London, then touring). p.[5].

'The horror! the horror!' – Conrad [on the paintings of Irving Petlin], in *Irving Petlin: Rubbings ...: the large paintings and the small pastels*. Purchase NY: Neuberger Museum (State University of New York); Chicago: Arts Club of Chicago, 1978 (catalogue of exhib.), p.[3].

[extracts from letters by R.B.K. dated 7 June 1977 and 4 April 1978], in [David Brown], R.B. Kitaj: 'The Orientalist', 1976–7. *The Tate Gallery 1976–8: illustrated catalogue of acquisitions*. London: Tate Gallery, 1979, p.101.

'The Autumn of Central Paris (after Walter Benjamin)', 1971, in *Art International*, March 1979, vol.22, no.10, pp.19–20 [this text was originally hung beside the painting when it was exhibited at the 1977 *Hayward Annual*, Hayward Gallery, London].

Introduction, in *The artist's eye: an exhibition selected by R.B. Kitaj at the National Gallery, London*. London: National Gallery, 1980, pp.[3–6].

[introductory text] in *Leland Bell: paintings*. London: Theo Waddington, 1980 (catalogue of exhibition), p.[4].

Glasgow sale of Whistlers [letter from John Golding, Richard Hamilton, R.B.K. and others, opposing proposed sale by University of Glasgow of 80 oils by Whistler], in *Times*, 12 July 1980, p.13.

R.B. Kitaj and two faces of Ezra Pound [on two photographs of Pound by Bill Brandt], in *Creative Camera*, June 1982, no.210, pp.536–7.

Foreword, in Michael Auping, *Jess: Paste-ups (and Assemblies) 1951–1983*. Sarasota FL: John and Mable Ringling Museum of Art, 1983 (catalogue of exhib.), pp.8–9.

[long statement by R.B.K.], in [David Brown], *R.B. Kitaj: 'The murder of Rosa Luxemburg', 1960–2. The Tate Gallery 1980–82: illustrated catalogue of acquisitions*. London: Tate Gallery, 1984, pp.156–7.

Jewish art – indictment and defence: a personal testimony, in *Jewish Chronicle Colour Magazine*, 30 Nov. 1984, pp.42–6 [based on a lecture delivered at the Oxford Synagogue, 25 Nov. 1983; greatly abbreviated].

Prefaces, in Marco Livingstone, *R.B. Kitaj*. Oxford: Phaidon, 1985, pp.145–54; repr. in 2nd (revised and expanded) ed., Kitaj. London: Phaidon, 1992, pp.161–72. [R.B.K.'s introductory text is dated 1984; the 'Prefaces' expound 16 of R.B.K.'s paintings; Livingstone's text makes extensive use of interviews and correspondence conducted between 1976 and 1984, with further correspondence for the revised edition from late 1991].

After Duncan, in *A Paris visit: five poems by Robert Duncan; drawings & afterword by R.B. Kitaj*. Grenfell Press, 1985, pp.[19–20, 22–3]; limited ed. of 130 signed copies, with 11 ill. by R.B.K. (incl. cover). Text and 6 ill. repr. in *Conjunctions* (New York: David R. Godine), 1985, no.8; text pp.19–21, ill. pp.8, 10, 12, 14, 16, 18.

Foreword: Still in praise of still photography, in *Lee Friedlander portraits*. Boston: Little, Brown, 1985 (A New York Graphic Society Book), pp.9–19.

Foreword, in *Degas monotypes*. London: Arts Council of Great Britain, 1985 (catalogue of exhib. at Hayward Gallery), pp.4–5.

A passion, in *R.B. Kitaj*. London: Marlborough Fine Art, 1985 (catalogue of exhib.), pp.II–III; repr. in *European Judaism*, 1987 [i.e. 1988], vol.21, no.2 (no.41) (1988 Conference issue. 'Remembering for the future: Holocaust and hope'), pp.33–4.

Hockney [one of 3 pieces on the occasion of David Hockney's 50th birthday], in *Vogue*, Aug. 1987, vol.144, no.2283 (no.8), pp.182–3.

Erstes Manifest des Diasporismus. Zurich: Arche Verlag, 1988. 144p., ill. [trans. from the English by Martina Moersberger; includes 'Biographische Notitzen', pp.138–44]. Subsequently publ. in English as *First Diasporist manifesto*, 1989 (see below).

Portrait [title from contents page], in *David Hockney: a retrospective*. Los Angeles: Los Angeles County Museum of Art, 1988 (catalogue of exhib., ed. by Maurice Tuchman and Stephanie Barron, travelling to Metropolitan Museum of Art, New York, and Tate Gallery, London), pp.[2–3].

[text on the work, previously publ. in Livingstone 1985], in [Judith Collins], *R.B. Kitaj: 'Cecil Court, London W.C.2 (The Refugees)', 1983–4, in The Tate Gallery 1984–86: illustrated catalogue of acquisitions*. London: Tate Gallery, 1988, p.198.

Letter from London / Brief aus London [English text with German trans.], in *Die Spur des Anderen: fünf jüdische Künstler aus London mit fünf deutschen Künstlern aus Hamburg im Dialog*. Hamburg: Heine Haus, 1988 (catalogue of exhib., ed. by Martin Roman Deppner), pp.8–12.

Two paintings: prefaces and postscripts [on 'Two brothers', 1987, and 'The Caféist', 1980–7; extracted from R.B.K.'s proposed book *Hints for young painters (prefaces and postscripts)*, to have been publ. in 1989], in *Art & Design*, 1988, vol.4, no.9–10, pp.22–5.

An uneasy participant in the tragicomedy of modern art, mad about drawing [on Degas's drawings], in *Burlington Magazine*, March 1988, vol.130, no.1020, p.179.

[one of 11 obituary reminiscences of the painter and singer Rory McEwen], appended to Nicholas Luard: 'The envy of his generation', in *Tatler*, May 1988, p.118.

Degas and the nude [review of Richard Thompson, *Degas: the nudes*], in *Modern Painters*, Summer 1988, vol.1, no.2, p.93.

First Diasporist manifesto. London; New York: Thames and Hudson, 1989. 128p., ill. [previously publ. in German trans., 1988; omits the biographical notes from German ed.; illustrations are rearranged. Based on material in R.B.K.'s 1983 Oxford lecture, also the basis of R.B.K.'s 1984 article in the *Jewish Chronicle Colour Magazine* (see above)].

Drancy, by Anne Atik and R.B. Kitaj. London: Victoria Miro, 1989. [21]p., ill. [incl. 3p. of text, incl. 'Notes from a trip to Drancy'; 2 ill. by R.B.K.. Publ. May 1989 in limited ed. of 300 signed copies].

Isabel Bishop [review of Helen Yglesias, *Isabel Bishop*]. *Modern Painters*, Summer 1989, vol.2, no.2, pp.116–7.

[one of 26 obituary tributes to Peter Fuller], in *Modern Painters*, June 1990, vol.3, no.2, p.11.

About the painting [title from contents page], in *R.B. Kitaj: 'The Sensualist', 1973–84*. Oslo: For Art, 1991 (vol.1, no.1), p.4 [main text by Timothy Hyman].

School of London [with Italian trans., 'La Scuola di Londra'], in *Da Bacon a oggi: l'outsider nella figurazione britannica / From Bacon to now: the outsider in British figuration*. Milan: Electa, 1991 (catalogue of exhib. in Florence, Palazzo Vecchio), pp.10–11.

'The Caféist' (1987) [notes on his painting, for the proposed Thames & Hudson book of 'prefaces']. *Antique and New Art*, Summer 1991, pp.234–5.

A painter's tales [on his lifelong obsession with films, film-books and film-magazines, and his meeting in 1970 with the director John Ford], in *Sight and Sound*, July 1991, vol.1 (n.s.), no.3, pp.30–1.

Art in sport: Boxing, in *Art Review*, Sept. 1993, vol.45, p.17.

'Automat', 1927, by Edward Hopper [in 'The best of America: favourite works from the art show of the season', works selected by 13 leading artists and collectors from the Royal Academy exhibition *American art of the twentieth century*], in *Telegraph Magazine*, 11 Sept. 1993, pp.36–7.

2 Interviews

The following abbreviated entries refer to articles, catalogue introductions and books containing substantial interview material: full entries can be found in the appropriate section.

Tuchman, 1965 Los Angeles solo catalogue.
Makins, *Sunday Times*, 28 Aug. 1966.
Glazebrook, *Studio International*, June 1967.
McNay, *Guardian*, 8 May 1970.
Tarshis, *Art News*, Oct. 1976.
Walker, *Artscribe*, Feb. 1977.
R.B.K. and MacBeth, *Art Monthly*, April 1977.
Berthoud, *Times*, 7 May 1977.
Hyman, *London Magazine*, Feb. 1980.
Wyndham, *Sunday Times Magazine*, 25 May 1980.
Kuhn, *Antique Dealer and Collectors' Guide*, Oct. 1980.
Tuten, *Artforum*, Jan. 1982.
Taylor, *Times*, 23 May 1983.
Plante, *Sulfur*, 1984.
Gee, *Inside Art*, June 1984.
Torrents, *Lapiz*, Oct. 1985.
Checkland, *Times*, 7 Nov. 1985.
Brighton, *Art in America*, June 1986.
Peppiatt, *Art International*, Autumn 1987.
Cumming, 1988 Royal College of Art group catalogue.
Cieszkowski, *Art Libraries Journal*, 1989.
Ríos, *Impresiones de Kitaj*, 1989.
Cohen, *R.A.: Royal Academy Magazine*, Winter 1990.
Robinson, *Alba*, Jan.–Feb. 1991.
Lambirth, *R.A.: Royal Academy Magazine*, Autumn 1991.
Benjamin, *Art and Design*, March–April 1992.
Bohm-Duchen, *Jewish Quarterly*, Summer 1992.
Lubbock, *Independent on Sunday, The Sunday Review*, 25 Oct. 1992.
Plante, *New Yorker*, 1 Nov. 1993.
Ríos, *Kitaj: pictures and conversations*, 1994.

3 Books on R.B. Kitaj

(including unpublished theses)

James Aulich. *The human clay: R.B. Kitaj 1932–1980 – the evolution of a figurative aesthetic*. unpubl. Ph.D. thesis, University of Manchester, 1985.

Marco Livingstone. *R.B. Kitaj*. Oxford: Phaidon; New York, Rizzoli, 1985. 160p., ill. 2nd (revised and expanded) ed. retitled: *Kitaj*. London: Phaidon, 1992. 192p., ill. Incl. texts by RBK, 'Prefaces', pp.145–54 (1985 ed.) and pp.161–71 (1992 ed.). [makes extensive use of interviews and correspondence with RBK, conducted between 1976 and 1984, with further correspondence for the revised edition in late 1991. The 2nd ed. has a 2nd preface, and an 'Index of works by Kitaj' and 'General index'; the text is expanded (new material pp.39–46) and reset, but the bibliography is not extended to 1992; there are 16p. of additional illustrations, nos.159–81, and there are some alterations in the arrangement of the figures illustrating the text].

Lynne Woolfson. *Jewish themes in the work of R.B. Kitaj, 1960–1985*. unpubl. M.A. report, Courtauld Institute of Art, London, 1987.

...... Deppner. *Zeichen und Bildwanderung: zum Ausdruck des 'Nicht-Sesshaften' im Werk R.B. Kitajs*. Ph.D. thesis, Universität Hamburg, 1988 [subsequently publ. by Lit Verlag, Münster, in 1992].

Julián Ríos. *Impresiones de Kitaj (La novela pintada)*. Madrid: Mondadori España, 1989. 577p., ill. [comprehensive study consisting largely of interviews with RBK, translated into Spanish; English-language edition, *Kitaj: pictures and conversations*, publ. 1994].

Olivia Carol Salus. *Four martyr icons of R.B. Kitaj: an analysis of their pictorial narratives*. unpubl. Ph.D. thesis, Ohio State University, Columbus OH, 1989.

Timothy Hyman. A note on R.B. Kitaj's The Sensualist (1973–84). *R.B. Kitaj: 'The Sensualist'. 1973–84*. Oslo: For Art, 1991 (vol.1, no.1); also incl. preface by RBK, 'About the painting'.

Martin Roman Deppner. *Zeichen und Bildwanderung: zum Ausdruck des 'Nicht-Sesshaften' im Werk R.B. Kitajs*. Münster: Lit Verlag, 1992 (Form und Interesse, Band 23). 292p., ill. [originally a Ph.D. thesis submitted in 1988 to Universität Hamburg].

Julián Ríos. *Kitaj: pictures and conversations*. London: Hamish Hamilton, 1994 (forthcoming). 288p., ill.; trans. Abner Stein. [abridged and revised English-language edition of *Impresiones de Kitaj (La novela pintada)*, publ. in Spanish in 1989; the interviews with RBK were conducted in English].

Jane Kinsman. *R.B. Kitaj's prints*. Aldershot: Scolar Press, 1994 (forthcoming). 160p.; ill.; incl. a number of 'Afterwords' by R.B.K..

see also catalogue of 1981 Washington, Hirshhorn Museum solo exhibition, republ. in 1983 as a monograph: John Ashbery, Joe Shannon, Jane Livingston, Timothy Hyman: *R.B. Kitaj: paintings, drawings, pastels*. London: Thames and Hudson, 1983 (repr. 1986).

4 Writings on R.B. Kitaj

This section does not include books or unpublished theses, nor texts published as introductions to catalogues of solo or group exhibitions; reviews are of solo exhibitions held in London unless otherwise stated; items marked with an asterisk are those which are the most interesting, substantial and original, in the view of the compiler of this bibliography.

Kenneth Frampton. Looking for Rosebud [review of *Young Contemporaries* exhib.]. *Art News and Review*, 11–25 Feb. 1961, vol.13, no.2, p.2.

Robert Melville. [incl. review of *Young Contemporaries* exhib.]. *Architectural Review*, May 1961, vol.129, no.771, p.352.

Keith Sutton. Round the London art galleries [incl. review of Tooth exhib.]. *Listener*, 19 Oct. 1961, vol.66, no.1699, p.615.

John Russell. Art news from London [incl. review of John Moores Liverpool exhib.]. *Art News*, Jan. 1962, vol.60, no.9, p.48.

Dennis Farr. The John Moores Liverpool Exhibition 3 [review]. *Burlington Magazine*, Jan. 1962, vol.104, no.706, pp.30–1.

*Jasia Reichardt. A return to the figurative? A new direction, indeed unforeseen: R.B. Kitaj. *Metro*, [June 1962], no.6, pp.94–7.

George Butcher. The anatomy of pop art. *Guardian*, 21 June 1962, p.6.

J.P. Hodin. Londres (Pop art or art) [incl. review of Marlborough exhib.]. *Quadrum*, 1963, no.14, p.161.

[Mary Chamot]. R.B. Kitaj: 'Isaac Babel riding with Budyonny', 1962. *The Tate Gallery: review of the period 1 April 1953 to 31 March 1963 including a report for the year 1 April 1962 to 31 March 1963*. London: Her Majesty's Stationery Office, 1963, p.70.

An eagerly awaited first exhibition [review of Marlborough exhib.]. *Times*, 7 Feb. 1963, p.16.

John Richardson. World of art [incl. review of Marlborough exhib.]. *Evening Standard*, 8 Feb. 1963, p.11.†

Michael Shepherd. Kitaj [review of Marlborough exhib.]. *Arts Review*, 9–23 Feb. 1963, vol.15, no.2, p.6.

Nigel Gosling. The shapes of the sixties [incl. review of Marlborough exhib.]. *Observer*, 10 Feb. 1963, p.21.

John Russell. The polemical painter [review of Marlborough exhib.]. *Sunday Times*, 10 Feb. 1963, p.33.

*Bryan Robertson. R.B. Kitaj: 'A fantastic conspiracy' [2nd article in series 'Painting now']. *Sunday Times Colour Magazine*, 10 Feb. 1963, pp.23–5.

Eric Newton. Kitaj exhibition at the New London Gallery [review of Marlborough exhib.]. *Guardian*, 12 Feb. 1963, p.9.

Literary references in the new figurative painting ['from a correspondent', on Marlborough exhib.]. *Times*, 12 Feb. 1963, p.14.

Edward Lucie-Smith. A village explainer [incl. review of Marlborough exhib.]. *Listener*, 21 Feb. 1963, vol.69, no.1769, p.342.

Denys Sutton. Two attitudes: Kitaj and Kossoff [incl. review of Marlborough exhib.]. *Financial Times*, 26 Feb. 1963.

Edwin Mullins. [incl. review of Marlborough exhib.]. *Apollo*, March 1963, vol.77, no.13 (n.s.), p.231.

John Russell. Kitaj [review of Marlborough exhib.]. *Art News*, March 1963, vol.62, no.1, p.46.

Keith Roberts. [incl. review of Marlborough exhib.]. *Burlington Magazine*, March 1963, vol.105, no.720, pp.136–7.

Robert Spira. Kitaj in der Londoner Galerie [review of Marlborough exhib.]. *Weltkunst*, 15 March 1963, vol.33, p.14.†

*Norbert Lynton. London letter [incl. review of Marlborough exhib.]. *Art International*, 25 March 1963, vol.7, no.3, pp.55–7.

Jane Harrison. Kitaj in London [incl. review of Marlborough exhib.]. *Arts Magazine*, April 1963, vol.37, no.7, pp.26–7.

Joseph Rykwert. La mostra di Kitaj a Londra [review of Marlborough exhib.; in English]. *Domus*, April 1963, no.401, pp.29–30.

G.S. Whittet. [incl. review of Marlborough exhib.]. *Studio*, April 1963, vol.165, no.840, p.170.

Michael Horovitz. London report [incl. review of Marlborough exhib.]. *Das Kunstwerk*, May–June 1963, vol.16 nos.11–12, pp.64–5.

*Robert Melville. [incl. review of Marlborough exhib.]. *Architectural Review*, June 1963, vol.133, no.796, pp.437–9.

Jasia Reichardt. Kitaj's drawings from life. *Connoisseur*, Oct. 1963, vol.154, no.620, pp.112–16.

John Russell. England: the advantage of being thirty [survey of a generation of young English artists]. *Art in America*, Nov.–Dec. 1963, vol.51, no.6, pp.92–7.

Robert Melville. English pop art. *Quadrum*, 1964, vol.17, pp.23–38 (esp. pp.36–8).

Robert Melville. [incl. review of Marlborough exhib.]. *Architectural Review*, April 1964, vol.135, no.806, p.293.

*Gene Baro. The British scene: Hockney and Kitaj [incl. review of Marlborough exhib.]. *Arts Magazine*, May–June 1964, vol.38, no.9, pp.94–101.

Painting: Britannia's new wave [survey of generation of young English artists]. *Time*, 9 Oct. 1964, vol.84, no.15, pp.74–9.

Bryan Robertson, John Russell, Lord Snowdon. *Private view*. London: Thomas Nelson, 1965, pp.193–7.

Robert Melville. [incl. review of Marlborough exhib.]. *Architectural Review*, Feb. 1965, vol.137, no.816, p.142.

Stuart Preston. Encyclopaedic Pop [review of New York exhib.]. *New York Times*, 7 Feb. 1965, section 2 p.19.†

Robert M. Coates. Chaos [incl. review of New York exhib.]. *New Yorker*, 13 Feb. 1965, vol.40, pp.132–4.†

Grace Glueck. Painter's painter [review of New York exhib.]. *New York Times*, 14 Feb. 1965, section 2 p.19.

Painting: literary collage [review of New York exhib.]. *Time*, 19 Feb. 1965, vol.85, no.8, p.72.

Norbert Lynton. London letter [incl. review of Marlborough exhib.]. *Art International*, March 1965. vol.8, no.3, pp.55–7.

L.C.[= Lawrence Campbell]. New names [incl. review of New York exhib.]. *Art News*, March 1965, vol.64, no.1, p.22.

D.J.[= Donald Judd]. [incl. review of New York exhib.]. *Arts Magazine*, March 1965, vol.39, no.6, pp.62–3.

John Canaday. The bandwaggon toboggan [incl. review of New York exhib.]. *New York Times*, 7 March 1965, p.17.†

Max Kozloff. R.J. [sic] Kitaj [review of New York exhib.]. *Nation*, 8 March 1965, vol.200, no.10, pp.263–4.

John Russell. London / NYC: a two-way traffic. *Art in America*, April 1965, vol.53, no.2, pp.126–36 (esp. pp.131, 134).

Lucy R. Lippard. New York letter [incl. review of New York exhib.]. *Art International*, April 1965, vol.9, no.3, pp.59–60.

*Dore Ashton. R.B. Kitaj and the scene. *Arts & Architecture*, April 1965, vol.82, no.4, pp.8–9, 34–5.

Sidney Tillim. Toward a literary revival? *Arts Magazine*, May–June 1965, vol.39, no.9, pp.30–3.

Nancy Marmer. [review of Los Angeles exhib.]. *Artforum*, Oct. 1965, vol.4, no.2, pp.10–11.

Jasia Reichardt. R.B. Kitaj. *Billedkunst*, 1966, vol.1, no.1, pp.12–19.

[article on R.B.K.]. *Mizue*, Jan. 1966, pp.26–7.

Larry Aldrich. New talent USA [selection of 37 artists]. *Art in America*, July–Aug. 1966, vol.54, no.4, p.35.

Virginia Makins. Americans in London: they like it here, but… [interviews with Americans living in London, incl. R.B.K.]. *Observer*, 28 Aug. 1966, colour supplement, pp.1, 19.

Edward Lucie-Smith. What ever happened to British Pop? *Art and Artists*, May 1967, vol.2, no.2, pp.16–18.

Mark Glazebrook. Lithographs and original prints: why do artists make prints? [questionnaire, incl. interview with R.B.K.]. *Studio International*, June 1967, vol.173, no.890, supplement pp.1–2.

*Robert Kudielka. R.B. Kitaj und die Schuld des Auges. *Das Kunstwerk*, Aug.–Sept. 1967, vol.20 nos.11–12, pp.3–12.

John Russell. Kitaj komedy [incl. review of Marlborough exhib. of prints]. *Art News*, Sept. 1967, vol.66, no.5, pp.60–1.

Robert Melville. The arresting image [incl. review of Marlborough exhib.]. *Architectural Review*, Oct. 1967, vol.142, no.848, pp.301–2.

Richard J. Boyle. Paintings of the later twentieth century [incl. catalogue-entry for R.B.K.'s 'Apotheosis of groundlessness', 1964]. *Cincinnati Art Museum Bulletin*, Oct. 1968, vol.8, no.4, p.17.

*Christopher Finch. Chapter 7: R.B. Kitaj, in *Image as language: aspects of British art 1950–1968*. Harmondsworth: Penguin Books, 1969; pp.80–5, and pl.31–5.

Frederic Tuten. Art and technology in California. *Vogue*, 15 April 1969, no.153, p.36.†

Grace Glueck. Coast art – Industry Project blossoms. *New York Times*, 17 April 1969, p.54.†

Heinz Ohff. R.B. Kitaj: das gesamte graphische Werk [review of Berlin exhib.]. *Das Kunstwerk*, June–July 1969, vol.22 nos.9–10, p.85.

Jun Miyagawa. Ronald B. Kitaj. *Mizue*, Oct. 1969, no.777, pp.72–87.

*Werner Haftmann. Kitaj's graphics 1963–1969 [incl. R.B.K.'s text 'Mainly about using photos; re: the prints', previously publ. in *R.B. Kitaj*, catalogue of exhib. at University of California, Berkeley, 1967, pp.9–12]. *Art and Artists*, Nov. 1969, vol.4, no.8, pp.24–9.

Elisabeth Novick. Spotlight on minds of invention: R.B. Kitaj. *Vogue* (U.K.), Nov. 1969, no.126, pp.162–3.

*[Richard Morphet]. R.B. Kitaj: 'Mahler becomes politics, Beisbol', 1964–7. *The Tate Gallery 1968–70*. London: Tate Gallery, 1970. pp.90–1.

Kitaj: neue Alchimie [review of Hanover exhib.]. *Der Spiegel*, 9 Feb. 1970, vol.24, no.7, pp.135–9.

John Russell: Separate directions [review of Marlborough exhib.]. *Sunday Times*, 19 April 1970, p.29.

Pierre Rouve. R.B. Kitaj. *Arts Review*, 25 April 1970, vol.22, no.8, pp.246, 261.

Nigel Gosling. Two sides to Kitaj [review of Marlborough exhib.]. *Observer*, 26 April 1970, p.28.

Guy Brett. Kitaj's spectres [review of Marlborough exhib.]. *Times*, 28 April 1970, p.7.

Marina Vaizey. R.B. Kitaj [review of Marlborough exhib.]. *Financial Times*, 29 April 1970, p.3.

James Burr. Philosopher painter [incl. review of Marlborough exhib.]. *Apollo*, May 1970, vol.91, no.99 (n.s.), p.393.

Robert Melville. Kitaj's thoughts [review of Marlborough exhib.]. *New Statesman*, 1 May 1970, vol.79, no.2042, pp.637–8.

Bryan Robertson. Golden oldies [review of Marlborough exhib.]. *Spectator*, 2 May 1970, vol.224, no.7401, pp.594–5.

John Russell. Discoveries [incl. review of Marlborough exhib.]. *Sunday Times*, 3 May 1970, p.32.

Simon Hodgson. Notes on Kitaj [review of Marlborough exhib.]. *Listener*, 7 May 1970, vol.83, no.2145, p.628.

Michael McNay. R.B. Kitaj in an interview with Michael McNay. *Guardian*, 8 May 1970, p.8.

Cor Blok. [incl. review of Rotterdam exhib.]. *Art International*, Summer 1970, vol.14, no.6, p.116.

Jasia Reichardt. Kitaj's pictures from an exhibition [review of Marlborough exhib.]. *Architectural Design*, June 1970, vol.40, p.269.†

Guy Brett. Artists and printers [incl. review of Marlborough exhib.]. *Times*, 23 June 1970, p.7.

Paul Hofmann. [incl. review of Marlborough exhib.]. *New York Times*, 24 June 1970, p.38.†

*John Willett. Where to stick it. *Art International*, Nov. 1970, vol.14, no.9, pp.28–36.

Robert Melville. English Pop Art. in J.P. Hodin [et al.]. *Figurative art since 1945*. London: Thames and Hudson, 1971, pp.179–200 (esp. pp.179–81).

*Gail R. Scott. R.B. Kitaj [on R.B.K.'s 1969 residency at the Lockheed plant at Burbank, as part of the LACMA 'Art and Technology' Program; incl. extensive quotations from R.B.K.'s letters]. *A report on the Art and Technology Program of the Los Angeles County Museum of Art 1967–1971*. Los Angeles: Los Angeles County Museum of Art, 1971 (main text by Maurice Tuchman, Jane Livingston). pp.147–63.

Contemporary art 1942–72: collection of the Albright–Knox Art Gallery. New York: Praeger; Buffalo NY: Albright-Knox Art Gallery, 1972, pp.132–4 (part of essay by John Russell), 147, 149 (incl. extract from letter from R.B.K., July 1968).

Van Deren Coke. *The painter and the photograph: from Delacroix to Warhol*. Albuquerque NM: University of New Mexico Press, 1972 (revised ed., originally publ. 1964), pp.125–8.

Robert F. Phillips. Ronald B. Kitaj's definition of nobody [on 'Notes towards a definition of

nobody', 1961]. *Toledo [Ohio] Museum of Art: Museum News*, 1974, vol.17 (n.s.), no.1, pp.19–22.

Richard Francis. 'The red banquet' by R.B. Kitaj. *Walker Art Gallery, Liverpool: Annual Reports and Bulletin*, 1971–4 [publ. 1974], vols.2–4, pp.84–90.

John Russell. Dream of perfection [incl. review of New York exhib.]. *Sunday Times*, 10 Feb. 1974, p.27.

Frederic Tuten. Kitaj [review of New York exhib.]. *Arts Magazine*, March 1974, vol.48, no.6, pp.70–1.

Gerrit Henry. [incl. review of New York exhib.]. *Art News*, April 1974, vol.73, no.4, p.96.

Phyllis Derfner. New York letter [incl. review of New York exhib.]. *Art International*, 20 April 1974, vol.18, no.4, pp.50–1.

John Ashbery. R.B. Kitaj at Marlborough [review of New York exhib.]. *Art in America*, May–June 1974, vol.64, no.3, p.103.

Robert Melville. With money to spend [incl. review of Marlborough exhib.]. *Architectural Review*, Dec. 1974, vol.156, no.934, p.390.

*[Anne Seymour]. R.B. Kitaj: 'The Man of the Woods and the Cat of the Mountains', 1973 [incl. extract from letter by R.B.K. dated 7 May 1974]. *The Tate Gallery 1972–4: biennial report and illustrated catalogue of acquisitions*. London: Tate Gallery, 1975. pp.181–3.

Erika Langmuir. The concert in European art [letter in response to exhib. review by Keith Roberts, Sept. 1974]. *Burlington Magazine*, Jan. 1975, vol.117, no.862, p.52.

Edward Gage. First Kitaj show in Scotland [review of Edinburgh exhib.]. *Scotsman*, 28 Aug. 1975.

Maurice Tuchman. European painting of the Seventies [explaining the ideas behind his Los Angeles exhib.]. *Art and Artists*, Nov. 1975, vol.10, no.8, pp.45–9.

Charles McCorquodale. Edinburgh – two exhibitions [incl. review of R.B.K.'s exhib.]. *Art International*, 20 Nov. 1975, vol.19, no.9, pp.26–8.

*Marco Livingstone. 'Young Contemporaries' at the Royal College of Art, 1959–1962: Derek Boshier, David Hockney, Allen Jones, R.B. Kitaj, Peter Phillips. unpubl. M.A. report, Courtauld Institute of Art, London, 1976 (esp. pp.12–28; transcript of interview on 11 April 1976 [revised Dec. 1976], pp.A51–5; footnotes 57–138, pp.A65–76; bibliog. entries 374–450; source illus. figs.1–7; plates 69–82).

Attilio Pizzeoni. La presenza polemica di Kitaj nella situazione inglese. *Artecontro*, 1976, no.15, pp.14–15.†

Peter Plagens. European painting in LA: a grab bag of well-worn issues. *Artforum*, Jan. 1976, vol.14, pp.40–4.

Richard Cork. Now what are those English up to? [review of Milan exhib.]. *Evening Standard*, 4 March 1976, p.24.

Iulian Mereuta. Serigrafii de R.B. Kitaj. *Arta* (Bucharest), May 1976, vol.33, no.5, p.24.

Toni del Renzio. Style, technique and iconography [extended English version of his introd. to

...terdam group exhib.]. *Art and Artists*, July 1976, vol.11, no.4, pp.34–9.

Lynda Morris. The human clay [review of Hayward Gallery exhib.]. *Listener*, 19 Aug. 1976, vol.96, no.2471, pp.218–9.

John Russell. A British show built of "human clay" [review of Hayward Gallery exhib.]. *New York Times*, 5 Sept. 1976, section 2 p.23.

*Jerome Tarshis. The 'fugitive passions' of R.B. Kitaj [incl. interview]. *Art News*, Oct. 1976, vol.75, no.8, pp.40–3.

Donald Hoffman. Things about modern art not said in public. *Kansas City Star*, 24 Oct. 1976, section D pp.1, 6.†

Robert Melville. The poetry of ordinariness [incl. review of Marlborough group exhib.]. *Architectural Review*, Nov. 1976, vol.160, no.957, pp.312–3.

John Russell. House miscellany. *New York Times*, 17 Dec. 1976, section C p.16.†

Suzi Gablik. Human clay [review of Hayward Gallery exhib.]. *Studio International*, Jan.–Feb. 1977, vol.193, no.985, pp.46–7.

*James Faure Walker. R.B. Kitaj interviewed by James Faure Walker. *Artscribe*, Feb. 1977, no.5, pp.4–5.

Marina Vaizey. Life classes. *Sunday Times*, 20 Feb. 1977, p.38.

*R.B. Kitaj and George MacBeth in dialogue [interview]. *Art Monthly*, April 1977, no.6, pp.8–10.

William Feaver. Alternative routes. *Vogue*, 15 April 1977.

William Feaver. Kitaj's characters [on Marlborough exhib.]. *Observer Magazine*, 24 April 1977, p.17.

Marina Vaizey. Private moments. *Sunday Times*, 24 April 1977, p.38.

M. and D. Ackerman. Dear Kitaj and David – the quality of the creation is more important than its content [on the Kitaj/Hockney dialogue in New Review, Jan.–Feb. 1977]. *Arts Review*, 29 April 1977, vol.29, no.9, pp.285–7.

Michael Shepherd. Kitaj observed. *Arts Review*, 29 April 1977, vol.29, no.9, pp.288–9.

Janet Daley. R.B. Kitaj [review of Marlborough exhib.]. *Arts Review*, 29 April 1977, vol.29, no.9, pp.289–291.

Caroline Tisdall. Figure reigns [incl. review of Marlborough exhib.]. *Guardian*, 29 April 1977, p.12.

Michael Horovitz. R.B. Kitaj [review of Marlborough exhib.]. *Art Monthly*, May 1977, no.7, pp.18–19.

William Feaver. Life class champion [review of Marlborough exhib.]. *Observer Review*, 1 May 1977, p.25.

Michael Shepherd. Art: authority and obscurity: figuring it out [review of Marlborough exhib.]. *Sunday Telegraph*, 1 May 1977, p.17.

Marina Vaizey. The week when the Americans took over [incl. review of Marlborough exhib.]. *Sunday Times*, 1 May 1977, p.39.

Richard Cork. People in the background [review of Marlborough exhib.]. *Evening Standard*, 5 May 1977, p.25.

Michael Shepherd. The 'mysterious' Kitaj [review of Marlborough exhib.]. *What's On In London*, 6 May 1977, p.34.

William Packer. Kitaj, Dine and Blake [incl. review of Marlborough exhib.]. *Financial Times*, 7 May 1977, p.9.

John McEwen. Mushy [review of Marlborough exhib.]. *Spectator*, 7 May 1977, pp.31–2.

*Roger Berthoud. A love for pictures and an enthusiasm for life [incl. interview]. *Times*, 7 May 1977, p.8.

Paul Overy. Filibuster for the figurative [review of Marlborough exhib.]. *Times*, 18 May 1977, p.12.

Christopher Butler. Figure-conscious [review of Marlborough exhib.]. *Times Literary Supplement*, 20 May 1977, no.3923, p.618.

David Anfam. Provocative pictures [review of Marlborough exhib.]. *Sennet* (University of London), 25 May 1977.

Lynda Morris. Popular front [review of Marlborough exhib.]. *Listener*, 26 May 1977, vol.97, no.2510, pp.692–3.

John Spurling. If not, what? [incl. review of Marlborough exhib.]. *New Statesman*, 27 May 1977, vol.93, no.2410, p.722.

Edward Lucie-Smith. R.B. Kitaj [review of Marlborough exhib.]. *Art and Artists*, July 1977, vol.12, no.4, p.6.

Roger Berthoud. A love for pictures and an enthusiasm for life [incl. interview]. *Times*, 7 July 1977, p.8.

Robert Melville. A mixture of survivals [incl. review of Marlborough exhib.]. *Architectural Review*, Aug. 1977, vol.162, no.966, pp.119–22.

Nikolaus Delacroix. R.B. Kitaj [review of Zurich exhib.]. *Das Kunstwerk*, Aug. 1977, vol.30, no.4, p.72.

*Timothy Hyman. R.B. Kitaj: avatar of Ezra [review of Marlborough exhib.]. *London Magazine*, Aug.–Sept. 1977, vol.17, no.3, pp.53–61.

Timothy Hyman. The big show: perspectives and polemics [review of Hayward Annual]. *London Magazine*, Nov. 1977, vol.17, no.5, pp.49–60.

Jean-Luc David. The image of culture. *Skira Annual*, 1978, no.4, pp.42–91.†

Robert Garrett. Kitaj lauds revival of the figurative artist. *Boston Herald American*, 30 May 1978, pp.11, 15.†

Jonathan Williams. *Portrait photographs*. London: Coracle Press, 1979, pp.[58–9], pl.23.

*Michael Podro. Some notes on Ron Kitaj. *Art International*, March 1979, vol.22, no.10, pp.18–26.

*Robert Creeley. Ecce Homo. *Art International*, March 1979, vol.22, no.10, pp.27–30; previously publ. as introd. to catalogue of exhibition, *R.B. Kitaj: pictures / Bilder*, London: Marlborough Fine Art; Zurich: Marlborough Galerie, 1977, pp.4–7 (English text with German translation).

Graham Stacy. Om R.B. Kitaj. *Paletten*, 1979, no.2, pp.35–8.

*[David Brown]. R.B. Kitaj: 'The Orientalist', 1976–7 [incl. extracts from letters by R.B.K. dated 4 April 1977 and 8 June 1977]. *The Tate Gallery 1976–8: illustrated catalogue of acquisitions*. London: Tate Gallery, 1979. p.101.

John Russell. Campaigner for figurative art [review of New York exhib.]. *New York Times*, 30 March 1979, section C p.19.

Hilton Kramer. R.B. Kitaj. *New York Times*, 6 April 1979, section C p.23.†

John Ashbery. Poetry in motion [review of New York exhib.]. *New York*, 16 April 1979, vol.12, no.16, pp.94–6.

Mark Stevens. The human factor [review of New York exhib.]. *Newsweek*, 16 April 1979, vol.93, no.16, p.79.

Robert Hughes. The last history painter: expatriate R.B. Kitaj brings home the Bacon. *Time*, 23 April 1979, vol.113, no.17, pp.70–1.

Eric Gibson. R.B. Kitaj [review of New York exhib.]. *Art International*, May 1979, vol.23, no.2, p.23.

*R.B. Kitaj: a return to London [interview with Timothy Hyman]. *London Magazine*, Feb. 1980, vol.19, no.11, pp.15–27; repr. in *R.B. Kitaj*. Washington: Smithsonian Institution, 1981 (catalogue of exhibition in Washington, Hirshhorn Museum and Sculpture Garden, 1981), pp.39–48.

Marina Vaizey. Back to earth [incl. review of National Gallery exhib.]. *Sunday Times*, 25 May 1980, p.40.

Francis Wyndham. The dream studio of R.B. Kitaj [on National Gallery exhib.; incl. interview]. *Sunday Times Magazine*, 25 May 1980, pp.59–62, 67.

William Packer. The artist's eye [review of National Gallery exhib.]. *Financial Times*, 27 May 1980.

Max Wykes-Joyce. R.B. Kitaj: a cat among the pigeons [review of National Gallery exhib.]. *International Herald Tribune*, 31 May – 1 June 1980, p.104.

Judith Bumpus. As a man sees [review of National Gallery exhib.]. *Art and Artists*, July 1980, vol.15, no.3, issue 172, pp.12–15.

Heidi Bürklin. Ein Künstler stöbert im Depot [review of National Gallery exhib.]. *Art: das Kunstmagazin*, July 1980, p.128.

*Marco Livingstone. Iconology as theme in the early work of R.B. Kitaj. *Burlington Magazine*, July 1980, vol.122, no.928, pp.488–97.

John McEwen. In principle [review of National Gallery exhib.]. *Spectator*, 12 July 1980, vol.245, no.7931, pp.26–7.

Guy Brett. What is the tradition? [polemic occasioned by R.B.K.'s National Gallery exhib.]. *Art Monthly*, July–Aug. 1980, no.38, p.2.

Joy Kuhn. The natural passage towards the other shore [review of Marlborough exhib.; incl. interview]. *Antique Dealer and Collectors Guide*, Oct. 1980, pp.68–71.

*Timothy Hyman. Kitaj: a prodigal returning. *Artscribe*, Oct. 1980, no.25, pp.37–41.

John Russell Taylor. Enigmatic images of gender and sexuality [incl. review of Marlborough exhib.]. *Times*, 14 Oct. 1980.

William Packer. Kitaj's pastels [review of Marlborough exhib.]. *Financial Times*, 21 Oct. 1980, p.23.

Steven Lavell. R.B. Kitaj [review of Marlborough exhib.]. *Arts Review*, 24 Oct. 1980, vol.32, no.21, p.481.

Michael McNay. R.B. Kitaj [review of Marlborough exhib.]. *Guardian*, 24 Oct. 1980, p.9.

Sara Selwood. Society nudes [review of Marlboroug exhib.]. *Times Literary Supplement*, 24 Oct. 1980, no.4047, p.1200.

Edward Lucie-Smith. London letter [incl. review of Marlborough exhib.]. *Art International*, Nov.–Dec. 1980, vol.24 nos.3–4, pp.174–7.

*[Richard Calvocoressi]. R.B. Kitaj: 'The rise of Fascism', 1975–9. *The Tate Gallery 1978–80: illustrated catalogue of acquisitions*. London: Tate Gallery, 1981. pp.107–8.

William Feaver. Shimmering dresses and Degas' deathbed [incl. review of Marlborough exhib.]. *Art News*, Jan. 1981, vol.80, no.1, pp.159–61.

Jeremy Wood. [review of National Gallery and Marlborough exhibs.]. *Pantheon*, Jan.–March 1981, vol.39, no.1, pp.26–7.

Richard Cork. Report from London: "The artist's eye" [review of National Gallery exhib.]. *Art in America*, Feb. 1981, vol.69, no.2, pp.43–55.

*Michael Peppiatt. R.B. Kitaj: le tableau comme un roman [review of Washington exhib.]. *Connaissance des Arts*, Sept. 1981, no.355, pp.36–43; also in English-language edition of *Connaissance des Arts*, 'R.B. Kitaj: pictures like novels', Sept. 1981, no.20, pp.28–35.

Paul Richard. Kitaj's turbulent kaleidoscope: the exhibit: a master of memory and pain [review of Washington exhib.]. *Washington Post*, 17 Sept. 1981, section C pp.1, 16.

*Hilton Kramer. Kitaj: the vision of an expatriate [review of Washington exhib.]. *New York Times*, 27 Sept. 1981, section D pp.33, 36; repr. in Kramer, *The revenge of the Philistines: art and culture, 1972–1984*. London: Secker & Warburg, 1985, pp.232–5.

Mark Stevens. Pictures that have a plot [review of Washington exhib.]. *Newsweek*, 28 Sept. 1981, vol.98, no.13, pp.96–7.

*Robert Hughes. Edgy footnotes to an era [review of Washington exhib.]. *Time*, 26 Oct. 1981, vol.118, no.17, pp.76–7; repr. as 'R.B. Kitaj' in Hughes, *Nothing if not critical: selected essays on art and artists*. London: Collins Harvill, 1990, pp.269–72.

Emerson Batdorff. R.B. Kitaj returns home in triumph. *Plain Dealer* (Cleveland), 16 Dec. 1981, section F pp.1, 11.

Elizabeth Price. Kinsman was home to painter R.B. Kitaj. *Plain Dealer* (Cleveland), 16 Dec. 1981, section F p.2.

Edward Lucie-Smith. R.B. Kitaj. *Art and Artists*, Jan. 1982, no.184, pp.34–5.

*John Ashbery. R.B. Kitaj; hunger and love. *Art in America*, Jan. 1982, vol.70, no.1, pp.130–6; previously publ. as 'Hunger and love in their variations' in *R.B. Kitaj*, Washington: Smithsonian Institution, 1981 (catalogue of exhib. in Hirshhorn Museum and Sculpture Garden, Washington, 1981), pp.11–17; repr. as 'R.B. Kitaj' in Ashbery, ed. David Bergman, *Reported sightings: art chronicles, 1957–1987*. Manchester: Carcanet, 1989, pp.299–308.

Franz Schulze. The Kitaj retrospective: too late or too early? [review of Washington exhib.]. *Art News*, Jan. 1982, vol.81, no.1, pp.122–5.

*Frederic Tuten. Neither fool, nor naive, nor poseur-saint: fragments on R.B. Kitaj [incl. interview]. *Artforum*, Jan. 1982, vol.20, no.5, pp.61–9.

Alfred Welti. Vorwärts zu den Alten Meistern [review of Düsseldorf exhib.]. *Art: das Kunstmagazin*, Feb. 1982, no.2, pp.136–7.

David Carrier. [incl. review of Washington exhib.]. *Artscribe*, Feb. 1982, no.33, pp.61–3.

Karl Diemer. Dem Dämon Fortschritt algeschworen [review of Düsseldorf exhib.]. *Stuttgarter Rundschau*, 8 Feb. 1982.

Simon Passmore. Juxtapositions [review of Düsseldorf exhib., mistitled 'Kitaj's compass']. *Times Literary Supplement*, 19 Feb. 1982, no.4116, p.186.

Karin Thomas. Der Atem des Zeitalters [review of Düsseldorf exhib.]. *Weltkunst*, 15 March 1982, vol.52, no.6, pp.780–1.

Clive Phillpot. Kitaj retrospective [review of Washington exhib.]. *Art Journal*, Spring 1982, vol.42, no.1, pp.55–7.

Peter Winter. R.B. Kitaj [review of Düsseldorf exhib.]. *Das Kunstwerk*, April 1982, vol.35, no.2, pp.61–3.

Michael Voggenauer. Düsseldorf: Kitaj at the Kunsthalle [review of exhib.]. *Burlington Magazine*, May 1982, vol.124, no.950, pp.320–1.

Mark Haworth-Booth. Kitaj / Brandt / Screenplay [on R.B.K.'s interest in Bill Brandt's photographs, and how this is reflected in R.B.K.'s work]. *Creative Camera*, June 1982, no.210, pp.546–9.

Edward B. Henning. R.B. Kitaj: 'The Garden'. *The Bulletin of the Cleveland Museum* of Art, Dec. 1982, vol.69, no.10, pp.309, 319–23.

Michael Peppiatt. R.B. Kitaj. *Kunst og Kultur*, 1983, vol.66, no.3, pp.166–175.

Will Hiley. [review of Thames & Hudson ed. of *R.B. Kitaj*]. *Blitz*, May 1983.

John Russell Taylor. Profile: R.B. Kitaj. The state of the artist [incl. interview]. *Times*, 23 May 1983, p.13.

Tom Phillips. Kitaj: Paintings, drawings, pastels [review of Thames & Hudson ed. of catalogue of 1981 Washington exhib.]. *R.A.: Royal Academy Magazine*, Sept. 1983, no.1, p.31.

Lucy Alexander. Mixed reactions to the new Kitaj painting [i.e. 'In the mountains']. *Friends of the S.A. National Gallery: Newsletter*, Dec. 1983, no.9, pp.13–16.

Martin Roman Deppner. Spuren geschichlicher Erfahrung: R.B. Kitajs 'Reflections on violence'. *Idea: Jahrbuch der Hamburger Kunsthalle*, 1984, vol.3, pp.139–66.

*[David Brown]. R.B. Kitaj: 'The murder of Rosa Luxemburg', 1960–2 [incl. long statement by R.B.K.]. *The Tate Gallery 1980–82: illustrated catalogue of acquisitions*. London: Tate Gallery, 1984. pp.156–7.

*David Plante. Paris, 1983 [interview with R.B.K.]. *Sulfur: a literary tri-quarterly of the whole art*, 1984, no.9, pp.96–110.

Krzysztof Z. Cieszkowski. No less mystifying [review of Thames & Hudson ed. of catalogue of 1981 Washington exhib.]. *Art Book Review*, Jan. 1984, vol.2, no.3, p.58.

Vivianne Barsky. R.B. Kitaj's 'Self-portrait in Saragossa'. *Israel Museum Journal*, Spring 1984, vol.3, pp.83–5.

Herman de Coninck. Portfolio: Kitaj. *NWT: Neuw Wereldtijdschrift* (Antwerp), May 1984, pp.40–7.

Charlie Gee. 'Life is short and art is long': painter R.B. Kitaj discusses his views with Charlie Gee [interview]. *Inside Art*, June 1984, no.5, p.6.

Catherine Klaus Schear. Photomontage in the early work of R.B. Kitaj. *Arts Magazine*, Sept. 1984, vol.59, no.1, pp.74–7.

Tom Phillips. Members. *R.A.: Royal Academy Magazine*, Summer 1985, no.7, p.19.

Nissa Torrents. Entrevista con R.B. Kitaj: 'la figura es casi sagrada'. *Lapiz*, Oct. 1985, vol.3, no.28, pp.22–7.

Sara Jane Checkland. The quiet approach [incl. interview]. *Times*, 7 Nov. 1985, p.10.

Waldemar Januszczak. Portrait of the artist as a Jew [review of Marlborough exhib.]. *Guardian*, 12 Nov. 1985, p.11.

John Russell Taylor. Organized spontaneity [incl. review of Marlborough exhib.]. *Times*, 12 Nov. 1985, p.10.

Sarah Kent. A Jewish passion [review of Marlborough exhib.]. *Time Out*, 14–20 Nov. 1985, no.795, p.41.

Barry Fealdman. An artist as a Jew [review of Marlborough exhib.]. *Jewish Chronicle*, 15 Nov. 1985.

William Feaver. [review of Marlborough exhib.]. *Observer*, 20 Nov. 1985.

Marina Vaizey. [incl. review of Marlborough exhib.]. *Sunday Times*, 20 Nov. 1985.

Monika Zimmermann. Traurig aus der Vergangenkeit [review of Marlborough exhib.]. *Frankfurter Allgemeine*, 21 Nov. 1985.

Mary Rose Beaumont. R.B. Kitaj at Marlborough Fine Art [review]. *Arts Review*, 22 Nov. 1985, vol.37, no.23, p.591.

Giles Auty. Enigma variations [incl. review of Marlborough exhib.]. *Spectator*, 23 Nov. 1985, vol.255, no.8211, p.36.

Alistair Hicks. A Jewish inheritance [review of Marlborough exhib.]. *Spectator*, 23 Nov. 1985, vol.255, no.8211, p.37.

Jacynth Ellerton. [review of Marlborough exhib.]. *Tablet*, 23 Nov. 1985.

William Packer. Kitaj: good, bad and remarkable [incl. review of Marlborough exhib.]. *Financial Times*, 26 Nov. 1985, p.17.

Michael Shepherd. Kitaj in Europe [review of Marlborough exhib.]. *Sunday Telegraph*, 27 Nov. 1985, p.16.

Max Wykes-Joyce. R.B. Kitaj [review of Marlborough exhib.]. *Art and Artists*, Dec. 1985, no.231, pp.32–3.

Richard Cork. Recovered identity [review of Marlborough exhib.]. *Listener*, 5 Dec. 1985, vol.114, no.2938, pp.40–1.

Michael Podro. Literary compounds [review of Marco Livingstone, *R.B. Kitaj*]. *Times Literary Supplement*, 6 Dec. 1985, no.4314, pp.1377, 1384.

Denis Thompson. Art and people [incl. review of Marco Livingstone, *R.B. Kitaj*]. *Listener*, 19 and 26 Dec. 1985, vol.114, no.2940, p.52.

*Peter Fuller. Kitaj at Christmas [review of Marlborough exhib.]. *Art Monthly*, Dec. 1985 / Jan. 1986, no.92, pp.11–14; repr. as 'R.B. Kitaj' in John McDonald (ed.). *Peter Fuller's modern painters: reflections on British art*. London: Methuen, 1993, pp.234–253.

*Marco Livingstone. Kitaj at Marlborough [review]. *Burlington Magazine*, Jan. 1986, vol.128, no.994, pp.50–3.

Caroline Collier. R.B. Kitaj [review of Marlborough exhib.]. *Flash Art*, Feb.–March 1986, no.126, pp.56–7.

Eric Parry. Places of reverie [article on artists' studios, and on recent house-conversions by M.J. Long for R.B.K. and Peter Blake]. *Architects' Journal*, 26 Feb. 1986, vol.183, no.9, pp.28–32.

*Israel Schenker. Always against the grain. *Art News*, March 1986, vol.85, no.3, pp.78–85.

Tony Godfrey [review of Marco Livingstone, *R.B. Kitaj*]. *Burlington Magazine*, March 1986, vol.128, no.996, pp.227–8.

John Russell. Into the labyrinth of dreams with Kitaj [review of New York exhib.]. *New York Times*, 16 March 1986, section H pp.31, 36.

Bill Zimmer. Gouged, frosted. sprayed [incl. review of New York exhib.]. *Village Voice*, 1 April 1986, vol.31, no.13, p.95.

Donald Kuspit. R.B. Kitaj [review of New York exhib.]. *Artforum*, Summer 1986, vol.24, no.10, pp.125–6.

*Andrew Brighton. Conversations with R.B. Kitaj. *Art in America*, June 1986, vol.74, no.6, pp.98–105.

Charles Jencks. Narrative classicism. *Art and Design*, 1987, vol.3 nos.9/10 (issue-title: British and American art), pp.45–64.

*Jim Aulich. The difficulty of living in an age of cultural decline and spiritual corruption: R.B. Kitaj 1965–1970. *Oxford Art Journal*, 1987, vol.10, no.2, pp.43–57.

R.B. Kitaj. *World art* (Beijing), 1987, no.3, pp.57–61.

*R.B. Kitaj: the Diaspora in London [interview with Michael Peppiatt]. *Art International*, Autumn 1987, no.1 (n.s.), pp.34–8.

Michael Peppiatt. Six new masters [the School of London]. *Connoisseur*, Sept. 1987, vol.217, no.907, pp.79–85.

John Griffiths. The School of London. *Art & Design*, 1988, vol.4, no.9–10, pp.6–13.

*David Cohen. R.B. Kitaj and the art of return: "My art has turned in the shadow of our infernal history". *Jewish Quarterly*, 1988, vol.35, no.2 (no.130), pp.32–6.

Carol Salus. Kitaj and Walter Benjamin. *Journal of Comparative Literature and Aesthetics*, 1988, vol.9 (special volume on The Frankfurt School Aesthetics).†

[Judith Collins]. R.B. Kitaj: 'Cecil Court, London W.C.2 (The Refugees)', 1983–4 [incl. text by R.B.K. on the work, previously publ. in Livingstone, 1985]. *The Tate Gallery 1984–86: illustrated catalogue of acquisitions*. London: Tate Gallery, 1988; pp.196–9.

*Katy Deepwell, Juliet Steyn. Readings of the Jewish artist in late Modernism [comparative studies of Mark Rothko and R.B.K.; incl. 'The loneliness of the long distance rider', on R.B.K., by Juliet Steyn]. *Art Monthly*, Feb. 1988, no.113, pp.6–9.

*Hans Platschek. Nichts passt, und doch stimmt alles. *Art: das Kunstmagazin*, May 1988, no.5, pp.32–46.

Michael Z. Wise. R.B. Kitaj and the Jewishness of Jewish art. *Midstream: a monthly Jewish review*, Dec. 1988, pp.37–9.

Alistair Hicks. *The School of London: the resurgence of contemporary painting*. Oxford: Phaidon, 1989, pp.32–7 and passim.

Alistair Hicks. *New British art in the Saatchi Collection*. London: Thames and Hudson, 1989, pp.11–12, 56–9.

Krzysztof Z. Cieszkowski. Problems in Kitaj, mostly iconographic [interview]. *Art Libraries Journal*, 1989, vol.14, no.2, pp.37–9.

Peter Rautmann. Zur Reflexion der Moderne in Kitajs Benjamin-Bild. *Die Horen: Zeitschrift für Literatur, Kunst und Kritik*, 1989, vol.34, no.1 (no.153), pp.50–70.

Hans Platschek. R.B. Kitaj. *Künstler: kritisches Lexikon der Gegenwartskunst*. Munich: Verlag Weltkunst und Bruckmann, 1989. Ausgabe 8.

Mary Rose Beaumont. Auerbach, Bacon, Kitaj [review of Marlborough group exhib.]. *Arts Review*, 13 Jan. 1989, vol.41, no.1, p.16.

Gabriel Josipovici. Kitaj's manifesto [review of *First Diasporist manifesto*]. *Modern Painters*, Summer 1989, vol.2, no.2, pp.115–6.

Brian Appleyard. School or scandal? [on the School of London]. *Sunday Times Magazine*, 9 July 1989, London section, pp.10–12.

John Russell. An American abroad undertakes a self–excavation [review of *First Diasporist manifesto*]. *New York Times*, 30 July 1989, section 2 pp.31, 33.

Agi Katz. Philosopher-painter puts us in the picture [review of *First Diapsorist manifesto*]. *Jewish Chronicle Literary Supplement*, 18 Aug. 1989, p.vii.

Ian Penman. Return to values [review of *First Diasporist manifesto*]. *Times*, 26 Aug. 1989, p.31.

Bryan Appleyard. Obsession of a black humorist: Bryan Appleyard talks to Peter Greenaway [incl. appreciation of R.B.K.'s influence on his work]. *Times*, 2 Sept. 1989, p.27.

Hilton Kramer. Memoir into myth [review of *First Diasporist manifesto*]. *Times Literary Supplement*, 8–14 Sept. 1989, no.4510, p.970.

Jed Perl. Diasporisms [review of *First Diasporist manifesto*]. *New Criterion*, Dec. 1989, vol.8, no.4, pp.51–4; repr. in Perl, *Four seasons in the art world*. San Diego; New York; London: Harcourt Brace Jovanovich, 1991, pp.315–321.

John A. Walker. Kitaj's memorial to a Socialist martyr [on 'The murder of Rosa Luxemburg',

1960; revised version of part of text of *Rosa Luxemburg and Karl Liebknecht: revolution, remembrance, representation* (exhib. catalogue), London: Pentonville Gallery, 1986]. *Studies in Iconography*, 1989–1990 [publ. 1992], vol.13, pp.258–262.

*Vivianne Barsky. "Home is where the heart is": Jewish themes in the art of R.B. Kitaj. Ezra Mendelsohn (ed.), *Art and its uses: the visual image and modern Jewish society*; symposium, ed. by Richard I. Cohen, in *Studies in Contemporary Jewry: an annual, IV*. New York; Oxford: Oxford University Press, for Institute of Contemporary Jewry, The Hebrew University of Jerusalem, 1990, pp.149–185.

Tony Godfrey. *Drawing today: draughtsmen in the Eighties*. Oxford: Phaidon; New York: Phaidon Universe, 1990, pp.57–60 and passim.

[section on proposed tapestry based on R.B.K.'s 'If not, not', 1975–6], in *'and some pictures have books': art for the new British Library*. London: British Library, 1990, pp.[10–11].

*Avram Kampf. *Chagall to Kitaj: Jewish experience in 20th century art*. London: Lund Humphries; Barbican Art Gallery, 1990, pp.105–112. (Revised ed. of *Jewish experience in 20th century art*, originally publ. in 1975; 1990 ed. publ. on occasion of exhib. at Barbican Art Gallery, London, 10 Oct. 1990 – 6 Jan. 1991).

Ulrich Krempel. Spurensuche und Vergangenheitbewältigung: Immendorff, Penck, Kitaj, Kiefer. *Funkkolleg: Moderne Kunst: Studienbegleitbrief 12*. Weinheim; Basel: Beltz Verlag (Tübingen: Deutsches Institut für Fernstudien an der Universität Tübingen), 1990; Band 29, pp.11–45 (esp. pp.32–9).

*Andrew Forge. At the Café Central [review of *First Diapsorist manifesto*]. *London Review of Books*, 22 March 1990, vol.12, no.6, pp.11–12.

Joan Stahl. [review of *First Diasporist manifesto*]. *Art Documentation*, Spring 1990, vol.9, no.1, p.27.

Carlos Jiménez. The iconographic sleuth [review of Julián Ríos, *Impresiones de Kitaj*]. *Lapiz*, April 1990, vol.8, no.67, pp.90–1.

Mary Blume. Artist R.B. Kitaj's route to Auschwitz [review of *Drancy*]. *International Herald Tribune*, 23 April 1990, p.14.

Max Ratino. I sei eremiti della Scuola di Londra. *Arte*, June 1990, vol.20, no.208, pp.68–75.

Dalya Alberge. Themes across frontiers [review of Barbican exhib.]. *Independent*, 2 Oct. 1990.

Marina Vaizey. Terrible visions in the eyes of the outsider [review of Barbican exhib.]. *Sunday Times Review*, 14 Oct. 1990, section 7, p.17.

David Cohen. The Viennese inspiration: in search of self [interview on the influence of Vienna on R.B.K.]. *R.A.: Royal Academy Magazine*, Winter 1990, no.29, pp.34–6.

David Cohen. Toward a definition [review of *First Diapsorist manifesto*]. *R.A.: Royal Academy Magazine*, Winter 1990, no.29, pp.63–9.

Robert Snell. Seeking a sense of belonging [review of Barbican exhib.]. *Times Literary Supplement*, 9–15 Nov. 1990, no.4571, p.1209.

*Dan Hofstadter. Annals of art: Dungeon masters [on the School of London]. *New Yorker*, 12 Nov. 1990, pp.53–92.

*Carol Salus. R.B. Kitaj's 'The murder of Rosa Luxemburg': a personal metaphor. *Jewish Art* (Center for Jewish Art, Hebrew University, Jerusalem), 1990–91, vols.16–17, pp.130–8.

Juliet Steyn. Which history? Chagall to Kitaj: Jewish experience in 20th century art [review of Barbican exhib.]. *Art Monthly*, Dec. 1990 / Jan. 1991, no.142, pp.22–3.

*Andrew Benjamin. Kitaj and the question of Jewish identity, in Benjamin, *Art, mimesis and the avant-garde: aspects of a philosophy of difference*. London; New York: Routledge, 1991, pp.85–97; republ. in German translation as 'Kitaj und die Frage nach der jüdischen Identität', in *Babylon: Beiträge zur jüdischen Gegenwart*, Oct. 1992, vol.10–11, pp.59–71.

Cecily Lowenthal. R.B. Kitaj: 'Cecil Court, London, W.C.2 (The Refugees)', 1983–84. Colin Naylor (ed.). *Contemporary masterworks*. Chicago; London: St James Press, 1991, pp.142–3.

*Carol Salus. R.B. Kitajs 'Go and get killed Comrade – we need a Byron in the Movement'. *Schatzkammer der deutschen Sprache, Dichtung und Geschichte*, 1991, vol.17, no.2, pp.21–9.

*Martin Roman Deppner. Bilder aus Kommentare: R.B. Kitaj und Aby Warburg. Horst Bredekamp, Michael Diers, Charlotte Schoell-Glass (hrsg.). *Aby Warburg: Akten des internationalen Symposions, Hamburg 1990*. Weinheim: V.C.H., Acta Humaniora, 1991 (Schriften des Warburg-Archivs im Kunstgeschichtlichen Seminar der Universität Hamburg, Bd.1), pp.236–260.

Hilary Robinson. Artists of a Diaspora: R.B. Kitaj interviewed by Hilary Robinson. *Alba*, Jan.–Feb. 1991, vol.1, no.1, pp.22–3.

Martin Roman Deppner, Doris von Drateln. Der Dialog mit dem Anderen: ein Einführung in den Dialog als Weltaspekt. *Kunstforum*, Jan.–Feb. 1991, no.111, pp.82–5.

*Klaus Herding. Kitaj: Weltkultur aus der Diaspora. *Kunstforum*, Jan.–Feb. 1991, no.111, pp.140–5.

*Martin Roman Deppner. Kitaj, Kiefer. *Kunstforum*, Jan.–Feb. 1991, no.111, pp.148–65.

Peter Greenaway. My great advantage over Veronese is that I can make the people move [interview, incl. discussion of R.B.K.'s 'Specimen musings of a Democrat']. *Art Newspaper*, June 1991, vol.2, no.9, pp.10–12 (ref. p.12).

British Library's £1m arts work in balance. *Evening Standard*, 2 Aug. 1991, p.17.

Andrew Lambirth. Pop goes the decade [on the Royal Academy exhib.; incl. interview]. *R.A.: Royal Academy Magazine*, Autumn 1991, no.32, pp.32–8.

Walter Grasskamp. Der Autor als Reproduktion. Ingrid und Konrad Scheurmann (hrsg.). *Für Walter Benjamin: Dokumente, Essays und ein Entwurf*. Frankfurt am Main: Suhrkamp Verlag, 1992; pp.195–209.

José Alvarez Lopera. R.B. Kitaj: 'Smyrna Greek (Nicos)' and 'A visit to London (Robert Creeley and Robert Duncan)', in *Modern masters: Thyssen-Bornemisza Museum*. Madrid: Thyssen-Bornemisza Museum, 1992, pp.54–6.

Andrew Benjamin. A guest in the house of art [interview]. *Art and Design*, March–April 1992,

vol.7 nos.3/4 (issue-title: Contemporary painting), pp.6–11.

R.B. Kitaj. *1992 yearbook of American Jewish Culture*. New York: National Foundation for Jewish Culture, 1992; p.8 (on occasion of presentation to R.B.K. of the Visual Arts Award at 3rd Annual Jewish Cultural Achievement Awards Ceremonies, New York, 14 May 1992).

*Monica Bohm-Duchen. The tribal passion: R.B. Kitaj interviewed by Monica Bohm-Duchen. *Jewish Quarterly*, Summer 1992, vol.39, no.2 (no.146), pp.17–23.

Andrew Benjamin. Kitaj und die Frage nach der jüdischen Identität. *Babylon: Beiträge zur jüdischen Gegenwart*, Oct. 1992, vol.10–11, pp.59–71; originally publ. as 'Kitaj and the question of Jewish identity' in Benjamin, *Art, mimesis and the avant-garde: aspects of a philosophy of difference*. London; New York: Routledge, 1991, pp.85–97.

Tom Lubbock. Grand designs of an unmodern man [incl. interview on the occasion of R.B.K.'s 60th birthday]. *Independent on Sunday, The Sunday Review*, 25 Oct. 1992, pp.18, 21.

Martin Roman Deppner. Das Zeigen und Verbergen der Wunden: zum sechzigsten Geburtstag des amerikanischen Malers R.B. Kitaj. *Frankfurter Allgemeine Zeitung*, 29 Oct. 1992, p.33.

Felice Maranz. Figures at an exhibition [review of Jerusalem group exhib.]. *Jerusalem Report*, 3 Dec. 1992, vol.3, no.15, pp.42–3.

*Ziva Amishai-Maisels. *Depiction and interpretation: the influence of the Holocaust on the visual arts*. Oxford: Pergamon, 1993; pp.318–23 and passim).

Candida Lycett Green. Fisher's tale [article on Sandra Fisher, on the occasion of her exhib. at Lefevre Gallery, London]. *Vogue*, May 1993, pp.150–3.

Martin Roman Deppner. Jewish School und London Diaspora. *Babylon: Beiträge zur jüdischen Gegenwart*, Oct. 1993, vol.12, pp.37–57.

Jed Perl. Figuring it out. *Vogue* (USA), Nov. 1993, pp.180–7.

David Plante. Bacon's instinct. *New Yorker*, 1 Nov. 1993, pp.93–108 [incl. extensive quotation from letter by R.B.K., assessing Bacon's stature, pp.96–7].

5 Solo exhibition catalogues

(including exhibitions selected by R.B. Kitaj)

R.B. Kitaj: pictures with commentary, pictures without commentary. London: Marlborough Fine Art, 1963. 35p., ill. 22 works. Notes and commentary by R.B.K.. Exhib. in New London Gallery, Feb. – 9 March 1963.

R.B. Kitaj. New York: Marlborough-Gerson Gallery, 1965. 32p., ill. 70 works. Incl. comments by R.B.K. and quotations from texts by others. Exhib. 7 Feb. – 6 March 1965.

Work of Ron Kitaj. Cleveland: Cleveland Museum of Art, 1967. [checklist]. 15 works. Exhib. 7 March – 2 April 1967.†

R.B. Kitaj: paintings and prints. Los Angeles: Los Angeles County Museum of Art, 1965. 35p., ill. 40 works. Introd. by Maurice Tuchman (incl. interview). Exhib. in Lytton Gallery, 11 Aug. – 12 Sept. 1965.

Kitaj: tekeningen en serigrafëen. Amsterdam: Stedelijk Museum, 1967. 8p., ill. 49 works. Introd. by John Russell (Dutch translation). Exhib. in Prentenkabinet, 11 May – 18 June 1967.

R.B. Kitaj. Berkeley: University of California, 1967. 15p., ill. 29 works. Introd. by R.B.K., 'Excerpts from an after-dinner speech delivered at London and entitled: This museum shows all kinds social disease and self abuse, young boys need it special' and 'Second part: (Mainly about using photos; re: the prints)'. Exhib. sponsored by University Art Museum and Department of Art, Berkeley; in Worth Ryder Art Gallery, 7 Oct. – 12 Nov. 1967.

R.B. Kitaj: Mahler becomes politics, Beisbol. London: Marlborough Graphics, 1967. 2p., ill. 15 works (screenprints). Exhib. 1967.

R.B. Kitaj: complete graphics 1963–69. Berlin: Galerie Mikro, 1969. 67p., ill. 52 works. Introd. by Werner Haftmann (German text with English translation); incl. text by R.B.K., 'Mainly about using photos; re: the prints' (English text; previously publ. in catalogue of 1967 Berkeley exhib.). Exhib. 10 May – 15 June 1969; travelling to Stuttgart, Württembergischer Kunstverein, July–Aug. 1969; Munich, Galerie van de Loo, 12 Sept. – 25 Oct. 1969; Düsseldorf, Galerie Niepel, 23 Jan. – 7 March 1970; Lübeck, Overbeck Gesellschaft, 22 March – 19 April 1970; Bonn, Städtische Kunstmuseum, May–June 1970.

R.B. Kitaj. Hanover: Kestner-Gesellschaft, 1970. 159p., ill. 40 works. Introd. by Wieland Schmied, 'Notizen zu R.B. Kitaj'; incl. texts by R.B.K., 'Mainly about using photos; re: the prints' (English text only; previously publ. in catalogues of 1967 Berkeley and 1969 Berlin exhibs.) and 're: The Mahler prints / A celebration and a crutch'. Incl. catalogue of complete graphics, and of important paintings not included in the exhibition. Exhib. 23 Jan. – 22 Feb. 1970; travelling to Rotterdam, Museum Boymans-van Beuningen, 28 Feb. – 5 April 1970 (Dutch-language ed. of catalogue publ. for Rotterdam show; omits R.B.K.'s text 're: The Mahler prints / A celebration and a crutch').

R.B. Kitaj: serigrafier. Høvikodden: Henie-Onstad Kunstsenter, 1970. 4p. 30 works. Exhib. 7 March – 12 April 1970.

R.B. Kitaj: pictures from an exhibition held at the Kestner-Gesellschaft, Hannover and the Boymans Museum, Rotterdam 1970. London: Marlborough Fine Art, 1970. [73]p., ill. 65 works. Exhib. in New London Gallery, 23 April – 23 May 1970.

R.B. Kitaj: Three sets. London: Marlborough Graphics, 1970. 15p., ill. 3 sets of screenprints: In our time, Struggle in the West, First series. Exhib. 1970.

R.B. Kitaj: screen prints, etchings. St Kilda (Victoria): Tolarino Galleries, 1970. 4p. 23 works. Exhib. 12–30 April 1972.

R.B. Kitaj: In our time – Mappenwerke und Grafik aus den Jahren 1969–1973. Berlin: Amerika Haus, 1973. 7p., ill. 17 works. Introd. by Mario Amaya (extracted from *Pop Art and after*, 1966); text by R.B.K., 'Über die Verbindung vom Texten und

Bildern (Fragment eines geplanten Vortrags...)'
(German trans. of 'On associating texts with
paintings', 1st publ. *Cambridge Opinion*, 1964).
Exhib. 14 April – 19 May 1973.

R.B. Kitaj: pictures. New York: Marlborough
Gallery, 1974. 40p., ill. 28 works. Introd. by
Frederic Tuten, 'On R.B. Kitaj: mainly personal,
heuristic and polemical'. Exhib. 2 – 23 Feb.
1974.

R.B. Kitaj: pictures. Edinburgh: New 57 Gallery,
1975. 16p., ill. 29 works. Exhib. 18 Aug. –
12 Sept. 1975 (Festival exhibition).

R.B. Kitaj: lithographs. New York: Petersburg
Press, 1975. [checklist]. 8 works. Exhib. Sept.
1975.†

R.B. Kitaj: The rash act A, B1, B2, B3. New York:
Petersburg Press, 1976. [checklist]. 1 work
(4 states). Exhib. March 1976.†

Ron B. Kitaj. Ljubljana: Mala Galerija, 1976. 23p.,
ill. 20 works. Text by R.B.K.: 'Mainly about using
photos; re: the prints', 1st publ. in 1967 Berkeley
catalogue; and Slovene translation, 'Predvsem o
uporati fotografij; zadeva: grafike'. Exhib.
24 March – 18 April 1976.

The human clay: an exhibition selected by R.B. Kitaj.
London: Arts Council of Great Britain, 1976.
64p.; ill. Introd. by R.B.K.. 1 unfin. work by
R.B.K. illustrated in the catalogue but not exhibited. Exhib. Hayward Gallery, London, 5–30 Aug.
1976, then travelling to Brighton, Gardner Centre Gallery, 28 Sept. – 28 Oct. 1976; Preston,
Polytechnic Art Centre, 17 Nov. – 11 Dec. 1976;
Leeds, Leeds Polytechnic, 5–27 Feb. 1977.
[R.B.K. was invited to buy works for the Art
Council Collection and to put together an exhibition consisting of these works and others on loan;
the introductory essay was the first to attempt to
define the 'School of London', a term
subsequently widely and variously used].

R.B. Kitaj: graphics. Birmingham: Ikon Gallery,
1977. [checklist]. 42 works. Exhib. Feb. 1977.†

R.B. Kitaj: pictures / Bilder. London: Marlborough
Fine Art; Zurich: Marlborough Galerie, 1977.
44p., ill. Introd. by Robert Creeley, 'Ecce Homo'
(English text, with German translation); republ.
in *Art International*, March 1979, vol.22, no.10,
pp.27–30 (English text only). 47 works. Exhib. in
London, April – 4 June 1977; in Zurich, 14 June
– 22 July 1977.

Open photography 1978 [3rd bi-annual open exhibition, selected by John Szarkowski and R.B.K.].
Nottingham: Midland Group, 1978. 129p., ill.
Introds. by John Szarkowski and R.B.K.. Exhib.
28 March – 6 May 1978; travelling to Serpentine
Gallery, London, 20 May – 11 June 1978, then
touring.

*R.B. Kitaj: fifty drawings and pastels, six oil
paintings*. New York: Marlborough Gallery, 1979.
64p., ill. Introd. by Timothy Hyman, 'R.B. Kitaj:
decadence and renewal'. 56 works. Exhib.
31 March – 28 April 1979.

*The artist's eye: an exhibition selected by R.B. Kitaj at
the National Gallery, London*. London: National
Gallery, 1980. 20p., ill. Introd. by R.B.K.. 2
works by R.B.K.. Exhib. 21 May – 21 July 1980.
[R.B.K. was the 4th artist invited to select works
from the collections of the National Gallery for an
exhibition there; he was invited to include two
works by himself – 'The Orientalist', 1975, and
'Degas', 1980].

R.B. Kitaj: pastels and drawings. London: Marlborough Fine Art, 1980. 59p., ill. 48 works. Introd.
by Stephen Spender, 'R.B. Kitaj'. Exhib. 8 Oct. –
7 Nov. 1980.

R.B. Kitaj. Washington: Smithsonian Institution
Press, 1981. 176p., ill. 108 works. Curated by
Joe Shannon. Foreword by Abram Lerner, pp.7–9;
texts by John Ashbery, 'Hunger and love in their
variations', pp.11–17 (repr. as 'R.B. Kitaj; hunger
and love', *Art in America*, June 1982, vol.70,
no.1, pp.130–6; and as 'R.B. Kitaj', in Ashbery,
ed. David Bergman, *Reported sightings: art chronicles, 1957–1987*. Manchester: Carcanet, 1989,
pp.299–308); Joe Shannon, 'The allegorists: Kitaj
and the viewer', pp.19–36; Jane Livingston, 'R.B.
Kitaj in the larger picture', pp.37–40; and Timothy Hyman, 'A return to London', pp.41–9 (interview; previously publ. in *London Magazine*, Feb.
1980, vol.19, no.11, pp.15–27); chronology;
extensive list of exhibitions and bibliography,
compiled by Anna Brooke. Exhib. Washington,
Hirshhorn Museum and Sculpture Garden, 17
Sept. – 15 Nov. 1981; travelling to Cleveland
Museum of Art, 15 Dec. 1981 – 25 Jan. 1982,
and (with additional works) to Städtische Kunsthalle Düsseldorf, 5 Feb. – 21 March 1982.
Repr. (without Foreword and chronology) as
Kitaj: paintings, drawings, pastels. London: Thames
and Hudson, 1983 (and reprinted 1986). (168p.;
all pages repaginated). German ed., *R.B. Kitaj*.
Düsseldorf: Kunsthalle Düsseldorf, 1982, 182p.
Incl. additional text by Jürgen Harten, 'Bonjour,
Mister Kitaj', pp.7–8 (all subsequent pages repagi-
nated).

R.B. Kitaj. London: Marlborough Fine Art, 1985.
76p. + 2-leaf insert (= pp.II–III), ill. 75 works.
Incl. text by R.B.K., 'A passion', pp.II–III. Exhib.
7 Nov. – Dec. 1985. Travelling to New York,
Marlborough Gallery, 6–29 March 1986.

R.B. Kitaj: Mahler becomes politics, Beisbol
[screen prints 1964–7]. Hamburg: Hamburger
Kunsthalle, 1990. Text by Martin Roman Deppner, 'Anigma und Rebus: die "Flucht der Bilder"
in Kitajs Mahler–Zyklus'. 15 works. Exhib. 9 Nov.
1990 – 3 Feb. 1991.

6 Group exhibition catalogues

Young Contemporaries 1958. London: Young Contemporaries, 1958. 1 work. Exhib. in R.B.A.
Galleries, 19 Feb. – 10 March 1958.

Young Contemporaries 1960. London: Young Contemporaries, 1960. 4 works. Introd. by Peter
Cresswell. Exhib. in R.B.A. Galleries, 14 March –
2 April 1960.

Young Contemporaries 1961. London: Young Contemporaries, 1961. 4 works. Introd. by Lawrence
Alloway. Exhib. in Royal College of Art,
8 – 25 Feb. 1961.

Recent developments in painting IV. London: Arthur
Tooth & Son, 1961. 2 works. Exhib. 3 – 21 Oct.
1961.

John Moores Liverpool Exhibition. Liverpool: Walker
Art Gallery, 1961. 1 work. Exhib. 16 Nov. 1961
– 14 Jan. 1962.

*Prizewinners of the John Moores Liverpool Exhibition
1961*. London: Institute of Contemporary Arts,
1962. 1 work. Exhib. 29 March – 28 April 1962.

*Kompas 2: hedendaagse schilderkunst uit Londen /
contemporary paintings in London*. Eindhoven:
Stedelijk Van Abbemuseum, 1962. 5 works.
Introd. by Ronald Alley. Exhib. 21 Oct. – 9 Dec.
1962.

*Towards art?: the contribution of the R.C.A. to the
Fine Arts 1952–62*. London: Royal College of Art,
1962. 2 works. Introd. by Carel Weight. Exhib.
7 Nov. – 1 Dec. 1962.

British painting in the Sixties. London: Contemporary Art Society, 1963. 3 works. Introd. by John
Sainsbury, etc. Exhib. in Tate Gallery and
Whitechapel Art Gallery, London, 1–30 June
1963.

*Premio Internacional de Pintura, Instituto Torcuato
Di Tella, 1963*. Buenos Aires: Museo de Artes
Visuales del Instituto Torcuato Di Tella, 1963.
5 works. Text by RKB, 'De los textos parafrasis,
comentarios, listas, notas y otro material manuscrito o impreso asociados con los cuadros', p.24.
Exhib. 12 Aug. – 8 Sept. 1963.

*Dunn International: an exhibition of contemporary
painting sponsored by the Sir James Dunn Foundation*.
Fredericton: Beaverbrook Art Gallery, 1963. 1
work. Exhib. 7 Sept. – 6 Oct. 1963; travelling to
London, Tate Gallery, 15 Nov. – 22 Dec. 1963.

John Moores Liverpool Exhibition. Liverpool: Walker
Art Gallery, 1963. 1 work. Exhib. 14 Nov. 1963
– 12 Jan. 1964.

Painting & sculpture of a decade: 54–64. London:
Calouste Gulbenkian Foundation, 1964. 4 works.
Introd. by Alan Bowness, &c. Exhib. in Tate
Gallery, 22 April – 28 June 1964.

Britische Malerei der Gegenwart. Düsseldorf: Kunstverein für die Rheinlande und Westfalen, 1964.
Exhib. 25 May – 5 July 1964.

Nieuwe Realisten. The Hague: Haags Gemeentemu-
seum, 1964. Introd. by Jasia Reichardt, 1964.
Exhib. 24 June – 31 Aug. 1964.

*Contemporary British painting and sculpture from the
collection of the Albright–Knox Art Gallery and
special loans*. Buffalo: Albright–Knox Art Gallery,
1964. 1 work. Exhib. 27 Oct. – 29 Nov. 1964.

The English eye. New York: Marlborough-Gerson
Gallery, 1965. 2 works. Introd. by Robert
Melville, Bryan Robertson. Exhib. Nov.–Dec.
1965.

John Moores Liverpool Exhibition. Liverpool: Walker
Art Gallery, 1965. 1 work. Exhib. 18 Nov. 1965
– 16 Jan. 1966.

*1965 annual exhibition of contemporary American
painting*. New York: Whitney Museum of American Art, 1965. 1 work. Exhib. 8 Dec. 1965 –
30 Jan. 1966.

Five Americans in Britain. London: U.S.I.S., American Embassy, 1966. 10 works. Introd. by Max
Wykes-Joyce. Exhib. 20 April – 6 May 1966.

John Moores Liverpool Exhibition 6. Liverpool:
Walker Art Gallery, 1967. 1 work. Exhib. 23
Nov. 1967 – 21 Jan. 1968.

Britische Kunst heute. Hamburg: Kunstverein,
1968. 15 works. Introd. by Hans Platte. Exhib.
30 March – 12 May 1968.

From Kitaj to Blake: non-abstract artists in Britain.
Oxford: Bear Lane Gallery, 1968. 6 works. Exhib.
8 – 29 June 1968.

Peintres européens d'aujourd'hui / European painters today. Paris: Musée des Arts Décoratifs; Mead Corporation, 1968. 1 work. Introd. by François Mathey. Exhib. 27 Sept. – 17 Nov. 1968; travelling to New York, Washington, Chicago, Atlanta and Dayton OH (to Dec. 1969).

A selection of 20th century British art. London: Marlborough Fine Art, 1969. 8 works. Exhib. in Cunard Marlborough London Gallery, on board Queen Elizabeth 2, from 2 May 1969.

Grafiek van Gene Davis, R.B. Kitaj en E. Paolozzi. Rotterdam: Museum Boymans-van Beuningen, 1969. 12 works. Exhib. 15 June – 3 Aug. 1969.

Information: Joe Tilson, Peter Phillips, Allen Jones, Eduardo Paolozzi, Ronald B. Kitaj, Richard Hamilton. Karlsruhe: Badischer Kunstverein, 1969. 13 works. Introd. by Peter F. Althaus. Exhib. 1 Aug. – 14 Sept. 1969.

Contemporary British art. Tokyo, National Museum of Modern Art, 1970. 3 works. Introd. by Andrew Causey. Exhib. 9 Sept. – 25 Oct. 1970.

Kunst und Politik. Basel: Kunsthalle, 1971. 5 works. Introd. by G. Bussmann, &c. Exhib. 24 Jan. – 21 Feb. 1971.

A report on the Art and Technology Program of the Los Angeles County Museum of Art, 1967–1971. Los Angeles: Los Angeles County Museum of Art, 1971. Text by Maurice Tuchman [repr. in *Studio International*, May 1971, vol.181, no.932, pp.173–180], Jane Livingston; text [on R.B.K.'s residency at the Lockheed plant at Burbank, 1969] by Gail R. Scott. Exhib. 14 May – 29 Aug. 1971.

Celebrate Ohio: fiftieth anniversary exhibition. Akron OH: Akron Art Institute, 1971. 7 works. Introd. by Alfred Radloff. Exhib. 27 Sept. – 7 Nov. 1971.

Dine, Kitaj: a two man exhibition. Cincinnati: Cincinnati Art Museum, 1973. 28 works. Introd. by Richard J. Boyle; texts by both artists. Exhib. 12 April – 13 May 1973.

Selected European masters of the 19th and 20th centuries. London: Marlborough Fine Art, 1973. 1 work. Exhib. Summer 1973.

An exhibition of contemporary British painters and sculptors. London: Lefebre Gallery, 1974. 2 works. Exhib. 18 April – 18 May 1974.

Drawings of people: an exhibition of drawings selected for the Arts Council by Patrick George. London: Arts Council of Great Britain, 1975. 2 works. Introd. by Patrick George. Touring exhib.

European painting in the Seventies: new work by sixteen artists. Los Angeles: Los Angeles County Museum of Art, 1975. 4 works. Introd. by Maurice Tuchman; statements by the artists (incl. R.B.K., p.73). Exhib. 30 Sept. – 23 Nov. 1975; travelling to St. Louis Art Museum, 16 March – 9 May 1976, and Madison WI, Elvehjem Art Center, 8 June – 1 Aug. 1976.

Arte inglese oggi 1960–76. Milan: Electa Editrice, 1976. 7 works. Introd. by Norbert Lynton, Richard Cork. Incl. text by R.B.K. (in English and in Italian trans.), p.128. Organised by Commune di Milano and British Council, London. Exhib. Milan, Palazzo Reale, Feb.–March 1976.

Pop Art in England: Anfänge einer neuen Figuration 1947–63 / Beginnings of a new figuration 1947–63. Hamburg: Kunstverein Hamburg, 1976. 5 works. Text by Uwe M. Schneede. Exhib. 7 Feb. –

21 March 1976; travelling to Munich and York (to July 1976).

Petersburg Press, London, 1968–1976. Paris: Galerie de France, 1976. 3 works. Introd. by Paul Cornwall-Jones, Véra Lindsay. Exhib. April–June 1976.

The two hundred and eighth Royal Academy of Arts summer exhibition. London: Royal Academy of Arts, 1976. 1 work. Exhib. 8 May – 1 Aug. 1976.

Peter Blake, Richard Hamilton, David Hockney, R.B. Kitaj, Eduardo Paolozzi. Rotterdam: Museum Boymans-van Beuningen, 1976. 19 works. Introd. by Toni del Renzio. Exhib. 20 May – 4 July 1976.

'Just what is it ...': Pop Art in England 1947–63. London: Arts Council of Great Britain, 1976. 6 works. Exhib. in York Art Gallery, 29 May – 4 July 1976.

American artists in Britain. Hull: University of Hull, Department of American Studies; North Humberside Area Centre, 1976. 3 works. Exhib. 2 – 19 Nov. 1976.

1977 Hayward Annual: current British art. London: Arts Council of Great Britain, 1977. 12 works. Introd. by Michael Compton. Exhib. (part two) in Hayward Gallery, London, 20 July – 4 Sept. 1977.

'The human clay': la figure humaine dans l'art britannique contemporain. Charleroi: Palais des Beaux-Arts, 1977. 1 work. Introd. by Robert Rousseau. Exhib. 11 Dec. 1977 – 8 Jan. 1978.

R.B. Kitaj: Grand Palais: FIAC 78: Marlborough. New York: Marlborough Gallery, 1978. Exhib. 1978.

Narrative paintings: figurative art of two generations. Bristol: Arnolfini, 1979. 2 works. Introd. by Timothy Hyman. Exhib. 1 Sept. – 20 Oct. 1979; travelling to London, Institute of Contemporary Arts, 26 Oct. – 25 Nov. 1979; Stoke-on-Trent, City Museum and Art Gallery, 5 Jan. – 2 Feb. 1980; Edinburgh, Fruit Market Gallery, 9 Feb. – 29 March 1980.

This knot of life: paintings and drawings by British artists. Venice CA: L.A. Louver Gallery, 1979. 6 works. Introd. by Peter Goulds. Exhib. (Part II) 27 Nov. – 22 Dec. 1979.

Kelpra Studio: an exhibition to commemorate the Rose and Chris Prater Gift. London: Tate Gallery, 1980. 16 works. Introd. by Pat Gilmour [ref. pp.32–4]. Exhib. 9 July – 25 Aug. 1980.

Twenty American artists. San Francisco: San Francisco Museum of Modern Art, 1980. 5 works. Introd. by Harry T. Hopkins. Exhib. 24 July – 7 Sept. 1980.

American drawing in black & white: 1970–1980. New York: Brooklyn Museum, 1980. 1 work. Introd. by Gene Baro. Exhib. 22 Nov. 1980 – 18 Jan. 1981.

A new spirit in painting. London: Royal Academy of Arts, 1981. 5 works. Introd. by Christos M. Joachimedes, Norman Rosenthal, Nicholas Serota. Exhib. 15 Jan. – 18 March 1981.

The Michael and Dorothy Blankfort Collection. Los Angeles: Los Angeles County Museum of Art, 1982. 17 works. Introd. by Maurice Tuchman, Michael Blankfort. Exhib. 1 April – 13 June 1982.

Exhibition of work by newly elected members and recipients of honors and awards. New York: American Academy and Institute of Arts and Letters, 1982. 6 works. Exhib. 19 May – 13 June 1982.

Britain salutes New York: paintings and sculpture by contemporary British artists. New York: Marlborough Gallery, 1983. 6 works. Exhib. 9 April – 3 May 1983.

Acquisition priorities: aspects of postwar painting in Europe. New York: Solomon R. Guggenheim Museum, 1983. 1 work. Exhib. 20 May – 4 Sept. 1983.

International masters of contemporary figuration. Tokyo: Marlborough Fine Art, 1984. 1 work. Exhib. 20 Feb. – 7 April 1984.

The hard-won image: traditional method and subject in recent British art. London: Tate Gallery, 1984. 5 works. Text by Richard Morphet. Exhib. 4 July – 9 Sept. 1984.

The British art show: old allegiances and new directions 1979–1984. London: Orbis; Arts Council of Great Britain, 1984. 1 work. Introd. by Jon Thompson, Alexander Moffatt, Marjorie Allthorpe-Guyton. Exhib. City of Birmingham Museum and Art Gallery, 2 Nov. – 22 Dec. 1984; Edinburgh, Royal Scottish Academy, 19 Jan. – 24 Feb. 1985; Sheffield, Mappin Art Gallery, 16 March – 4 May 1985; Southampton Art Gallery, 18 May – 30 June 1985.

Master drawings 1879–1984. New York: Janie C. Lee Master Drawings, 1984. 1 work. Exhib. 13 Nov. 1984.

The proper study: contemporary figurative paintings from Britain. London: British Council, 1984. 6 works. Introd. by Norbert Lynton; introd. to work of R.B.K. by Marco Livingstone, p.89. Exhib. in Delhi, Lalit Kala Akademi, 1 – 31 Dec. 1984; Bombay, Jehangir Nicholson Museum of Modern Art, 1 – 28 Feb. 1985.

The two hundred and seventeenth Royal Academy of Arts summer exhibition. London: Royal Academy of Arts, 1985. 1 work. Exhib. 1 June – 25 Aug. 1985.

Charcoal drawings 1880–1985. Houston: Janie C. Lee Gallery, 1985. 1 work. Exhib. Oct. – Nov. 1985.

Studies of the nude. London: Marlborough Fine Art, 1986. 2 works. Introd. by William Packer. Exhib. 19 March – 2 May. 1986.

The two hundred and eighteenth Royal Academy of Arts summer exhibition. London: Royal Academy of Arts, 1986. 1 work. Exhib. 31 May – 24 Aug. 1986.

Artist and model. Manchester: Whitworth Art Gallery, 1986. 6 works. Text by Julian Tomlin. Exhib. 23 May – 19 July 1986.

One hundred works on paper from the collection of the Israel Museum, Jerusalem. Jerusalem: Israel Museum, 1986. 1 work. Text by Meira Perry-Lehmann. Exhib. June 1986.

Rosa Luxemburg and Karl Liebknecht: revolution, remembrance, representation. London: Pentonville Gallery, 1986. 1 work. Text by John A. Walker (esp. pp.38–41). Exhib. 11 Oct. – 22 Nov. 1986.

British art of the 20th century: the Modern Movement. Munich: Prestel-Verlag, 1987. 4 works. Text ed. by Susan Compton; incl. essay by Norman Rosenthal, 'Three painters of this time:

Hodgkin, Kitaj and Morley', pp.382–4. Exhib. in London, Royal Academy of Arts, 15 Jan. – 5 April 1987; travelling to Staatsgalerie Stuttgart.

Current affairs: British painting and sculpture in the 1980s. Oxford: Museum of Modern Art, 1987. 3 works. Introd. by Lewis Biggs, David Elliott, Andrew Brighton. Exhib. 1 – 29 March 1987; toured by British Council to Budapest, Prague and Warsaw (to Oct. 1987).

A School of London: six figurative painters. London: British Council, 1987. 12 works. Introd. by Michael Peppiatt. Exhib. in Oslo, Kunstnernes Hus, 9 May – 14 June 1987; Humlebaek, Louisiana Museum of Modern Art, 27 June – 16 Aug. 1987; Venice, Museo d'Arte Moderna, Ca' Pesaro, 5 Sept. – 18 Oct. 1987; Kunstmuseum Düsseldorf, 6 Nov. 1987 – 10 Jan. 1988.

The two hundred and nineteenth Royal Academy of Arts summer exhibition. London: Royal Academy of Arts, 1987. 1 work. Exhib. 6 June – 23 Aug. 1987.

Art of our time: the Saatchi Collection. Edinburgh: Royal Scottish Academy, 1987. 3 works. Introd. by Alastair Hicks. Exhib. 7 Aug. – 5 Sept. 1987.

Art history: artists look at contemporary Britain. London: South Bank Board, 1987. 1 work. Introd. by Richard Cork. Exhib. in Hayward Gallery, London, 29 Oct. 1987 – 10 Jan. 1988.

British season: Joe Tilson and R.B. Kitaj: A change of He(art). Canberra: Australian National Gallery, 1987. 64 works. Text by Pat Gilmour, Cathy Leahy, Jane Kinsman. Exhib. 19 Dec. 1987 – 13 March 1988.

The British picture. Venice CA: L.A. Louver, 1988. 2 works. Introd. by Catherine Lampert, William Feaver. Marina Vaizey. Exhib. 5 Feb. – 5 March 1988.

Exhibition Road: painters at the Royal College of Art. London: Phaidon; Christie's; Royal College of Art, 1988. 3 works. Text ed. by Paul Huxley; incl. interview with Robert Cumming, p.90. Exhib. March–April 1988.

The Sunday Times Mother & Child exhibition at the Lefevre Gallery in aid of Birthright. London: Sunday Times, 1988. 1 work. Exhib. 11–26 May 1988.

Die Spur des Anderen: fünf jüdische Künstler aus London mit fünf deutschen Künstlern aus Hamburg im Dialog. Hamburg: Heine Haus, 1988. 2 works. Text ed. by Martin Roman Deppner; incl. text by R.B.K., 'Letter from London'/'Brief aus London' (English text with German translation), pp.8–12. Exhib. 30 Sept. – 22 Oct. 1988.

Golem!: danger, deliverance and art. New York: Jewish Museum, 1988. 1 work. Text ed. by Emily D. Bliski. Exhib. 20 Nov. 1988 – 2 April 1989.

On view: new paintings: Auerbach, Bacon, Kitaj. London: Marlborough Fine Art, 1989. 1 work. Exhib. 6 Jan. – 10 Feb. 1989.

Blasphemies, ecstasies, cries. London: Serpentine Gallery, 1989. 1 work. Introd. by Andrew Brighton, Andrea Schlieker. Exhib. 18 Jan. – 26 Feb. 1989; travelling to Norwich and Llandudno (to July 1989).

The two hundred and twenty-first Royal Academy of Arts summer exhibition. London: Royal Academy of Arts, 1989. 2 works. Exhib. 10 June – 20 Aug. 1989.

School of London: works on paper. London: Odette Gilbert Gallery, 1989. 1 work. Introd. by Alistair Hicks. Exhib. 20 Sept. – 4 Nov. 1989.

Master drawings, 1859–1989. New York: Janie C Lee Master Drawings, 1989. 1 work. Exhib. Oct.–Dec. 1989.

Glasgow's Great British exhibition. Glasgow: Glasgow Museums and Art Galleries, 1990. 2 works. Introd. by Julian Spalding, Andrew Patrizio. Exhib. 27 March – 9 May 1990.

The two hundred and twenty–second Royal Academy of Arts summer exhibition. London: Royal Academy of Arts, 1990. 2 works. Exhib. 9 June – 19 Aug. 1990.

Chagall to Kitaj: Jewish experience in 20th century art. London: Lund Humphries; Barbican Art Gallery, 1990. 4 works. Text by Avram Kampf (revised ed. of book originally publ. in 1975). Exhib. in Barbican Art Gallery, London, 10 Oct. 1990 – 6 Jan. 1991.

Tribute to Peter Fuller. Bath: Beaux Arts, 1990. 1 work. Exhib. 20 Oct. – 20 Nov. 1990.

The two hundred and twenty-third Royal Academy of Arts summer exhibition. London: Royal Academy of Arts, 1991. 1 work. Exhib. 9 June – 18 Aug. 1991.

Pop Art. London: Weidenfeld & Nicolson; Royal Academy of Arts, 1991. 3 works. Text ed. by Marco Livingstone. Exhib. London, Royal Academy of Arts, 13 Sept. – 15 Dec. 1991; Cologne, Museum Ludwig, 23 Jan. – 19 April 1992; Madrid, Centro d'Arte Reina Sofia, 16 June – 14 Sept. 1992.

Da Bacon a oggi: l'outsider nella figurazione britannica / From Bacon to now: the outsider in British figuration. Milan: Electa, 1991. 3 works. Introd. by Keith Patrick; text by R.B.K., 'The School of London', p.10 (with Italian translation, 'La Scuola di Londra', p.11). Exhib. in Florence, Palazzo Vecchio, Sala d'Arme, 7 Dec. 1991 – 16 Feb. 1992.

The two hundred and twenty-fourth Royal Academy of Arts summer exhibition. London: Royal Academy of Arts, 1992. 1 work. Exhib. 7 June – 14 Aug. 1992.

Le portrait dans l'art contemporain 1945–1992. Nice: Musée d'Art Moderne et d'Art Contemporain, 1992. 1 work. Exhib. 3 July – 29 Sept. 1992.

British figurative painting of the 20th century. Jerusalem: Israel Museum, 1992. 2 works. Introd. by Yigael Zalmona. Exhib. Nov. 1992 – Feb. 1993.

The sixties art scene in London. London: Phaidon; Barbican Art Gallery, 1993. 2 works. Text by David Mellor. Exhib. 11 March – 13 June 1993.

The two hundred and twenty-fifth Royal Academy of Arts summer exhibition. London: Royal Academy of Arts, 1993. 2 works. Exhib. 6 June – 15 Aug. 1993.

Seven British painters: selected masters of Post-War British art. London: Marlborough Fine Art, 1993. 3 works. Exhib. 18 June – 4 Sept. 1993.

Arikha, Auerbach, Kitaj: obra reciente. Madrid: Galeria Marlborough, 1993. 7 works. Introd. by Francisco Calvo Serraller. Exhib. Sept.–Oct. 1993.

Åstrup Fearnley Museet for Moderne Kunst: Apningsutstilling. Oslo: Astrup Fearnley Museet for Moderne Kunst, 1993. 31 works. Text by Gunnar Sörensen (ref. pp.46–51, 73–7). Exhib. Oct. 1993 – April 1994.

The portrait now. London: National Portrait Gallery, 1993. 1 work. Introd. by Robin Gibson. Exhib. 19 Nov. 1993 – 6 Feb. 1994.

Lenders

Diane L. Ackerman 42
Albright-Knox Art Gallery Buffalo, New York
15
Astrup Fearnley Museum of Modern Art,
Oslo 17, 36, 56, 69, 71
High Museum of Art, Atlanta, Georgia 2

Mrs Edwin Bergman 37, 47
Staatliche Museen zu Berlin, Nationalgalerie
16
Michael and Dorothy Blankfort Collection
14
Museum Boymans-van Beuningen,
Rotterdam 30
Trustees of the British Museum, London 48

Cincinnati Art Museum 11
The Cleveland Museum of Art 58
Nan and Gene Corman 26, 70

Scottish National Gallery of Modern Art,
Edinburgh 29, 49

Sandra Fisher 113
Fondation du Judaisme Français, Paris 76

Hamburger Kunsthalle, Hamburg 10

Mrs David G. Kangesser 61
The artist 3, 4, 5, 9, 13, 18, 31, 38, 39,
44, 46, 50, 52, 53, 60, 62, 63, 74, 91
Dominie Kitaj 35

Mr and Mrs Francis Lloyd 19, 84, 86
National Portrait Gallery, London 77
Ludwig Collection, Aix-la-Chapelle 21

Marlborough International Fine Art 23
Marlborough Fine Art (London) Ltd 72, 87,
92, 93, 94, 95, 96, 97, 98, 99, 100, 101,
103, 104, 106, 107, 108, 110, 112,
114, 115
The Metropolitan Museum of Art 66, 85
Achim Moeller Fine Art, New York 24
The Museum of Modern Art, New York 12

The Foundation FOR ART and The National
Museum of Contemporary Art, Oslo 64

Private collections 1, 8, 25, 27, 28, 32, 40,
41, 43, 54, 57, 59, 67, 73, 75, 78, 80,
81, 82, 83, 89, 90, 105, 111

Saatchi Collection, London 79
Dr and Mrs Jerry Sherman 88

Tate Gallery 6, 22, 33, 51, 65, 102
Fundación Colección Thyssen-Bornemisza,
Madrid 34, 45

Whitney Museum of American Art, New
York 68
Colin St John Wilson 7, 20
Richard Wookey, Toronto, Canada 109

Works not exhibited:
21, 25, 43, 45, 55, 77, 87, 115

Photographic Credits

Albright-Knox Art Gallery, Buffalo
Arts Council Collection, London
Astrup Fearnley Museum of Modern Art,
    Oslo
Staatliche Museen zu Berlin, Nationalgalerie
Museum Boymans-van Beuningen,
    Rotterdam
British Museum, London
Chester Brummel
Cincinnati Art Museum
Geoffrey Clements
Cleveland Museum of Art
A.C. Cooper Ltd
Prudence Cuming Associates Limited
Kunstmuseum, Düsseldorf
Thomas Gibson Fine Art
Hamburger Kunsthalle
High Museum of Art, Atlanta
Israel Museum, Jerusalem
Jacques Lathion
National Portrait Gallery, London
Los Angeles County Museum of Art
Ludwig Museum Koblenz
    Deutschherrenhaus

Museo Nacional Centro de Arte Reina Sofia,
    Madrid
Marlborough Fine Art (London) Ltd
Minneapolis Institute of Arts
Metropolitan Museum of Art, New York
Achim Moeller Fine Art, New York
Henry Moore Fondation
Museum of Modern Art, New York
Nasjonalgalleriert Oslo
Antonia Reeve
Tore H. Royneland
Scottish National Gallery of Modern Art,
    Edinburgh
Sotheby's New York
Tate Gallery
Fundación Colección Thyssen-Bornemisza,
    Madrid
O. Væring
Elke Walford
Whitney Museum of American Art,
    New York

Copyright Credits

Illustrated works of art are copyright as follows:

R.B. Kitaj © The artist 1994
Willem De Kooning, Pablo Picasso © DACS 1994
Sandra Fisher © The artist 1994
David Hockney © Tradhart 1994
Leonard McComb © The artist 1994
Henry Moore © The Henry Moore Foundation 1994

Ways of Giving to the Tate Gallery

The Tate Gallery attracts funds from the private sector to support its programme of activities in London, Liverpool and St Ives. Support is raised from the business community, individuals, trusts and foundations, and includes sponsorships, donations, bequests and gifts of works of art. The Tate Gallery is recognised as a charity under Inland Revenue reference number x780551.

Donations

There are a variety of ways through which you can make a donation to the Tate Gallery.

Donations All donations, however small, will be gratefully received and acknowledged by the Tate Gallery.

Covenants A Deed of Covenant, which must be taken out for a minimum of four years, will enable the Tate Gallery to claim back tax on your charitable donation. For example, a covenant for £100 per annum will allow the Gallery to claim a further £33 at present tax rates.

Gift-Aid For individuals and companies wishing to make donations of £250 and above, Gift-Aid allows the gallery to claim back tax on your charitable donation. In addition, if you are a higher rate taxpayer you will be able to claim tax relief on the donation. A Gift-Aid form and explanatory leaflet can be sent to you if you require further information.

Bequests You may wish to remember the Tate Gallery in your will or make a specific donation In Memoriam. A bequest may take the form of either a specific cash sum, a residual proportion of your estate or a specific item of property, such as a work of art. Certain tax advantages can be obtained by making a legacy in favour of the Tate Gallery. Please check with the Tate Gallery when you draw up your will that it is able to accept your bequest.

American Fund for the Tate Gallery The American Fund was formed in 1986 to facilitate gifts of works of art, donations and bequests to the Tate Gallery from the United States residents. It receives full tax exempt status from the IRS.

Individual Membership Programmes

FRIENDS OF THE TATE GALLERY

Share in the life of the Gallery and contribute towards the purchase of important works of art for the Tate.

Privileges include free unlimited entry with a guest to exhibitions; *tate: the art magazine*; previews, events and art courses; 'Late at the Tate' evening openings; exclusive Friends Room. Annual rates range from £22 to £30.

Tate Friends St Ives offers a local events programme and full membership of the Friends of the Tate Gallery.

FELLOWS

The Fellows support the acquisition of works of art for the British and Modern Collections of the Tate Gallery. Privileges include invitations to Tate Gallery receptions, curatorial talks and behind-the-scene tours, complimentary catalogues and full membership of the Friends. Annual membership ranges from £100 to £500.

The Friends of the Tate Gallery are supported by Tate & Lyle PLC.

Further details on the Friends and Fellows in London and St Ives may be obtained from:

Friends of the Tate Gallery
Tate Gallery
Millbank
London SW1P 4RG

Tel: 071-887 8752

PATRONS OF THE TATE GALLERY

The Patrons of British Art support British painting and sculpture from the Elizabethan period through to the early twentieth century in the Tate Gallery's collection. They encourage knowledge and awareness of British art by providing an opportunity to study Britain's cultural heritage.

The Patrons of New Art support contemporary art in the Tate Gallery's collection. They promote a lively and informed interest in contemporary art and are associated with the Turner Prize, one of the most prestigious awards for the visual arts.

Annual membership of the Patrons ranges from £350 to £750, and funds the purchase of works of art for the Tate Gallery's collection.

Privileges for both groups include invitations to Tate Gallery receptions, an opportunity to sit on the Patrons' acquisitions committees, special events including visits to private and corporate collections and complimentary catalogues of Tate Gallery exhibitions.

Further details on the Patrons may be obtained from:

The Development Office
Tate Gallery
Millbank
London SW1P 4RG

Tel: 071-887 8743

Corporate Membership Programme

Membership of the Tate Gallery's Corporate Membership Programme oVers companies outstanding value-for-money and provides opportunities for every employee to enjoy a closer knowledge of the Gallery, its collection and exhibitions.

Membership benefits are specifically geared to business needs and include private views for company employees, free and discount admission to exhibitions, discount in the Gallery shop, out-of-hours Gallery visits, behind-the-scenes tours, exclusive use of the Gallery for corporate entertainment, invitations to VIP events, copies of Gallery literature and acknowledgement in Gallery publications.

TATE GALLERY CORPORATE MEMBERS

Partners
ADT Group PLC
The British Petroleum Company plc
Ernst & Young
Glaxo Holdings p.l.c.
Manpower PLC
Unilever

Associates
BUPA
Drivers Jonas
Global Asset Management
Herbert Smith
Lazard Brothers & Co Limited
Linklaters & Paines
Merrill Lynch
Refco Overseas Ltd
Salomon Brothers
Schroders plc
S.G. Warburg Group
THORN EMI

Corporate sponsorship

The Tate Gallery works closely with sponsors to ensure that their business interests are well served, and has a reputation for developing imaginative fund-raising initiatives. Sponsorships can range from a few thousand pounds to considerable investment in long-term programmes; small businesses as well as multi-national corporations have benefited from the high profile and prestige of Tate Gallery sponsorship.

Opportunities available at Tate Gallery London, Liverpool and St Ives include exhibitions (some also tour the UK), education, conservation and research programmes, audience development, visitor access to the Collection and special events. Sponsorship benefits include national and regional publicity, targeted marketing to niche audiences, exclusive corporate entertainment, employee benefits and acknowledgment in Tate Gallery publications.

TATE GALLERY LONDON: PRINCIPAL CORPORATE SPONSORS
(alphabetical order)

Barclays Bank PLC
  1991, *Constable*
The British Land Company PLC
  1993, *Ben Nicholson**
The British Petroleum Company plc
  1990–4, *New Displays*

Channel 4 Television
  1991–3, The Turner Prize
Daimler-Benz AG
  1991, Max Ernst
Ernst & Young
  1994, Picasso: Sculptor/Painter*
Pearson plc
  1992–5, Elizabethan Curator Post
Reed Elsevier
  1994, Whistler
Tate & Lyle PLC
  1991–5, Friends Relaunch
  Marketing Programme
Volkswagen
  1991–4, The Turner Scholarships

TATE GALLERY LONDON:
CORPORATE SPONSORS
(alphabetical order)

ABN AMRO Bank
  1994, Turner's Holland
AFAA, Association Française d'Action
Artistique, Ministère de AVaires
Etrangères, The Cultural Service of
the French Embassy, London
  1993, Paris Post War: Art and
  Existentialism 1945–55
Agfa Graphic Systems Group
  1992, Turner: The Fifth Decade*
Beck's
  1994, Rebecca Horn
  1992, Otto Dix
Blackwall Green Ltd
  1991, International Conference on
  the Packing and Transportation of
  Paintings
  1994, Frames Conservation
Borghi Transporti Spedizioni SPA
  1991, International Conference on
  the Packing and Transportation of
  Paintings
Calor Gas
  1994, Turner's Holland
James Bourlets & Sons
  1991, International Conference on
  the Packing and Transportation of
  Paintings
Clifton Nurseries
  1991–4, Christmas Tree (in kind)
D'Art Kunstspedition GmbH
  1991, International Conference on
  the Packing and Transportation of
  Paintings
Deutsche Bank A.G.
  1994, Rebecca Horn
Digital Equipment Co Limited
  1991–2, From Turner's Studio
  1993, Library and Archive
  Computerisation
Alfred Dunhill Limited
  1993, Sir Edward Burne-Jones:
  Watercolours and Drawings
Gander and White Shipping Ltd
  1991, International Conference on
  the Packing and Transportation of
  Paintings
Gerlach Art Packers & Shippers
  1991, International Conference on
  the Packing and Transportation of
  Paintings
The German Government
  1992, Otto Dix
Harsch Transports
  1991, International Conference on
  the Packing and Transportation of
  Paintings
Hasenkamp Internationle Transporte
  1991, International Conference on

the Packing and Transportation of
  Paintings
The Independent
  1992, Otto Dix (in kind)
  1993, Paris Post War: Art and
  Existentialism 1945–55
KPMG Management Consulting
  1991, Anthony Caro: Sculpture
  towards Architecture*
Kunsttrans Antiquitaten
  1991, International Conference on
  the Packing and Transportation of
  Paintings
Lloyd's of London
  1991, Friends Room
Makro
  1994, Turner's Holland
Martinspeed Ltd
  1991, International Conference on
  the Packing and Transportation of
  Paintings
Masterpiece International Ltd
  1991, International Conference on
  the Packing and Transportation of
  Paintings
Mat Securitas Express AG
  1991, International Conference on
  the Packing and Transportation of
  Paintings
Mobel Transport AG
  1991, International Conference on
  the Packing and Transportation of
  Paintings
MOMART plc
  1991, International Conference on
  the Packing and Transportation of
  Paintings
Nuclear Electric plc
  1993, Turner: The Final Years
  1994, The Essential Turner
Propileo Transport
  1991, International Conference on
  the Packing and Transportation of
  Paintings
Rees Martin Art Service
  1991, International Conference on
  the Packing and Transportation of
  Paintings
SRU Limited
  1992, Richard Hamilton*
Sun Life Assurance Society plc
  1993, Robert Vernon's Gift
THORN EMI
  1993 Turner's Painting Techniques
TSB Group plc
  1992, Turner and Byron
  1992–5, William Blake display
  series
Wingate & Johnston Ltd
  1991, International Conference on
  the Packing and Transportation of
  Paintings

TATE GALLERY LIVERPOOL:
CORPORATE SPONSORS
(alphabetical order)

AIB Bank
  1991, Strongholds
American Airlines
  1993, David Hockney
Beck's
  1993, Robert Gober
British Alcan Aluminium plc
  1991, Dynamism
  1991, Giacometti
Canadian High Commission, London
and Government of Canada
  1993, Elective Affinities

Cultural Relations Committee, Department of Foreign Affairs, Ireland
  1991, Strongholds
David M Robinson Jewellery
  1994, Venus Re-Defined
English Estates
  1991, Mobile Art Programme
Ibstock Building Products Ltd
  1993, Antony Gormley
Korean Air
  1992, Working with Nature (in
  kind)
The Littlewoods Organisation plc
  1992–5, New Realities
Merseyside Development Corporation
  1992, Myth-Making
  1992, Stanley Spencer
MOMART plc
  1991–4, The Momart Fellowship
NSK Bearings Europe Ltd
  1991, A Cabinet of Signs: Contemporary Art from Post-Modern Japan
North West Water Group PLC
  1994, Corporate Membership
  Brochure
Ryanair
  1991, Strongholds (in kind)
Samsung Electronics
  1992, Working With Nature
Volkswagen
  1991, Mobile Art Programme (in
  kind)

TATE GALLERY ST IVES:
CORPORATE SPONSORS

First Class Pullman, InterCity*
  1993–4, Annual Displays
South Western Electricity plc (SWEB)*
  1993–4, Education Programme

*denotes a sponsorship in the arts,
recognised by an award under the
Government's Business Sponsorship
Incentive Scheme, administered by
the Association for Business Sponsorship of the Arts.

Tate Gallery Founding Benefactors
(date order)

Sir Henry Tate
Sir Joseph Duveen
Lord Duveen
The Clore Foundation

Tate Gallery Principal Benefactors
(alphabetical order)

American Fund for the Tate Gallery
Calouste Gulbenkian Foundation
Friends of the Tate Gallery
The Henry Moore Foundation
National Art Collections Fund
National Heritage Memorial Fund
The Nomura Securities Co., Ltd
Patrons of New Art
Dr Mortimer and Theresa Sackler
  Foundation
St Ives Tate Action Group
The Wolfson Foundation and Family
  Charitable Trust

Tate Gallery Benefactors
(alphabetical order)

The Baring Foundation
Bernard Sunley Charitable
  Foundation
Gilbert and Janet de Botton
Mr Edwin C. Cohen
The Eleanor Rathbone Charitable
  Trust
Esmée Fairbairn Charitable Trust
Foundation for Sport and the Arts
GEC Plessey Telecommunications
The Getty Grant Program
Granada Group plc
The Paul Hamlyn Foundation
John and Olivia Hughes
The John S. Cohen Foundation
The John Ellerman Foundation
The Kreitman Foundation
John Lewis Partnership
The Leverhulme Trust
Museums and Galleries Improvement
  Fund
Ocean Group plc (P.H. Holt Trust)
Patrons of British Art
Peter Moores Foundation
The Pilgrim Trust
Mr John Ritblat
The Sainsbury Family Charitable
  Trusts
Save & Prosper Educational Trust
SRU Limited
Weinberg Foundation

Tate Gallery Donors
(alphabetical order)

LONDON

Professor Abbott
The Andy Warhol Foundation for the
  Visual Arts, Inc
Lord Attenborough CBE
BAA plc
Friends of Nancy Balfour OBE
Balmuir Holdings
The Hon. Robin Baring
B.A.T. Industries plc
Nancy Bateman Charitable Trust
Mr Tom Bendhem
Mr Alexander Bernstein
Michael and Marcia Blakenham
Miss Mary Boone
The Britwell Trust
Card Aid
Carlsberg Brewery
Mr Vincent Carrozza
Mrs Beryl Carpenter
Cazenove & Co
Charlotte Bonham Carter Charitable
  Trust
Christie, Manson & Woods Ltd
The Claire Hunter Charitable Trust
The Clothworkers Foundation
Mrs Elisabeth Collins
Mr R.N. Collins
Giles and Sonia Coode-Adams
Mrs Dagny Corcoran
C.T. Bowring (Charitable Trust) Ltd
Cognac Courvoisier
Mr Edwin Cox
Anthony d'Offay Gallery
Mr and Mrs Kenneth Dayton
Mr Damon and The Hon. Mrs de
  Laszlo
Madame Gustava de Rothschild
Baroness Liliane de Rothschild

Miss W.A. Donner
Mr Paul Dupee
Mrs Maurice Dwek
Elephant Trust
Eli Broad Family Foundation
Elizabeth Arden Ltd
European Arts Festival
Evelyn, Lady Downshire's Trust Fund
Roberto Fainello Art Advisers Ltd
The Flow Foundation
First Boston Corporation
Foreign & Colonial
    Management Limited
Miss Kate Ganz
Mr Henry Geldzahler
Mr and Mrs David Gilmour
The German Government
Goethe Institut
Sir Nicholas and Lady Goodison
    Charitable Settlement
Mr William Govett
Mr and Mrs Richard Grogan
Gytha Trust
Mr and Mrs Rupert Hambro
Miriam and Peter Haas Foundation
Mrs Sue Hammerson
The Hon. Lady Hastings
The Hedley Foundation
Mr and Mrs Michael Heseltine
Mr Rupert Heseltine
Horace W. Goldsmith Foundation
Mr Robert Horton
Hurry Armour Trust
Idlewild Trust
The Italian Government
Sir Anthony and Lady Jacobs
Mrs Gabrielle Keiller
Mr James Kirkman
Knapping Fund
Mr and Mrs Richard Knight
Mr and Mrs Jan Krugier
The Leche Trust
Robert Lehman Foundation, Inc
The Helena and Kenneth Levy
    Bequest
Mr and Mrs Gilbert Lloyd
Mr and Mrs Lawrence Lowenthal
Mail on Sunday
Mr Alexander Marchessini
The Mayor Gallery
Midland Bank Artscard
Mr and Mrs Robert Mnuchin
The Monument Trust
Mr Peter Nahum
Mr and Mrs Philip Niarchos
Dr Andreas Papadakis
The Paradina Trust
Mr William Pegrum
Philips Fine Art Auctioneers
The Earl of Plymouth
Old Possum's Practical Trust
The Hon. Mrs Olga Polizzi
Paul Nash Trust
Peter Samuel Charitable Trust
Mr Jean Pigozzi
Sir Gordon Reece
Reed International P.L.C.
Richard Green Fine Paintings
Mrs Jill Ritblat
Rothschild Bank AG
Mrs Jean Sainsbury
The Hon. Simon Sainsbury
Sebastian de Ferranti Trust
Schroder Charity Trust
Ms Dasha Shenkman
South Square Trust
Mr A. Speelman
Standard Chartered Bank
Mr and Mrs Bernhard Starkmann

The Swan Trust
Sir Adrian and Lady Judith Swire
Mrs Barbara Thomas
Time-Life International Ltd
The 29th May 1961 Charitable Trust
Lady Juliet Townsend
Mr Barry and The Hon. Mrs Townsley
The Triangle Trust
U.K. Charity Lotteries Ltd
Mrs Anne Uribe-Mosquera
Visiting Arts
Mr and Mrs Leslie Waddington
Waley-Cohen Charitable Trust
Mr Mark Weiss
Weltkunst Foundation
Mrs Alexandra Williams
Nina and Graham Williams
Willis Faber plc
Mr Andrew Wilton
Thomas and Odette Worrell
The Worshipful Company of
    Fishmongers
The Worshipful Company of
    Goldsmiths
The Worshipful Company of Grocers
The Worshipful Company of Mercers
Mrs Jayne Wrightsman

and those donors who wish to remain
anonymous

LIVERPOOL (alphabetical order)

The Baring Foundation
David and Ruth Behrend Trust
Ivor Braka Ltd
The British Council
British Telecom plc
Calouste Gulbenkian Foundation
Mr and Mrs Henry Cotton
English Estates
European Arts Festival
Goethe Institut, Manchester
Mrs Sue Hammerson OBE
Mr John Heyman
Liverpool Council for Voluntary
    Services
Merseyside Development Corporation
Momart plc
The Henry Moore Foundation
Ocean Group plc (P.H. Holt Trust)
Eleanor Rathbone Charitable Trust
Tate Gallery Liverpool Supporters
Bernard Sunley Charitable
    Foundation
Unilever
Visiting Arts

and those donors who wish to remain
anonymous

ST IVES (alphabetical order)

Donors to the Appeal coordinated by
the Steering Group for the Tate
Gallery St Ives and the St Ives Action
Group.

Viscount Amory Charitable Trust
Barbinder Trust
Barclays Bank PLC
The Baring Foundation
BICC Group
Patricia, Lady Boyd and Viscount
    Boyd
British Telecom plc
Cable and Wireless plc
Carlton Communications

Mr Francis Carnwath
Christie, Manson & Woods Ltd
Mr Peter Cocks
John S. Cohen Foundation
Miss Jean Cooper
D'Oyly Carte Charitable Trust
David Messum Fine Paintings
Dewhurst House
Dixons Group plc
Mr Alan Driscoll
The John Ellerman Foundation
English China Clays Group
Esmee Fairbairn Charitable Trust
Foundation for Sport and the Arts
J. Paul Getty Jr Charitable Trust
Gimpel Fils
Grand Metropolitan Trust
Ms Judith Hodgson
Sir Geoffrey and Lady Holland
Mr and Mrs Philip Hughes
Mr Bernard Jacobson
Mr John Kilby
Lloyds Bank plc
Lord Leverhulme's Trust
The Manifold Trust
The Mayor Gallery
Marlborough Fine Art
Mercury Asset Management plc
Meyer International plc
The Henry Moore Foundation
National Westminster Bank plc
New Art Centre
Pall European Limited
The Pilgrim Trust
The Joseph Rank (1942) Charitable
    Trust
Mr Roy Ray
The Rayne Foundation
Royal Bank of Scotland
The Sainsbury Family Charitable
    Trusts
Mr Nicholas Serota
Mr Roger Slack
Trustees of the Carew Pole Family
    Trust
Trustees of H.E.W. Spurr Deceased
South West British Gas
South West Water plc
South Western Electricity plc
Sun Alliance Group
Television South West
The TSB Foundation for England and
    Wales
Unilever
Mrs Angela Verren Taunt
Weinberg Foundation
Wembley plc
Western Morning News, West Briton,
    Cornish Guardian and The
    Cornishman
Westlake & Co
Mr and Mrs Derek White
Mr and Mrs Graham Williams
Wingate Charitable Trust
The Worshipful Company of
    Fishmongers
The Worshipful Company of Mercers
Mrs Monica Wynter

and those donors who wish to remain
anonymous

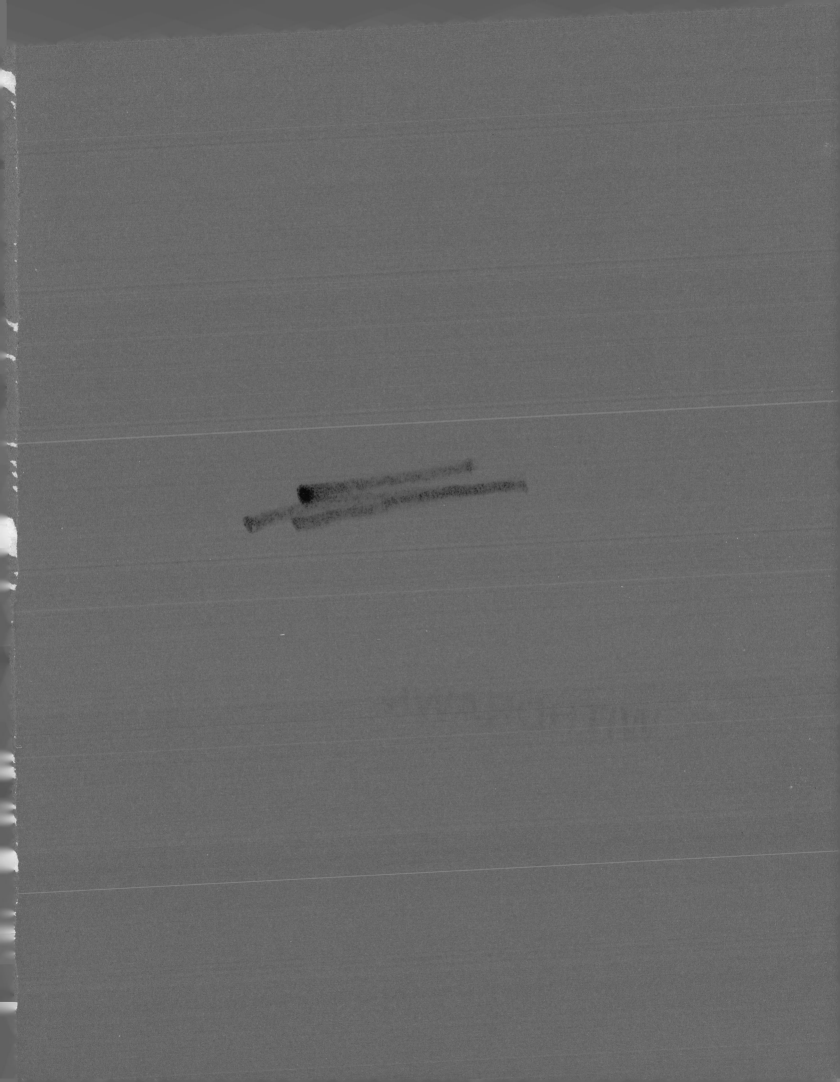

WITHDRAWN